So You Think You Know Baseball?

A FAN'S GUIDE TO THE OFFICIAL RULES

Peter E. Meltzer

W. W. NORTON & COMPANY

New York • London

Printed in the United States of America
First Edition

Manufacturing by Quad Graphics
Book design by Chris Welch
Production manager: Louise Mattarelliano

Library of Congress Cataloging-in-Publication Data

Meltzer, Peter E., 1958–
So you think you know baseball? : a fan's guide to the official rules / Peter E. Meltzer. —
First edition.
pages cm
Includes bibliographical references and index.
ISBN 978-0-393-34438-7 (pbk.)
1. Baseball—Rules. I. Title.
GV877.M43 2013
796.357—dc23
2013001520

W. W. Norton & Company, Inc.
500 Fifth Avenue, New York, N.Y. 10110
www.wwnorton.com

W. W. Norton & Company Ltd.
Castle House, 75/76 Wells Street, London W1T 3QT

1 2 3 4 5 6 7 8 9 0

So You Think You Know Baseball?

ALSO BY PETER E. MELTZER

The Thinker's Thesaurus:
Sophisticated Alternatives to Common Words

So You Think You Know the Presidents?
Fascinating Facts about Our Chief Executives

To Aaron, Joel, Mark, Mike, and Steve
Five mensches with five wonderful wives

CONTENTS

PART ONE
RULES ON THE FIELD

ACKNOWLEDGMENTS

I have ably been assisted in this endeavor by two of the foremost experts in the country on the Major League Baseball rulebook. One is Rich Marazzi, who reviewed the material on sections 2 through 9 of the rulebook, the on-the-field rules, which are the province of the umpires. His biography is at the end of his foreword. He is one of the foremost experts on the rules of baseball. I was also assisted regarding section 10—the official scorer—by a gentleman who must remain anonymous but whose credentials with respect to that section are just as impeccable as Mr. Marazzi's. I cannot thank these two men enough for their wisdom and insights, not to mention the countless hours of their time they both spent with me. The baseball rulebook can be difficult terrain to navigate, and I could not have had better guides than these two cognoscenti.

Thanks to Major League Baseball for allowing me to quote from the *Official Baseball Rules*. I would also like to thank Mark Schneider for tips and suggestions he offered all along the way and for lots more. Thanks also to my fine agent, Regina Ryan, and to my wonderful team at Norton on this, our second go-round, including my editors, Amy Cherry and Tori Leventhal. They are all a pleasure to work with. I am also most appreciative for the assistance of Steve

Boldt, possibly the most thorough copyeditor ever. This book has a large number of game facts, dates, and names (many Hispanic, which means lots of accents), and he went through the painstaking task of double-checking every last one.

I am most grateful for the unwavering support of my mom, my sisters, my brother, and all of my Buffalo in-laws. I am always grateful to my wife, Deirdre, who tolerates my book writing (this is number four) with remarkable good humor and cheer, despite that she would probably prefer that I do fun tasks such as tar the driveway, rotate the tires, and regrout the bathtub. Finally, a shout-out to my children, Thomas and Charlotte, who are as magical to me as Game 5 of the 2008 World Series.

I must emphasize that, unless I'm quoting others, all opinions and conclusions expressed in the book are mine alone, and if there are any "errors" (pun intended), they are certainly mine alone as well.

FOREWORD

Rich Marazzi

When Peter Meltzer approached me about this book project, I was apprehensive about getting involved. I knew he was taking on a massive undertaking since the *Official Baseball Rules* has historically created challenges for the best baseball minds in the game.

I was aware that Peter's game plan to identify, explain, and assess most rules was a daunting task. But after careful review, I believe that he has met the challenge through a uniquely written format that triggers the thinking of the reader through a plethora of questions and an opinionated analysis of baseball's playing and scoring rules.

The reader is quizzed about the rules through a series of pertinent questions drawn from actual plays that have occurred in a major league game as opposed to mere hypotheticals. To my knowledge, this is the first baseball book ever written that contains this feature. In my opinion this is the book's greatest asset as the author engages the reader throughout. His carefully designed questions based on actual plays are a valuable learning technique that is absent from most previously written rules-related books.

In my thirty-five years or so as a rules columnist, and now rules consultant for several major league teams, I have never encountered such a book that not only teaches the reader about the rules of the game, but explores the intricacies and nuances of the more common rules as well as the obscure.

While any analysis of the *Official Baseball Rules* is subject to individual interpretation, it is my opinion after reviewing Peter's efforts that all rules-related questions are appropriate and answered with accuracy.

The smooth flow of the book enables the reader to maintain a high level of interest about a subject that is loaded with complexities and nuances often subject to interpretation. I have often said that a rule is often like an onion because there are so many layers. Meltzer uncovers the layers through his practical examples and evaluation of the rule.

If you enjoy being challenged and want to have some fun, sit back, relax, and enjoy an exciting journey through the hills and valleys of the *Official Baseball Rules*.

ABOUT RICH MARAZZI

Rich Marazzi has served as the rules consultant for various Major League Baseball organizations, including the New York Yankees, Boston Red Sox, Toronto Blue Jays, Cleveland Indians, Arizona Diamondbacks, and Houston Astros, and is considered the first rules consultant in Major League Baseball history. He has authored five baseball books, including *The Rules and Lore of Baseball*. He has been a monthly rules columnist for *Baseball Digest* since 1988 and has also served in the same capacity for *Yankees Magazine* and *Referee* magazine over the years. Rich is also currently a rules columnist for *USA Today Sports Weekly*, *New England Baseball Journal*, the ABUA Web site (www.umpire.org), and *Collegiate Baseball*. He also hosts a weekly baseball radio talk show on 97.9 ESPN and ESPN Radio 1300 in Connecticut.

INTRODUCTION

Every sport has its rabid fans, but none enjoy discussing the rules of their sport so much as baseball fans. Virtually anytime a play occurs in a major league game that involves interpretation of a baseball rule, one can be sure that the next day's newspapers (and even more so the blogosphere) will have a full analysis of the play, the rule it brought into question, and especially whether or not the umpire (or the official scorer) got the call right. We are a nation of armchair umpires.

Why the fascination with baseball rules? Numbers and statistics are part of it. Baseball has a rich history of capturing every aspect of the performance of every player ever since the game began.

The Major League Baseball rulebook (the *Official Baseball Rules*) has two components. The first (sections 2 through 9) relates to the action on the field that can affect the outcome of the game and how umpires should deal with game situations. Did the ball hit the runner? Does the infield fly rule apply to that pop-up? Didn't the fielder obstruct the runner? Does that run count even though the third out occurred on the play? Can the batter run to first after the catcher did not catch strike three?

The second component (section 10) relates specifically to how the action on the field should be scored—i.e., the statistical component. Should that mental mistake by the fielder have been counted as an error? Does the runner get credit for a stolen base on a wild throw? Does the hitter get credit for an RBI even though he hit into a double play? Does the pitcher get credit for a save even though his team was up by 5 runs?

Though part of the same rulebook, the two sections are entirely distinct from one another: one is the province of the umpires on the field, the other is the province of the "official scorer." Indeed, they are so distinct that a Major League Baseball umpire is neither required nor presumed to have any specialized expertise regarding the official scorer rules, and the official scorer is neither required nor presumed to have any specialized expertise regarding the umpiring rules.

The official scorer section demonstrates another way in which the sport of baseball is unique. Statistics are a far more important part of baseball than of any other sport.

Consider the following: On June 2, 2010, the Tigers' Armando Galarraga retired the first twenty-six Cleveland Indians batters he faced. Had he retired the next batter, Jason Donald, he would have thrown a perfect game. Donald hit a grounder to the first baseman, Miguel Cabrera, who threw to Galarraga, who was covering first. Although Donald was clearly out on the play, umpire Jim Joyce mistakenly called him safe, thus ruining Galarraga's perfect game (Joyce admitted as much the moment he saw the replay after the game). Galarraga retired the next batter, and the Tigers won 3–0.

A Google search of this play just a few days after it occurred turned up over half a million hits from around the world, discussing it from every angle. Of course, blown umpire or referee calls are nothing new in sports, with plenty of famous (or infamous) instances of such blown calls in every sport. But, only in baseball could there be such a firestorm over a blown call *that had no effect on the outcome of the game at all*. The Tigers won the game immediately afterward anyway. Every time there has been a controversy about a blown call in other sports it is because that call had an impact on the result of the game. In this case, the blown call made no difference whatsoever in that respect. It was important only statistically—perfect games are rare in baseball, and because fans of the game pay attention to statistics and history, Joyce's blown call mattered.

This book is unique in three respects. First, it is the only book that focuses on actual Major League Baseball plays as opposed to dry hypotheticals invented by the author. This brings the plays to life and lets the reader know that umpires (or official scorers) actually had to deal with the situations at hand. It is more entertaining to analyze plays that have actually occurred as opposed to those created by the writer. (It is also much more time-consuming—it has taken over three years to locate all the plays and situations in this book.) Second, it is the only book that analyzes every baseball rule that has been the subject of interpretation. It does not merely consider a random rule here and there, in hodgepodge fashion. Third, it is the only book that analyzes both the "action on the field" rules and the "official scorer" rules.

Some books have been written in the past (and there are Web sites) regarding the baseball rules. However, (1) they analyze the rules sporadically and randomly, and not comprehensively (often without any specific references to the rules at all), (2) they are not based on actual plays, (3) they ignore the official scorer rules, and (4) they were written before a number of significant amendments to the rules. In addition, most of these books are simply a narrative about the rules. However, I favor the quiz approach because it provides readers with an interactive experience that encourages them to test their knowledge, as opposed to a passive experience.

The typical question found in other books on the baseball rules goes something like this:

Based loaded, one out. Batting team has runners on first (R1) and third (R3). Batter hits grounder to the second baseman (2B). He intended to tag R1 and throw to first for the double play. However, R1 sized up the situation and stopped between first and second, where 2B couldn't tag him. Thus 2B threw to first to retire the batter and 1B threw to SS, who tagged R1 to complete the inning-ending double play. While all this was going on, R3 crossed home plate. Does the run count?

The question is thus presented in a clinical and lifeless way, and it may not ever actually have occurred. (In this case, it did, and an actual play based on these facts is analyzed in this book.)

The plays range from the older (in 1917, a relief pitcher came in—for Babe Ruth!—after the first batter had walked. The batter was thrown out trying to steal, and the relief pitcher retired the next twenty-six batters. Does he get credit for a perfect game?) to the present day. Also, while focusing solely on how plays would be ruled under the major league rulebook, we examine minor league plays, plays from other countries (such as the Netherlands), and even a Bugs Bunny cartoon.

My own fascination with the rules of baseball goes back many years. Virtually every time I have come across an article discussing a play involving a rules or scoring controversy, I have cataloged it. Many of the plays described in this book come out of that catalog.

I hope that readers enjoy testing their knowledge of the rules as much as I enjoyed writing the book.

NOTE

The Commissioner of Baseball is the owner of the copyright in the *Official Baseball Rules*. This book is not intended in any way as a substitute for the *Official Baseball Rules*.

PART ONE: RULES ON THE FIELD

Chapter 1

Equipment

1.1 Player's uniforms

On June 7, 1938, the Indians and Red Sox met at Fenway Park. A part of the short sleeve of Cleveland pitcher Johnny Allen dangled when he pitched. Umpire Bill McGowan ordered Allen to cut off the dangling threads. Allen, known for his volatile temper, refused McGowan's directive. The stubborn hurler stormed off the mound, refusing to pitch. His ragged shirt now hangs in the Hall of Fame at Cooperstown, New York.

1: Was McGowan authorized to order Allen to cut off part of his sleeve?

Yes. Rule 1.11(c)(2) specifically prohibits ragged or fraying sleeves.

2: On June 12, 1988, the Blue Jays hosted the Red Sox. In the bottom of the fifth inning, Blue Jays skipper Jimy Williams asked home plate empire Chuck Meriwether to order Sox pitcher Dennis "Oil Can" Boyd to remove a gold chain and large medallion from his neck. Boyd

argued vehemently against Meriwether's demand that he remove the jewelry but eventually gave in. Was Boyd right to complain?

No. Rule 1.11(f) prohibits glass buttons and polished metal on a uniform. While one could question whether Boyd's jewelry was "on a uniform," he was likely violating Rule 1.11(f). The idea is that players (usually hitters) should not be distracted by something on the uniform of an opposing player (typically the pitcher). The issue usually arises when one team complains to the umpire, as happened above. Another example is Rule 1.15(a), which specifically prohibits the pitcher from using a glove with a distracting appearance, such as an unusual color.

3: More than 50 percent of Toronto Blue Jays pitcher Justin Miller's body (including most of his arms) is covered with body art. MLB thought that the tattoos were distracting and ordered him to wear long-sleeved shirts under his uniform when he pitched. Was the league within its rights?

The rulebook does not contain any specific reference to tattoos. Nevertheless, if MLB believes anything about Miller's overall appearance is distracting to opposing teams, it has discretion to take action. In 2004, Major League Baseball established a rule that forced Miller to wear long sleeves whenever he played. "I didn't want to stare him up and down, but we'll see during the course of his stay here how many tattoos he has," said Marlins manager Fredi González on his first encounter with his newest pitcher. Miller said at the time of MLB's ruling that he was worried the sleeves would be uncomfortable, especially when it was hot. Three years later, though, he had grown accustomed to the extra clothing and said he actually liked it. How does it feel to tell people you've got a baseball rule named after you? "I don't know," he said, laughing. "They just said it's the 'Justin Miller Rule.'"

4: On July 27, 2010, the San Francisco Giants were playing the Florida Marlins. Giants pitcher Brian Wilson was wearing orange shoes, as he had done in the All-Star Game. Marlins manager Edwin Rodríguez complained to the umpires about the bright color being a distraction for his team. Wilson was fined $1,000. Were Miller's shoes prohibited by the rules as being distracting?

Not by the rules but by the *Major League Manual*. Rule 1.11(a)(3) does prohibit a player from wearing a "uniform" that does not conform to that of his teammates. The only rule that specifically references shoes is 1.11(g), which provides in part that shoes with pointed spikes similar to golf or track shoes are prohibited. However, MLB does require that a player's cleats be at least 50 percent of the team's dominant color, which in the Giants' case would be black. Therefore, Wilson subsequently painted half of his cleats black and dubbed them "Nike Air Sharpies." Asked about the situation—and Rodríguez calling the shoes "too flashy"—Wilson gave a pretty amusing answer: "Too flashy. I didn't know that's in the rulebook. Oh, it's *not* in the rulebook. The fact that he thinks these shoes throw ninety-seven to one hundred with cut might be a little far-fetched. I guess we should have these checked as performance-enhancing shoes."

5: In 1997, Deion Sanders of the Reds wanted to honor Jackie Robinson by shortening his sleeves several inches in an effort to replicate the uniform worn by Robinson when he broke the Major League Baseball color barrier fifty years earlier. Was he permitted to do so?

No. National League senior vice president Katy Feeney said Sanders had to adhere to Rule 1.11(a)(1), which requires players on a team to wear uniforms identical in color, trim, and style. If a player's uniform does not conform, he may not participate in the game. "We obviously appreciate that he wants to honor Jackie Robinson, but that's what the whole season is about," Feeney said. "Jackie always wore the uniform the rest of his teammates wore." Interestingly, Feeney said that although many players wear altered uniform pants, which come just below the knee, as well as solid socks instead of stirrups, those kinds of variations are not prohibited by the rule.

Similarly, in 1997, Yankees pitcher David Wells was forced to remove a hat worn by Babe Ruth in 1934, which Wells bought for $35,000. The interlocking *NY* on the old Yankees hats is considerably smaller than the current letters.

6: True or false? No part of a player's uniform may have a pattern that looks like a baseball.

True. Rule 1.11(g).

1.2 Appearance of glove

On May 1, 2010, the Yankees hosted the White Sox. As Yankee right-hander Javy Vázquez walked out to the mound to start the third inning, he was stopped by umpire Jerry Meals. Meals wanted Vázquez to use a different glove because he felt that Vázquez's two-tone glove (light and dark brown) was distracting.

1: Did the umpire have a right to force Vázquez to change gloves?

Yes. This is permitted by Rule 1.15. Vázquez said he was caught "off guard because I've been using the same glove for three or four years. Exactly the same glove." White and gray gloves are prohibited as well (exclusive of piping) whether distracting or not. In spring training, Meals was asked by Florida minor league pitcher Taylor Tankersley, who uses the same glove as Vázquez, whether the model was okay.

Meals took a picture of the glove and sent it to MLB officials, who ruled it was illegal.

2: What if, instead of umpire Meals, the White Sox manager felt that the glove was distracting? Could he request that Vázquez use a different glove?

Yes, he could request it, but whether it would have to be removed is up to the umpire in chief.

1.3 Using pine tar on a bat

On July 24, 1983, the Kansas City Royals were playing the New York Yankees at Yankee Stadium. In the top of the ninth inning, the Royals were trailing 4–3. With two out, and U L Washington on first, George Brett hit a home run off Goose Gossage to put the Royals up 5–4. However, after Brett crossed home plate and had returned to the dugout, Yankees manager Billy Martin argued that the rules prevented any foreign substance on a bat that extended farther than eighteen inches from the knob—and Brett's bat had a substantial amount of pine tar on it, maybe beyond eighteen inches.

Pine tar is a substance legally used by hitters to improve their grip on the bat. The umpires measured the pine tar on Brett's bat (by laying it across home plate, which is seventeen inches wide) and found that it extended well past eighteen inches. The home plate umpire, Tim McClelland, in his first year as a major league umpire, signaled that the bat was in violation of the rules and called Brett out, which meant that the game ended as a Yankees win. An irate Brett charged out of the dugout to protest the call, but to no avail. Writing about the game the next day, *Kansas City Star* reporter Mike McKenzie wrote, "Brett has become the first player in history to hit a game-*losing* home run."

The Royals protested the game, and American League president Lee

MacPhail upheld the protest, reasoning that the pine tar had no effect on the distance a ball would travel and that the intent and spirit of the rule had not been violated. He also said that the bat should have been excluded from future use but the home run should not have been nullified. Amid much controversy, the game was resumed on August 18, from just after the point of Brett's home run, and ended with a 5–4 Royals win.

1: At the time of McClelland's ruling, the rules did prohibit the use of a bat with as much pine tar as Brett's had, but did not specify the consequences (thus leading to years of controversy regarding both McClelland's ruling and MacPhail's decision to overturn the ruling). However, the question for our purposes is, if the play had unfolded the exact same way under today's rules, what would be the outcome?

Based on a Comment that was added to Rule 1.10(c) before the 2010 season, it is now made explicit that excessive pine tar on the bat is grounds for removing the bat from the game (if discovered before or during the time at bat), but it is not grounds for declaring the batter out or being ejected from the game. Therefore, under the rules today, Brett's home run would stand. While the Comment refers to the umpire "discovering" the nonconforming bat, presumably anyone is free to bring the issue to the umpire's attention. Generally speaking, however, virtually no one protests nonconforming bats anymore.

2: True or false? The reason this rule originally came into being was to prevent a hitter from using a bat that would give him an unfair advantage.

False. An advantage to the hitter had nothing to do with it. The real reason was money. Calvin Griffith, the very frugal (some would say cheap) owner of the Minnesota Twins, who was also on the rules committee, was concerned that baseballs were becoming discolored from contact with pine tar, making it necessary to throw them out. Therefore, he reasoned that less pine tar on the bats meant less chance of discoloration and fewer balls would have to be replaced. He caused Rule 1.10(b), now 1.10(c), to be added to the rules.

Note also the significant distinction between a nonconforming bat and an illegal bat. Brett's was nonconforming, which is less serious. An illegal bat, such as a corked bat, has been altered in such a way as to improve the distance the ball flies. Use of illegal bats has more serious consequences and is the subject of a different rule—6.06(d)—discussed below.

Chapter 2

Definitions

2.1 Definition of "force play"

On August 30, 2006, the Astros were playing the Brewers in Houston. In the bottom of the ninth in a scoreless game and one out, the Astros had the bases loaded with Mike Lamb at third. Aubrey Huff hit a grounder down the line that first baseman Jeff Cirillo grabbed with a dive. He touched first, then threw to catcher Damian Miller, who stepped on the plate just before Lamb touched home plate.

1: Time for extra innings?

No, the game is over, and the Astros win 1–0. By retiring Huff first, the force on Lamb was removed and he would have had to be tagged out. Whenever the batter-runner or a preceding runner is retired on what would have otherwise been a force play, the force is no longer in effect on subsequent runners. This important rule is sometimes forgotten even at the major league level. With Huff out at first, Lamb would have had to be tagged to be retired, and Miller made no effort to do so. This rule can also be important when it comes to "time" plays, which we will discuss in chapter 13.

2.2 Definition of "foul ball"

On August 5, 2010, the Marlins were playing the Phillies in Miami. In the bottom of the ninth, with the score tied 4–4 and Hanley Ramírez of the Marlins on second base, Gaby Sánchez hit a shot down the third-base line. The ball hit the chalk line before reaching third base, hopped in the air as it passed third base, then bounced in fair territory. The ball then rolled into the left-field corner. Had it been ruled fair, Ramírez would have scored easily for the game-winning run. However, third-base umpire Bob Davidson ruled that it was foul. Marlins manager Edwin Rodríguez stormed out of the dugout to protest the call, but to no avail. He later said, "That was one of the worst calls I've ever seen in my thirty years of professional baseball."

1: Did Davidson make the proper call?

A. No, because the ball bounced in fair territory before reaching third base.

B. No, because the chalk line is considered fair territory.

C. Yes, if the ball was in foul territory as it passed over third base before hooking back into fair territory.

D. Yes, because the chalk line is considered foul territory.

The correct answer is C, and Davidson used this justification for his call, even though this would have required the ball to go from fair territory before reaching third base, then to foul as it hopped over the bag, and then to fair again after third base. If a ball is foul as it passes over first or third base, then it is a foul ball, even if it is fair before or after that. Thus, despite the fact that the ball would have traveled an unlikely path, Davidson was correct that only the location of the ball as it passed over third base was relevant. Note that choice B is correct in the sense that chalk line is considered fair territory, but the relevant consideration is the location of the ball when it passes third base.

2: Say that Sánchez's shot landed in foul territory before passing third base, but then spun back into fair territory. Which of the following statements is true?

A. It's a fair ball no matter what.

B. It's a foul ball no matter what.

C. It's a foul ball if it rolls back into fair territory before reaching third base.

D. It's a fair ball if it rolls back into fair territory before reaching third base.

The correct answer is D. The definition of "foul ball" does not specifically address this situation, but the definition of "fair ball" includes a ball that settles in fair territory between home and first or home and third or one that is in fair territory when bouncing to the outfield. Therefore, choice D would be correct even if the ball initially landed in foul territory.

3: Say that Sánchez's hit struck the pitcher's rubber and then ricocheted into foul territory. No player touched the ball while it was in fair territory. Which of the following statements is true?

A. It's a fair ball no matter what.

B. It's a foul ball no matter what.

C. It's a fair ball if it hits the ground before hitting the rubber and if it rolls back into fair territory before reaching third base.

D. It's a foul ball if it goes into foul territory before reaching first or third base.

Even though the ball would clearly have been fair had it not hit the pitcher's rubber, the correct answer is D. This is treated the same as any other ball that rolls from fair territory to foul territory. Thus, if the ball rolls out while in the infield, it's a foul ball, and if it rolls out only after first or third base, it's a fair ball.

4: What if Sánchez's hit passed third base on the fly while in fair territory, but then hooked foul afterward so that the initial bounce was in foul territory. Fair or foul?

This would be a foul ball because its first contact with the ground was past third base and in foul territory.

5: Suppose a fielder overruns a fly ball and is standing completely in foul territory when he catches a ball that would otherwise have landed and settled in fair territory. Fair or foul?

Fair. The positioning of the fielder is irrelevant. The position of the ball is what determines whether a ball is fair or foul.

2.3 Definition of "in flight"

In a May 10, 1977, game at Montreal's Olympic Stadium, Warren Cromartie of the Expos slammed a long drive to center against the Dodgers. Center fielder Rick Monday chased the ball but was unable

Carlos Martínez of the Indians hit a shot to right field that bounced off the top of José Canseco's head and went over the fence. Is Martínez awarded a double or a home run? *Ron Kuntz Collection/Getty Images*

to reach it. The ball caromed off the wall, struck Monday on the head, and then bounced over the wall.

1: Does Cromartie get credit for a home run? If not, where does he wind up?

He only is awarded two bases. Rule 6.09(g) provides that the batter becomes a runner when "any bounding fair ball is deflected by the fielder into the stands . . . in which case the batter and all runners shall be entitled to advance two bases." Because the Cromartie hit "bounded over" the wall into the stands, he only gets two bases.

2: On May 26, 1993, the Cleveland Indians were playing the Texas Rangers. Carlos Martínez of the Indians hit a shot to right field that bounced off the top of José Canseco's head and went over the fence, helping the Tribe to a 7–6 win. The next day, the *Cleveland Plain Dealer* bannered, "CONK! The Tribe Wins by a Head." Does Martínez get credit for a home run? If not, where does he wind up?

He gets credit for a home run. Rule 6.09(h) provides that if a "fair fly ball" (as opposed to a "bounding fair ball") is deflected into the stands or over the fence into fair territory, it's a home run. This was the case with Martínez's hit.

Also, though not mentioned in Rules 6.09(g) or 6.09(h), we need to consider the definition of a ball's being "in flight." This is a defined term in section 2.00 as "a batted, thrown, or pitched ball which has not yet touched the ground or some object other than a fielder." So what difference does it make whether a ball is "in flight" or not? Because a "catch" is defined as "the act of a fielder in getting secure possession in his hand or glove of a ball *in flight* and firmly holding it." In other words, if the ball is not "in flight," it cannot be a "catch," and if it cannot be a "catch," it cannot be an out.

So let's return to the above plays. Cromartie's ball would not be considered "in flight" because it *did* first hit "an object other than a fielder" before it hit Monday, namely the fence. Therefore, it would be considered a "bounding ball [being] deflected by the fielder into the stands" under Rule 6.09(g) and would be considered the same as a ground-rule double. If, on the other hand, Monday had actually caught the ball on the carom off the fence, it would still not be "in flight" and he would simply have to play the ball.

With the (comical) Canseco play on the other hand, the ball hit his head *before* hitting anything else, so it would be considered "in flight." This means it was a "fair fly ball" for purposes of Rule 6.09(h). Therefore, when it went into the stands, it became a home run. The same would be the case if the ball hit Canseco's equipment or any other part of his body.

3: Let's say on the Martínez/Canseco play that the ball had bounced off Canseco's head (or his glove) into foul territory. What would be the result for Martínez?

Under Rule 6.09(h), he would be entitled to second base. Indeed the result would be the same even if he reached over the fence and used his glove to swat the ball into foul territory.

4: On April 12, 1987, in the third inning of a game between the Atlanta Braves and the New York Mets, Dion James hit a routine fly to left field. As New York's Kevin McReynolds drifted under the ball, it suddenly collided with—and killed—a dove in flight. Shortstop Rafael Santana collected the bird from the outfield grass and handed it to the ball girl. Reluctantly, she took it and deposited it under the stands.

"I didn't know what had happened," McReynolds said. "It was that time of game when the sun was in my eyes. The only thing I could think right off was the ball went in the sun and I just lost it. Then all of

a sudden, I saw two objects falling." Would this have been a live ball or a dead ball?

It's a live ball, so if McReynolds had caught the dove-killing ball, the batter would have been out. That did not occur; James wound up with a double.

Should this have been the result? Let's return to the definition of "in flight": "a batted, thrown, or pitched ball which has not yet touched the ground *or some object other than a fielder.*" It would seem that a dove would be considered "some object other than a fielder." Nevertheless, baseball people consider these types of hits as being "in flight," and birds and speakers are not considered "objects" for purposes of the definition. "In flight" is interpreted to mean only objects that are part of the baseball field itself (such as the outfield fence), rather than "alien" objects, such as a bird.

5: On July 10, 1974, the Phils were playing the Astros in the old Astrodome. Mike Schmidt of the Phillies hit a towering drive that struck the bottom of a speaker suspended 117 feet over center field and 329 feet from home plate. Dave Cash, who was on base at the time, said, "I took one look and knew it was gone. Then I took another look and it was coming down in front of César Cedeño." Would the result of this play be different from that of the previous play since Schmidt's ball hit a speaker instead of a dove?

No. It would be the same result and for the same reason. A speaker is treated the same as a bird. On this play, Cedeño did not catch the ball and Schmidt wound up with a long single. In domed stadiums, batted balls that strike speakers in foul territory are no longer "in flight" and are considered foul balls.

6: What is the result if a ball hits an infielder in fair territory and flies into the stands?

It's a double and all runners advance two bases, despite the fact that the ball never left the infield in fair territory. Although such a scenario may seem fantastical, it has happened. On August 3, 2007, Melky Cabrera of the Yankees hit a shot off Royals pitcher Ryan Braun's foot in the sixth inning. The ball caromed into the stands over the Yankees dugout, resulting in perhaps the shortest double ever.

7: On April 11, 2009, the Red Sox and the Angels played in Anaheim. The Angels' Torii Hunter hit a shot deep to left that popped out of Jason Bay's glove, bounced off the wall, and landed back in his glove. Similarly, on June 5, 2007, the Cards hosted the Reds. In the top of the fifth inning, the Reds had two outs and a runner on first when Adam Dunn hit a shot in the direction of Cards' left fielder Chris Duncan. Duncan gloved the ball momentarily before it popped out and struck the wall. The ball then landed back in Duncan's glove, where he secured it before it ever hit the ground. In both cases, the batter was called out. Was that the right call?

No. Once the ball made contact with the wall, it was no longer legally "in flight" and a legal catch could not be made. This type of play is not reviewable even though the umpire is at a far distance from the play.

Chapter 3

Starting and Ending the Game

3.1 Starting the game

1: Which of the following statements is true?

A. A Major League Baseball game cannot start until the umpire calls, "play."

B. A Major League Baseball game cannot start until the umpire calls, "Play ball."

C. There are no specific words that an umpire has to say before a game can start.

D. An umpire has to say specific words before a game can start, but A and B are incorrect.

I suspect that the most popular answer would be B, followed by C, but the correct answer is A, per rule 4.02. "Believe it or not, every one of them simply says, 'Play,'" said Ralph E. Nelson Jr., vice president of umpiring for Major League Baseball. The origins of "play ball" are murky, but it appears in print at least as far back as 1901.

3.2 Determining rainouts

On June 18, 2009, the Yankees were scheduled to play the lowly Nationals in an interleague game starting at 1:05 in Yankee Stadium. However, due to torrential downpours, the game could not start on time. Rather than rescheduling the game, the umpires delayed the start for five hours and twenty-six minutes before it finally got under way. Michael Kay, the Yankees play-by-play man, repeatedly explained to the audience that the decision on calling the game was in the umpires' hands.

1: Was Kay correct?

No. While most people assume that this would be an umpire's call, Rule 3.10(a) provides that the home team manager is the "sole judge" on whether to start a game because of "unsuitable weather conditions." Some unwritten exceptions exist to this rule, but they did not apply here. As crew chief Charlie Reliford stated, "I had no say in this. Not until after the All-Star break." Reliford meant that, although not explicitly stated in the *Official Baseball Rules*, the umpires can make the decision if the game occurs after the All-Star break and is the final series of the season between two teams. To add insult to injury and complete a truly miserable day for Yankees fans, the Nationals shut out the Yankees.

2: Say that the downpour started between games of a doubleheader. Would that make a difference?

Yes. Rule 3.10(b) provides that in this instance the decision is left up to the umpire in chief of the first game. The rules do not make clear why the decision-maker changes between games of a doubleheader. Of course, in this day and age, doubleheaders are virtually nonexistent anyway, except when a team is forced to schedule one because of a previously canceled game.

3.3 Regulation and suspended games

On June 1, 2001, the Yankees played the Indians in New York. The line score looked like this:

	1	2	3	4	5	6	R	H	E
Indians	0	0	0	1	4	2	**X**	**10**	**3**
Yankees	1	1	1	1	0	0	**4**	**5**	**2**

The Indians pitching lines looked like this:

	IP	H	R	ER	BB	SO
CC Sabathia	4	4	4	3	5	2
Ricardo Rincón	1	1	0	0	0	0

Indians reliever Ricardo Rincón was pitching to the first batter in the bottom of the sixth when the game was called because of rain. The Yankees thus did not bat in the bottom of the sixth.

1: Which of the following is correct?

A. The Indians win because they were ahead after the last complete inning.

B. It's not an official game because the Indians had an extra half-inning and scored in that half-inning.

C. The game gets replayed in its entirety.

D. The game picks up exactly where it left off.

E. The game picks up as if five full innings had been played.

The correct answer is A. Under Rule 4.10(c), a called game is a regulation game (1) if five innings have been completed; (2) if the home team has scored more runs in four or four and a fraction half-innings than the visiting team has scored in five completed half-innings; (3) if the home team scores one or more runs in its half of the fifth inning to tie the score. From this, we may conclude that this was a regulation game because it went more than five innings. While it is true that the Indians scored two runs in the top of the sixth, that made no difference because they were ahead 5–4 after five full innings.

2: Note that an "X" was placed where the Indians' run total should be. Should that "X" be a five or a seven?

It should be a seven. We know that the game is a regulation game, and under Rule 4.11, the score of a regulation game is the total number of runs scored by each team at the moment the game ends.

3: On June 28, 2007, the Yankees were playing the Orioles in Baltimore. In the top of the eighth, Derek Jeter was on second with two outs when the rains came. The umpires decided that the game could not be completed that night. The box score at the time looked like this:

	1	2	3	4	5	6	7	8	R
NYY	1	0	1	1	0	0	1	4	**8**
BAL	2	0	0	0	0	0	4		**6**

Which of the following is correct?

A. The Orioles win because they were ahead after the last complete inning.

B. The Yankees win because five full innings had been played.

C. The game should be replayed in its entirety.

D. The game should pick up exactly where it left off.

E. The game should pick up as if seven full innings had been played.

The correct answer is D. We start with the question of whether the game was a "regulation game" to begin with. Under Rule 4.10(c), if a game is called, it is a regulation game, if (1) five innings have been completed or if the home team has scored more runs in four or four and a fraction half-innings than the visiting team has scored in five completed half-innings; or (2) if the home team scores one or more runs in its half of the fifth inning to tie the score. From this, we may conclude that it was a regulation game because it went more than five innings.

We then turn to Rule 4.12(a)(5), which provides that a game becomes a suspended game to be completed at a future date if the game is terminated by "weather, if a regulation game is called while an inning is in progress and before the inning is completed, and the visiting team has scored one or more runs to take the lead, and the home team has not retaken the lead." This is just what happened in the Orioles-Yankees game—the Yankees were trailing after seven complete innings but had taken the lead in the top of the eighth. Therefore, it's treated as a suspended game.

Finally, we turn to the new Rule 4.12(c), which answers the question by providing that a suspended game is resumed exactly where the original game left off, as if the original game had continued.

Rules 4.10 and 4.12 were also involved in the fifth game of the 2008 World Series between the Phillies and the Tampa Rays. Although the Phillies were leading 2–1 after five complete innings in a driving rainstorm, the umpires decided that the game should continue. The Rays scored a run in the top of the sixth to tie the game, but the officials decided that the weather was simply too inclement to continue past the top of the sixth.

Rule 4.10(d) provides that if a regulation game is called with the score tied (which was not the Yankees-Orioles situation), it becomes a suspended game under Rule 4.12. Therefore, the final innings were played two nights later and the game picked up exactly where it left off, with the Phils batting in the bottom of the sixth. They wound up winning only their second championship in over 125 years.

In an interesting footnote to the Phils-Rays World Series, say that the top of the sixth had not been played. One would think that, given Rule 4.10(c) mentioned above, since the Phils were leading 2–1 after five full innings, the game would have been considered a regulation game and the Phils would have won it right then and there. But Commissioner Bud Selig in essence threw out the rule-book and indicated that the game would have to be completed no matter what. Selig said that he made a judgment call before the game began and informed officials of both teams that he would not allow a rain-shortened game to take place in the World Series, no matter how long it meant waiting. "I have to use my judgment. It's not a way to end the World Series," Selig said. However, in postgame interviews both teams made it clear that neither was aware that Selig had made this unilateral pregame rule modification.

3.4 Game-ending scoring rules

On October 16, 2008, the Red Sox were playing the Rays in Game 5 of the American League Championship Series in Fenway Park, with the Rays ahead three games to one. Going into the bottom of the seventh, the Red Sox were trailing 7–0 but came back to tie it 7–7 with 4 runs in the seventh and 3 in the eighth. With the score tied in the bottom of the ninth and two outs, the Red Sox had Kevin Youkilis on second and Jason Bay on first. J. D. Drew then hit a book-rule double that bounced over the right-field fence.

1: What is the final score of the game? Would the answer be different if there had been runners on second and third instead?

The final score would be 8–7 in both cases. Under Rule 4.11(c), the game would end immediately when the winning run was scored.

2: In the first situation above, what if Drew had hit a home run, and in his excitement, he passed Bay on the base path? Who is credited with what and what is the final score?

It depends on whether the run scored before or after Drew passed Bay. If before, then Youkilis's run would count and the Sox would win 8–7. While the rule is not clear on this point, Drew would presumably be credited for the last base he legally touched before overtaking Bay, even though he hit the ball out of the park. If Drew passed Bay before the run scored, then that would be the third out of the inning and no runs would be deemed to have scored, per Rule 7.08(h).

3: On August 19, 2011, the Nationals were playing the Phillies. With the score tied 4–4 in the bottom of the ninth, and the bases loaded, Ryan Zimmerman hit a home run. What was the final score of the game?

It would be 8–4. Under an exception to Rule 4.11(c), when a home run is hit in this situation, all runs would score.

3.5 Suspended games

On June 24, 1994, the Yankees were playing the Indians in Cleveland. It was a dark and stormy night! Three rain delays totaled over three hours. After seven full innings, the Yanks were ahead 9–5 and the clock had rolled past 1:00 a.m. The umps called it a suspended game. The next day (in an even harder rainstorm) the Yanks won the completed game 11–6. In the early-morning hours between the two parts of the game, the Indians had placed pitcher Steve Farr on the disabled list and recalled pitcher Jerry DiPoto to take his place. DiPoto had been recovering from thyroid cancer all season.

1: Were the Indians permitted to use DiPoto when the game resumed given that he was not on their roster when the game started?

Not only were the Indians permitted to use DiPoto (over the Yankees' objections), but they did. Not that it mattered much. He pitched the ninth and gave up two earned runs. Rule 4.12(c) specifically permits in these circumstances the use of a player who was not with the club when the game started.

2: Would it have made a difference if Farr—the player whom DiPoto replaced—had already been used in the game and thus was ineligible?

It would have made no difference. In fact, the Indians *had* used Farr earlier in the game. Rule 4.12(c) specifies that the new player can be used even if the player he is replacing is no longer eligible.

3: Why wouldn't the game have been considered a regulation game in the first place, since the teams had played seven full innings by the time it was called?

Although the game had repeatedly been delayed due to poor weather, the reason the game was suspended was not because of the weather—it was not raining then—but because Rule 4.12(a)(2) permits each league to establish a time limit. In the American League, a rule provided that no inning could start past 1:00 a.m. If the game was called because of poor weather, it would have been a regulation nonsuspended game. The only exception to this rule is if the regulation game is called on account of weather during an inning in which the visiting team has taken the lead and the home team has not retaken the lead, per Rule 4.12(a)(5). This is exactly what took place in the Orioles-Yankees game discussed above.

3.6 Forfeits

A game can be forfeited for a number of reasons, including unfitness of the playing field (Rule 3.11); unauthorized persons entering the playing field during a game and not leaving (Rule 3.18); and failing to appear on the field after the umpire in chief has called "Play" or refusing to continue play during a game (Rule 4.15).

1: Which of the following has not been the basis for a forfeited game in the last fifty years?

A. A team mistakenly believed that a day game was scheduled as a night game and thus failed to appear at the proper time.

B. The home team was offering ten-cent beers and drunken fans swarmed the field and attacked an opposing player.

C. A manager pulled his team off the field and refused to let them play again after an umpire refused to remove a tarpaulin from the bullpen area.

D. On a ball-giveaway day, hundreds of balls were thrown onto the field after a disputed call by the umpire.

E. To protest disco music, hundreds of fans rushed onto the field after a DJ set off a bonfire of disco records in center field.

The correct answer is A. The details of the last five forfeits (the last four of which are mentioned above) are as follows (quoting from www.retrosheet.org/forfeits.htm):

September 30, 1971—New York at Washington—AL. The last American League game played in Washington ended in a forfeit win for the New York Yankees. The Senators were leading 7–5 with two out in the ninth inning when souvenir hunters stormed onto the field. The field could not be cleared, and the umpire had no choice but to call the game. The fans had been unruly most of the night since the club was moving to Texas for the 1972 season. Some had run onto the field in the eighth inning, delaying the game.

June 4, 1974—Texas at Cleveland—AL. It was ten-cent beer night in Cleveland. The Indians had just tied the score at 5 in the ninth inning and had the winning run at third when hundreds of fans jumped the right-field fence and attacked Rangers right fielder Jeff Burroughs and other players. Umpire in chief Nestor Chylak, who was struck on the head, declared the game a forfeit win for Texas. Six fans were arrested.

September 15, 1977—Baltimore at Toronto—AL. The Orioles were behind 4–0 in the bottom of the fifth inning when manager Earl Weaver asked umpire Marty Springstead to remove a tarpaulin that was covering the Toronto bullpen area. The game was being played in a light rain, and Weaver felt that the tarpaulin posed an injury risk to his left fielder. The umpire refused, and Weaver pulled his team from the field. Springstead waited fifteen minutes for the team to retake the field before declaring the forfeit.

July 12, 1979—Detroit at Chicago—AL. In the most ill-fated promotion in baseball history, thousands of fans overran the Comiskey Park playing field during "Disco Demolition Night" between games of a doubleheader. They caused the Chicago White Sox to forfeit the second game, after having lost to Detroit 4–1 in the first. Umpire Dave Phillips declared the field unplayable after an hour-and-sixteen-minute delay and postponed the game. Later, American League president Lee MacPhail ruled the game a forfeit win for the Tigers.

August 10, 1995—St. Louis at Los Angeles—NL. Baseballs were distributed to fans as they entered Dodger Stadium. The game was delayed in the seventh inning when some fans started throwing their souvenir baseballs onto the field. In the bottom of the ninth with St. Louis leading 2–1, the first batter, Raúl Mondesí, was called out on strikes. He started to complain to umpire Jim Quick and was ejected. Dodger manager Tommy Lasorda was ejected as well. The fans became upset and started throwing the balls onto the field again. The umpires brought the Cardinal team in from the field while the grounds crew cleared the field. When play resumed, the fans again bombarded the field, and the umpires forfeited the game in favor of St. Louis.

2: What is the score of a forfeited game?

A. No score is given and the nonforfeiting team is simply given credit for the win.

B. 1–0.

C. 9–0.

D. The actual score if the nonforfeiting team is ahead; otherwise no score given.

The answer is C, based on the definition of a forfeited game.

3.7 Obligation of groundskeepers to cover field

On April 30, 2005, the Mets were playing the Nationals in Washington. This was Washington's first year back in baseball after a thirty-five-year hiatus. The game was played at the decrepit RFK Stadium. The weather was poor, and in the sixth inning the umpires called a thirty-minute rain delay. The game then resumed, but between the eighth and ninth innings, with the Nationals leading 5–3, a downpour began. The grounds crew fought hard, but with little success, to wrestle the waterlogged tarp onto the field. The efforts of the grounds crew to cover the field drew laughter and applause from the crowd. Finally, after thirty-eight minutes, the tarp was on, but the damage had been done. The game was called just six minutes later. Adding to the Mets' agitation, the rain stopped shortly afterward. "I just thought that they were understaffed and undermanned. If they could have gotten the tarp back on, anything could have happened," said Mets manager Willie Randolph. The Mets filed a protest with the National League.

1: What remedy were the Mets seeking that could theoretically be supported by the rules?

A. That the Nationals forfeit the entire game.

B. That the game be halted and completed at a later date, picking up at the point it left off.

C. That the game be replayed in its entirety.

D. That the game be replayed from the sixth inning, which is when the first rain delay occurred, which caused the field to be covered.

The answer is A. The Mets cited Rule 4.16, which provides that a game is forfeited to the visitors if, after it has been halted, the groundskeepers fail to prepare the field to resume play when ordered by the umpires to do so. (The rule actually uses the word "suspended" rather than "halted," but presumably means "halted" since suspension of play is not the same as a suspended game.) Of course, this game had not actually been suspended, but the Mets argued that there should be no difference between the failure of the groundskeepers to prepare the field whether in a suspended game or a postponed game. Though the Mets had a good argument on this point, their protest was denied.

As noted, Rule 4.16 by its terms only applies to "suspended" games. However, a game that has merely been temporarily called due to bad weather, such as the Mets-Nationals game, is not a suspended game but a halted game. Based on Rule 4.12(b)(1), a game that has been "suspended" does not even resume until just before the next scheduled game between the two clubs. This could mean the next day (at a minimum) or perhaps weeks or months in the future.

Chapter 4

Putting the Ball in Play

4.1 Ball touching/hitting base coach/umpire

On April 22, 2002, the White Sox were playing the Indians. When Omar Vizquel of the Tribe tried to steal second, White Sox catcher Sandy Alomar's throw bounced off second base umpire Brian Runge and caromed away. Vizquel continued on to third base. Runge ruled the play dead the instant the ball touched him and ordered Vizquel back to second. To make sure that Runge got the call right, the whole umpiring crew, led by chief Chuck Meriwether, held an impromptu meeting. After consulting with one another, they stuck by their call.

1: Did they get the call right?

No. Rule 5.08 clearly provides that if a pitched or thrown ball touches an umpire, the ball remains alive and in play. Umpires are treated as part of the ground. After discovering their error, Meriwether called Tribe manager Charlie Manuel to apologize the next day.

2: What if instead, Vizquel had been trying to steal third, and Alomar's throw hit the third-base coach and again bounced away. Could Vizquel continue on and score?

If it accidentally hit him, it's the same situation as if it hit the umpire. However, if it's considered intentional, then it's called coach's interference and the runner is out.

3: Section (c) of the definition of "interference" provides in part that umpire's interference occurs when "(1) a plate umpire hinders, impedes or prevents a catcher's throw attempting to prevent a stolen base or (2) when a fair ball touches an umpire before touching a fielder." Doesn't that mean that the umpiring crew got the call right in the Alomar/Vizquel play above? After all, Runge inadvertently hindered, impeded, or prevented Alomar's throw from reaching second base. Also, the ball touched Runge.

No, for two reasons. When reading the above definition of "interference," it would appear that it applies to the Alomar/Vizquel play. However, it is clear that the first part of the definition refers to the home plate umpire only. It refers to interfering with the catcher while he is making the throw—not when a cleanly thrown ball arrives at a given base. The second part of the definition of "interference" requires being hit by a batted ball and not by a thrown ball. In addition, as a practical matter, the second part of the definition applies only to the second-base umpire, since he positions himself on the infield side of second base on steal situations. The "wing" umpires (first and third) are always behind the infielders.

4.2 Ball hitting player or umpire

In Game 6 of the 1998 ALCS between the Indians and Yankees, in the top of the fifth inning, Cleveland had Kenny Lofton on first and Enrique Wilson on third. Omar Vizquel hit a shot up the middle that struck Ted Hendry, the second-base umpire, who was standing on the infield side of second base.

1: Which of the following statements is correct?

A. The ball is live and the Yankee fielders have to track it down.

B. The information about where Hendry was standing is irrelevant.

C. The ball is dead, Vizquel gets first base, and all other runners advance.

D. The ball is dead, Vizquel gets first base, and only Lofton advances.

The correct answer is D by virtue of Rule 5.09(f), which provides that "the ball becomes dead and runners advance one base, or return to their bases, without liability to be put out when . . . a fair ball touches a runner or an umpire on fair territory before it touches an infielder including the pitcher, or touches an umpire before it is passed an infielder other than the pitcher; runners advance, if forced." Only Lofton advances because he is the only runner forced to advance on the play. B is not correct because the Comment to Rule 5.09(f) states that if a fair ball touches an umpire working in the infield after it has bounded past, or over, the pitcher, it is a dead ball. C is not correct because Wilson was not forced to advance. Rule 7.04(b) states that runners advance only when forced when umpire's interference is called.

2: Would the result be different if the ball had ricocheted off the pitcher and then hit the umpire?

Yes. If the ball hits the pitcher *before* hitting the umpire, that constitutes an exception to the "dead ball" rule set forth set forth in Rule in 5.09(f). In that situation, the ball remains alive and in play.

As a side note, the Comment to Rule 5.09(f) states that the ball is dead if it hits an umpire "working in the infield." However, Rule 5.09(f) itself makes no reference to where the umpire is standing and requires only that the ball touch the umpire "before it has passed an infielder." Presumably, if a shift is on, and the second baseman is playing in the short outfield, the second base umpire may no longer be "working in the infield" but is nevertheless in front of the second baseman. Presumably the Rule 5.09(f) applies here as well.

4.3 Ball getting caught in mask or gear

On August 9, 2005, the Indians were playing the Royals. In the third inning, with two outs, with the Royals' Ángel Berroa on third and Donnie Murphy at bat, Indians pitcher Cliff Lee threw a pitch that got stuck in the chest protector of catcher Víctor Martínez.

1: Assuming Murphy did not swing at the ball, and it wasn't strike three or ball four, what is the result of the play?

Berroa scores on the play. Rule 5.09(g). This rule provides that when a pitched ball lodges in the umpire's or the catcher's mask or paraphernalia, and remains out of play, the ball becomes dead and runners advance one base.

2: Would the answer be different if the ball stuck in the umpire's mask instead?

No.

3: Say that Murphy swung and missed with two strikes and the ball lodged in the umpire's gear. Is it a strikeout?

No. The Comment to Rule 5.09(g) explains that if on the third strike, a pitch lodges in the umpire's or the catcher's mask or paraphernalia and remains out of play, then the batter is entitled to first base and all runners advance one base. If, however, the same situation had occurred on a foul tip, it would simply be a foul ball.

4.4 Positioning of fielders

1: True or false? When the ball is put in play, all fielders must be positioned entirely in fair territory.

The answer is false because the catcher's box is entirely in foul territory. However, it is true as to all other fielders.

Chapter 5

The Batter

5.1 Stepping out of the batter's box

On June 23, 2007, the Red Sox were playing the Padres. Sox catcher Doug Mirabelli stepped into the batter's box for his first at bat of the evening and waited for the first offering from Padre starter Chris Young. Greeted with a chorus of boos from the hometown fans, Mirabelli held up his hand for "time" and stepped out of the batter's box. Young delivered a belt-high fastball and home plate umpire Doug Eddings signaled strike one.

1: Did Eddings act within his authority?

Yes. Under the Comment to Rule 6.02(b), the batter leaves the batter's box at the risk of having a strike delivered and called, unless he requests and gets the umpire to call "time." The batter cannot step in and out of the batter's box at will. It should also be noted that no one other than an umpire has a right to call "time." While a batter certainly has the right to request that the umpire call "time," the umpire can grant or deny that request at his discretion. It's not automatic.

In the above play, as Mirabelli was reminded, the batter *requests* time-out; the umpire actually calls it. Once the pitcher comes set, a batter steps out at risk of having a pitch called a strike. This rule serves several functions, including keeping up the pace of the game, avoiding intentional delays of the game, and, perhaps most important, avoiding injury to a pitcher attempting to shut down a pitch while in motion.

Rule 6.02(b) comes up anytime a batter steps out of the box without "time" being called. In *The Rules and Lore of Baseball*, Rich Marazzi points to a number of instances in which the rule was invoked. Frank Robinson got called out on strikes after stepping out of the box to argue a previous call on June 1, 1956. And in 1920, the year Ray Chapman became the first and only major leaguer to die in a game, he was called out after he walked to the dugout with two strikes while facing Walter Johnson's heat. Ump Billy Evans yelled to Chapman, "You got another strike coming." Chapman allegedly responded, "You can have it. It wouldn't do me any good."

2: Could one of the Padre fielders have asked for "time" just before the pitch was thrown, thus nullifying the strike?

The *Official Baseball Rules* does not prohibit a player from asking for time. Rule 5.10 lists a series of events for which the umpire "shall call time," but the request of a player is not one of those events. This is up to the umpire's discretion. In addition, while the Comment to Rule 6.02(b) above discusses a batter's request for time, there is no equivalent provision in the rules for fielders or runners. We know in practice, however, that runners ask for (and receive) time routinely, especially after just having stolen a base. It would appear that fielders have the same right.

In some situations a fielder's request for "time" has altered the course of a game. A noteworthy example occurred on April 10, 1976, when the Brewers were playing the Yankees. Milwaukee was trailing, 9–6, going into the bottom of the ninth inning at County Stadium, when Don Money hit a bases-loaded blast off Yankee pitcher Dave Pagan. The Brewers and their fans were jumping for joy, thinking they had won the game on Money's walk-off home run. But the party came to an abrupt end when they realized that first-base ump Jim McKean had granted Yankee first baseman Chris Chambliss "time" just prior to the pitch.

After a wild argument between the Brewers and the umps, Money hit a sacrifice fly to make it 9-7, which became the final score.

5.2 Batter not taking position in batter's box

1: Is it possible for a game to end under the following circumstances: (1) The pitcher does not throw a pitch (i.e., no walk-off hit, no bases-loaded walk, no balk, no passed ball, no wild pitch); (2) there are no base runners (i.e., no pickoff, no steal of home, no appeal of base-running errors, etc.); and (3) the game is not forfeited or called because of weather or shortened for any reason (i.e., there are a full twenty-seven outs)?

Hint before answer: The above situation nearly occurred on April 19, 2002, when the Mets were playing the Expos in Montreal. In the top of the ninth, with Montreal ahead 5–3 and two outs, Timo Pérez was at bat for the Mets. With a 1-1 count, pitcher Matt Herges threw a pitch that Pérez thought was out of the strike zone, but home plate umpire Mark Carlson called a strike.

Under Rule 6.02(c), if the batter refuses to take his position in the batter's box, the umpire shall call a strike on him. In the above situation, after Carlson called the 1-1 pitch a strike, Pérez turned away in disbelief. He stood outside the batter's box, signaling with his left hand how low he thought the pitch had been. Carlson then ordered Pérez to get back in the box. Pérez did, but then stepped out again. Carlson said he directed Pérez to step back in, and when Pérez did not comply, Carlson ordered Herges to pitch.

Pérez heard his bench yell for him to get in the box. Perez stepped in, raised his head just as Herges was in his windup, and fouled off the pitch. He eventually hit a double, but the next hitter grounded out to end the game. Crew chief John Hirschbeck later said that it was decided not to call an automatic strike on Pérez because he judged Pérez to have entered the box simultaneously with Carlson's directive to Herges. Had that not occurred, however, Carlson could have called an automatic strike on Pérez, which would have been the third strike, the third out, and the end of the game. Under the prior rules, the pitcher would have had to at least throw to the batter, but now the umpire can call an automatic strikeout.

On April 25, 2007, in Baltimore, Red Sox batter Julio Lugo did not return to the batter's box when directed to do so by plate umpire Ángel Hernández. Hernández ordered the O's pitcher, Daniel Cabrera, to pitch and called a strike on Lugo. Again, Lugo refused to enter the box, and Hernández ordered Cabrera to pitch and called, "Strike two." Finally, Lugo stepped in. As noted, Hernández did not have to order Cabrera to pitch since, under new legislation for the 2007 season, the plate umpire is empowered to call an automatic strike on a batter who refuses to enter the box.

5.3 Third strike not caught by catcher

On April 29, 2007, the Mariners were playing the Royals. In the seventh inning, with two out and runners on second and third, Seattle second baseman Willie Bloomquist fouled a pitch back on a 3-2 count. The ball lodged in the chest protector of the Royals' catcher, John Buck, who then picked it out. The ball never touched the ground.

1: Is it a strikeout?

No, it is a foul ball. Rule 6.05(b) provides that a batter is out if a third strike is "legally caught" by the catcher. But what does that mean? The Comment to the rule explains that if the ball lodges in the catcher's clothing or paraphernalia, it's not a legal catch. That's what happened here, and that was the call made by home plate umpire Chris Guccione after conferring with his crew. It was a key moment in the game. After Guccione's call, Bloomquist hit a double, which scored the two base runners with what stood up as the winning runs.

2: What if the pitch had hit the umpire and was caught by the catcher on the rebound?

Still no third strike. This would be a foul ball.

3: What if Buck had smothered the ball against his chest protector without the ball hitting the ground? Which of the following answers is correct?

A. It's a strikeout.

B. It's not a strikeout.

C. It's a strikeout only if the ball touched Buck's hand or mitt first.

D. None of the above.

The correct answer is C. Under the Comment to the rule, a ball smothered against the catcher's body or chest protector is an out only if it touches the catcher's glove or hand first.

5.4 Third strike not caught with runner on first and less than two outs

On August 3, 2005, the Phils were playing the Cubs. The Phils had the bases loaded and one out with the score tied 3–3. Pat Burrell of the Phils, batting with a full count, swung and missed a pitch that got past Cubs catcher Michael Barrett.

1: Is Burrell out?

A. Yes.

B. Not if he can beat the throw to first.

The answer is A. Rule 6.05(c) provides that the batter is automatically out on a play like this, namely if first base is occupied and there are less than two outs.

2: Since Burrell is out, is there any purpose to his running to first base?

Yes. If the catcher is unaware of the rule and makes an errant throw to first in trying to throw out Burrell, the other runners could advance. In these situations, the onus is on the defense to know that the batter-runner is out.

3: In the above play, Jimmy Rollins, the runner on third, broke for home, then stopped halfway down the line, perhaps unsure of what he should be doing. Which one or more of the following statements is true?

A. Barrett can simply step on home plate to force out Rollins.

B. Barrett can throw down to third, and if the ball gets there before Rollins gets back to third and Rollins is tagged, then Rollins would be retired.

C. The play is considered dead.

The correct answer is B. Choice A is not correct because it's not a force play. Since Burrell is out anyway, Rollins is not forced to run, but if he does, he must be tagged out by Barrett. (Later that evening on ESPN's *Baseball Tonight*, Harold Reynolds, apparently confused about the rule, stated that Barrett should have stepped on the plate to retire Rollins, which is choice A above and incorrect.) Choice C is not correct because the ball remains alive. While not forced to run, the runners are free to go at their peril. Whether Rollins hesitated between third and home because he was uncertain about the rules is anyone's guess. As it happens, he scored on the play, and because it was the bottom of the ninth, the Phillies won, 4–3.

Note that Rule 6.05(c) only applies if there are less than two outs and a runner on first.

The purpose of this rule is similar to the purpose of the infield fly rule, namely to prevent a fielder (in this case the catcher) from intentionally dropping the ball with men on base and thus setting up a double-play situation. Without the rule, Barrett could have intentionally dropped the ball, retrieved it, stepped on home plate to retire Rollins (being forced to run), then fired down to first to complete the easy double play on Burrell.

Strategy for catchers: Clever catchers, if aware of this rule, have opportunities to trap unsuspecting base runners, especially in a bases-loaded situation or other perceived force situations. If the catcher lets the ball roll away a little, the runner on third may think he's forced to run home. If he does, it's not a force play, and the catcher can simply tag the runner when he arrives at home.

5.5 Ball hitting batter who swings

On April 22, 2001, the Dodgers were playing the Padres in Los Angeles. With the score tied 6–6 in the bottom of the tenth and the bases loaded and two outs, San Diego's Jay Witasick threw a two-strike breaking ball to Tom Goodwin. The ball hit Goodwin but he swung at it.

1: Which of the following is the result of the play?

A. It's a strikeout.

B. It's a strikeout only if the umpire decides, in his discretion, that Goodwin did not make a good faith effort to get out of the way of the ball.

On September 23, 2008, Mets pitcher Johan Santana squared to bunt but instead swung away. The bat broke on Santana's swing. Both the ball and a portion of the broken bat flew past the pitcher's mound. As Cubs shortstop Ronny Cedeño was about to field the ball, it hit the rolling bat again and bounced away from Cedeño. Is Santana safe or out? *New York Daily News Archive/Getty Images*

C. Whether he swings or not, Goodwin is awarded first base and the winning run scores.

D. It's treated the same as a third strike that gets by the catcher, who then has the opportunity to retrieve the ball and throw out Goodwin at first, which would end the inning.

The answer is A, per Rule 6.05(f). Being hit by a pitch makes no difference if the batter swings and misses, regardless of the count. When the umpire judges that the batter offered at the pitch and he is hit by it, the "offering," or the swing, takes precedence over the hit-by-pitch. If there are two strikes on the batter, he is out and the ball is dead.

5.6 Ball hitting bat a second time

On September 23, 2008, the Mets were playing the Cubs at Shea Stadium. With one out in the fifth inning and a man on base, Mets pitcher Johan Santana came to the plate. He saw the corner infielders move in, squared to bunt, but instead swung away. The bat broke on Santana's swing. Both the ball and a portion of the broken bat flew past the pitcher's mound. As shortstop Ronny Cedeño was about to field the ball, it hit the rolling bat again and bounced away from Cedeño.

1: Is Santana safe or out?

He is safe. While a batter is expected to have control over his whole bat, he is not expected to have control over a broken bat, which is like an act of God. Because a broken bat cannot cause interference, the ball is alive and in play. Santana therefore had a single. A video of the play can be seen on the Internet.

2: What if Santana's bat had not broken?

When the bat hits the ball a second time in fair territory, the batter is out due to interference per Rule 6.05(h). The batter is expected to control his whole bat. The ball is dead and no runners may advance. Note also that Santana's intent is irrelevant. He is out regardless.

3: Would it make any difference if the (unbroken) bat had come to a complete stop and the ball then rolled into it? Would that still be interference on the batter?

No. In this case, the ball is alive and in play. A good example of this happened in the first game of the 2010 NLDS between the Phillies and the Reds. Roy Halladay had a no-hitter going for the Phils through 8⅔ innings. The last Reds batter, Brandon Phillips, hit a dribbler that rolled a few feet in front of home plate. Phillips dropped his bat on the way to first, and it came to a stop a few feet away from home plate just before the ball rolled into it. In this case, since the ball hit a bat that had come to a stop, it remained alive and in play. However, Phils catcher Carlos Ruiz made the adjustment and threw out Phillips to complete the no-hitter.

4: Say a batted ball hits a batting helmet in fair territory. Which of the following statements is true?

A. The ball is considered dead when it hits the helmet and no runners can advance farther.

B. The ball is not dead and the runners can continue to advance as far as they are able.

The correct answer is B. If the batted ball had hit the helmet in foul territory, it would be considered a foul ball.

5: A thrown ball hits a batting helmet. Which of the following statements is true?

A. The ball is considered dead when it hits the helmet and no runners can advance farther.

B. The ball is not dead and the runners can continue to advance as far as they are able.

C. It depends on whether the ball hit the helmet in fair or foul territory.

The correct answer is still B, as it was with the previous quiz. The third choice was thrown in as a red herring.

5.7 Tie goes to the batter-runner?

On July 8, 2009, the Dodgers were playing the Mets. Mark Loretta of the Dodgers ripped a ground ball down the first-base line. It hit first base and popped high in the air. Mets first baseman Daniel Murphy reacted quickly to the deflection. He ran toward second base, picked up the ball with his right hand, and, in an incredible move, flipped it behind his back to pitcher Bobby Parnell, who was covering first base. The ball and Loretta appeared to arrive at first base at the exact same moment.

1: Is Loretta safe or out?

The fact that the ball hit first base is not an issue since the bases are clearly in fair territory. What about the tie? One of the favorite topics in the baseball blogosphere is the derivation of the maxim "tie goes to the runner." Putting aside the esoteric issue of whether there can be an "exact" tie, nowhere in the rules will one find "ties goes to the runner." In umpiring, there is no such thing as a tie. The concept is nevertheless in the rules, though by implication only. Rule 6.05(j) provides that a batter is out when "after a third strike or after he hits a fair ball, he or first base is tagged before he touches first base." In my view, if first base has to be tagged "before" the batter-runner gets there, it stands to reason that if the batter-runner and the ball arrive at the same time, then the batter-runner must be safe. In the above play, Loretta was actually called out. Murphy's great play can be seen on the Internet, and it really is too close to call.

5.8 Not having both feet in the batter's box

On August 6, 1992, the Red Sox were playing the Yankees. In the seventh inning, with John Marzano on first, Sox shortstop John Valentin came up and hit the ball in fair territory. Home plate umpire Tim McClelland called him out without a fielder ever making a play on the ball.

1: Assuming no interference issues and no issues with Valentin's bat, how is this possible?

Hint: Valentin was attempting a bunt and run, trying not only to advance Marzano but also to get on base himself.

The umpire ruled that one of Valentin's feet was on the ground outside the batter's box, and under Rule 6.06(a), a batter is out when he hits the ball with one or both feet outside the batter's box. The batter's foot must be completely outside the box (and on the ground) for this rule to apply. The lines are part of the box. Similarly, in the top of the third inning of the Phils-Padres game on April 20, 2012, Juan Pierre was called out for making contact with the ball with one foot outside the batter's box.

Batter's boxes have measured six feet by four feet since Grover Cleveland was president in 1886. They have been around as long as peanuts, popcorn, and Cracker Jack. Their purpose is to restrict the batter from taking unfair advantage of the pitcher or the defensive team.

Rule 6.06(a) is not frequently invoked. When it is, it tends to be on bunt plays, when the batter is trying to get out of the batter's box as quickly as possible and is not taking a full swing at the ball. On May 22, 2011, the Nationals were playing the Orioles. The Nationals' Roger Bernadina led off the game with what appeared to be a drag-bunt single, but plate umpire Todd Tichenor overturned it because Bernadina had made contact with the ball with a foot on home plate. Nationals' manager Jim Riggleman argued the call and was ejected. Following the game Riggleman said, "That's a call you never see get made. I got irritated." Riggleman is right, but it is a call that should be made more frequently.

Ironically, two of baseball's greatest sluggers—Hank Aaron and Babe Ruth—violated this rule. Aaron, playing for the Milwaukee Braves, lost a home run on August 18, 1965, while facing St. Louis Cardinals southpaw Curt Simmons at Sportsman's Park in St. Louis. Simmons delivered a slow breaking pitch and Hammerin' Hank walked up on the pitch and went yard. By doing so, he took unfair advantage of the pitcher since he could hit the pitch before it possibly broke. Plate umpire Chris Pelekoudas judged that Aaron's left foot was on the ground, completely out of the batter's box, when he hit the pitch, and thus he called the Braves' slugger out. "His left foot was at least three feet out when he swung," said Pelekoudas. The infraction caused Aaron to finish his career with 755 home runs rather than 756.

As for Ruth, let's go back to July 26, 1926, when the Cleveland Indians played the New York Yankees. Indians pitcher Joe Shaute tried to give Ruth an intentional bases-loaded walk with two outs in the sixth inning. But the Babe impatiently and foolishly stepped across the plate and fouled off what would have been ball four. Umpire Brick Owens called him out for making contact with the ball with one foot on the ground outside the batter's box.

2: Would the call have been different if McClellan believed that Valentin's foot was directly on the chalk line?

Yes. The rule requires that the batter's foot (or feet) be entirely outside the box and on the ground for the batter to be out.

3: Would the call have been different if McClellan thought that Valentin's foot was completely outside the batter's box but in midair?

Yes. The batter's foot must be on the ground completely outside the box for the rule to apply.

4: What if part of the batter's foot is on the line of the batter's box and the other part is touching home plate when he makes contact with a pitched ball? Should the batter be called out?

No. As long as part of the batter's foot is touching the batter's box, he is legal.

On occasion, the batter's boxes have not been properly chalked in relation to home plate. On April 13, 2012, the Chicago White Sox hosted the Detroit Tigers at U.S. Cellular Field. Miguel Cabrera of the Tigers is known to prefer standing deep in the box. He stepped to the plate with two outs in the top of the first inning and took his normal position in relation to the plate. But his back foot was entirely out of the batter's box, a violation of the rule that states that the batter must have both feet entirely within the box when he assumes his position. In addition, no part of either foot may extend beyond the outer edge of the lines defining the box.

White Sox catcher A. J. Pierzynski was quick to point out Cabrera's illegal position to plate umpire Adrian Johnson. Cabrera, a skilled and experienced hitter, claimed the boxes were not properly aligned. He was right. Crew chief Gary Cederstrom confirmed that the box was drawn too far forward and stopped the game for the grounds crew to rechalk the lines.

The position of the batter's box is important to a hitter who wants to stay as far back as possible so as to have an extra split second to react to the pitch. Or, in some cases, a hitter might want to be as far up toward the pitcher as possible to get an early start on a breaking pitch.

Once the grounds crew finally had it right, Cabrera stepped to the plate and flew out to right on the first pitch. Was this simply an error by the grounds crew, or was it intentional so as to keep Cabrera up in the box? This could have been an honest mistake, but it would be no surprise if the White Sox did some creative batter's-box tailoring in an attempt to neutralize Cabrera.

5.9 Hitter switching sides during an at bat/ambidextrous pitcher

On June 19, 2008, in a minor league game, the Staten Island Yankees were playing their crosstown rivals, the Brooklyn Cyclones. In the ninth inning, with Staten Island ahead 7–2, switch-hitter Ralph Henriquez came to the plate for the Cyclones with two outs and a man on first. On the mound for the Yankees, making his first minor league appearance, was Pat Venditte, who has the distinction of being the only "switch pitcher" in professional baseball. He had a glove specially made for him that has room for both a right thumb and a left thumb—i.e., a six-fingered glove. Henriquez took his place in the right-handed batter's box. When he saw this, Venditte put the glove on his left hand so he could pitch right-handed. Henriquez then walked over to the left-handed batter's box so he could hit left-handed. So Venditte prepared to pitch to Henriquez as a left-hander . . . and Henriquez switched back. The game was delayed for eight minutes while the pitcher and the hitter did their little dance and the umpires tried to sort it out. They ultimately ruled that Henriquez must first select the side of the plate from which he intended to hit, then Venditte could decide with which arm to pitch. It wound up being a righty-righty matchup. Venditte subsequently struck out a frustrated Henriquez (who slammed his bat against the dirt in anger) on four pitches to end the game.

1: How do the major league rules address this situation?

The most directly applicable Rule is 8.01(f), which requires the pitcher to indicate the hand with which he intends to pitch to the umpire in chief, the batter, and any runners. He may convey this by wearing his glove on the other hand while touching the pitcher's plate. The pitcher must then continue to throw with the same hand until the batter is retired or reaches base, or the pitcher suffers an injury. If injured, the pitcher cannot switch back again for the remainder of the game.

Some rules touch on the "switching" situation from the batter's perspective. Rule 6.06(b) says a batter is out for an illegal action if "he steps from the batter's box to the other side while the pitcher is in position ready to pitch." In addition, Rule 6.02(b) states that the batter shall not leave his position in the batter's box after the pitcher comes to set position or starts his windup. The "penalty" for this is simply that the pitcher can pitch and the umpire "shall call ball or strike as the case may be." However, Rule 6.06(b) provides that the batter is actually out if he steps from one batter's box to the other while the pitcher is in position and ready to pitch. Admittedly, if a batter simply steps backward out of the box, that would invoke Rule 6.02(b) and not Rule 6.06(b). However, if he crossed from one side of the plate to the other, it would invoke both rules. Then, under 6.02(b), the pitcher is free to pitch, but under Rule 6.06(b), the batter is out.

5.10 Using illegal bat

One June 3, 2003, the Cubs were playing Tampa (then known as the Devil Rays instead of the Rays). In the first inning, Sammy Sosa was up and his bat splintered as he hit a ground ball to second base.

Player	Team	Date	Suspension	Offense
Sammy Sosa	Chicago Cubs	June 3, 2003	8 games	Corked bat
Wilton Guerrero	Los Angeles Dodgers	June 1, 1997	8 games	Corked bat
Chris Sabo	Cincinnati Reds	July 29, 1996	7 games; Reds fined $25,000	Rubber balls in bat
Albert Belle	Cleveland Indians	July 15, 1994	7 games	Corked bat
Billy Hatcher	Houston Astros	August 31, 1987	10 days	Corked bat
Graig Nettles	New York Yankees	September 7, 1974	10 days	6 super balls in bat

Catcher Toby Hall retrieved the pieces and showed them to plate umpire Tim McClelland.

After huddling with his crew, McClelland said he saw a half-dollar-size piece of cork in the bat about halfway down the barrel. McClelland ejected the Cubs superstar for using a corked bat. Sosa said he had used the corked bat only in batting practice "to put on a show for the fans." Sosa said, "I'm just trying to go and get ready for the game, and I picked the wrong bat." Major league officials collected all seventy-six bats in Sosa's locker for inspection. Sosa guaranteed they would not find another corked bat. He was correct.

1: What are the umpire's options or obligations in such a situation?

He has no "options" per se. Sosa is automatically out and ejected from the game. Rule 6.06(d) prevents the use of any bat that the umpire feels "has been altered or tampered with in such a way to improve the distance factor or cause an unusual reaction on the baseball. This includes bats that are filled, flat surfaced, nailed, hollowed, grooved or covered with a substance such as paraffin, wax, etc." Interestingly, cork is not specifically mentioned.

2: On Sosa's grounder, a runner scored on the play. However, it did not count because the rule prohibits advancement on the bases. Say, however, that Sosa had instead hit into a double play when it was discovered that his bat was illegal. What would be the result then?

The double play would stand. All outs made on play involving an illegal bat stand.

3: Say that Sosa was up to bat and discovered to be using an illegal bat before the first pitch was thrown to him. Would this have made a difference?

No. Under the Comment to the rule, a batter shall be deemed to have attempted to use an illegal bat if he brings it to the batter's box.

4: Say that Sosa was in the on-deck circle and discovered to be using an illegal bat before the first pitch was thrown to him. Would this have made a difference?

Yes. By implication based on the Comment, if he has not brought the bat to the batter's box, he has not yet used an illegal bat.

Since 1970, six players have been caught using illegal bats.

In addition, former player and major league manager Phil Garner admitted in January of 2010 on a Houston radio station that he used a corked bat against Gaylord Perry and hit a home run with it.

Does a corked bat actually help a hitter? The August 8, 2007, episode of the TV show *MythBusters* concluded that the answer was no and that corked bats in fact had the opposite effect. Using a corked bat is based on the assumption that such bats can be swung faster because of their lighter weight, and that the springiness of the cork could propel the ball farther. Using a pressurized air cannon, tests on the show showed regulation bats could propel the ball away at 80 mph, while corked bats could only propel it 40 mph. That's because corked bats have less mass to transfer force into the ball, and the cork actually absorbs some of the ball's impact.

Therefore, major league batters who were caught using cork-filled bats risked their careers for nothing. The show also noted that while filling a bat with cork makes it lighter, nothing in the rulebook prevents a player from simply using a lighter uncorked bat.

One wonders whether the absence of any (discovered) corked bats since 2007 is due to sudden honesty by baseball players or because they all saw or heard about the *MythBusters* show.

5.11 Getting hit by pitch

On May 31, 1968, the Dodgers were playing the Giants. Dodgers pitcher Don Drysdale was in the middle of a record streak of 58⅔ scoreless innings that ran from May 14 to June 8. In the ninth inning, Drysdale was working on his fourth consecutive shutout, and the streak was already national news. With none out, bases loaded, and a 2-2 count, Drysdale's pitch hit Giants catcher Dick Dietz. That should have plated a run and ended Drysdale's streak. However, home plate umpire Harry Wendelstedt famously called "ball three," and Dietz eventually flied out. Drysdale's streak remained intact. (His record was eventually broken by another Dodgers pitcher, Orel Hershiser, in 1988.)

1: Assuming there was no question that Dietz was hit by the pitch, what was the basis for Wendelstedt's call?

He ruled that Dietz made no effort to get out of the way of the pitch. Rule 6.08(b) allows a batter to go to first base when hit by a pitch "unless [he] makes no attempt to avoid being touched by the ball." This rule is often not enforced, as those who have pitched against the likes of Craig Biggio, Jason Kendall, Don Baylor, Ron Hunt, and Chase Utley can attest. Because they are (or were) all masters at standing close to the plate and not moving their bodies on inside pitches, they are among the career leaders for being hit by pitches.

On May 20, 2007, the Mets played the Yankees. In the top of the seventh inning, the Yankees' Doug Mientkiewicz was hit by a pitch from Pedro Feliciano of the Mets but was not awarded first base by umpire Tony Randazzo because Randazzo ruled that Mientkiewicz made no attempt to avoid the pitch.

2: What if Dietz had tried to get out of the way of the ball but it hit him in the strike zone?

Then it's a strike. Rule 6.08(b).

3: Say in the first situation above that the ball had skidded away from the catcher. Could the runners have advanced?

No. In either of the above situations, the ball is considered dead and the runners cannot advance.

4: Is there any way in which a batter is not awarded first base if (1) he is hit by a pitch that is not in the strike zone and (2) the umpire does not rule that he made no attempt to get out of the way of the ball?

There are actually two ways. The first is if he offers at the pitch. Rule 6.08(b) provides that a batter hit by a pitch "which he is not attempting to hit" is awarded first base. Therefore, if he swings at the pitch, even if inadvertently, then it's merely a strike. (Rule 6.05(f) also specifically provides that a batter is out when he attempts to hit a third strike and the ball touches him.) This has happened from time to time.

On May 18, 2002, the Yankees hosted the Twins. In the top of the sixth inning, Minnesota third baseman Casey Blake was up with runners on first and second and two out. With two strikes, Blake was hit in the shin by Ted Lilly's pitch. Blake moved his bat, and plate umpire Gary Darling ruled that Blake had offered at the pitch, thus negating the hit-by-pitch. The ball got by Yankees catcher Alberto Castillo, but the play was ruled dead the moment Blake offered at the pitch and was hit.

As noted above, Rule 6.08(b) provides that the batter is awarded first base if he is hit by a pitch "which he is not attempting to hit." Rule 6.05(f) similarly references the "attempt" to hit a third strike. However, in plenty of instances the hitter's bat inadvertently passes through home plate (especially on an inside pitch, such as the Blake situation) when he is not "attempting" to hit the ball at all. The rules cover this situation as well.

A second scenario in which this can occur is as follows: There is a runner on second base with a 2-2 count. The pitcher is in the set position and balks, but pitches following the balk and hits the batter. In this case, the hit-by-pitch would be considered a nonevent (as if the pitch had never been thrown), and the runner on second would go to third. This is because not all runners were forced to advance in this situation. Similarly, if there were runners on first and third, the runner on first would go to second, the runner on third would score, and the hit-by-pitch would be ignored. The only time the batter would be awarded first base in this situation is if every base runner was forced to advance by virtue of the batter's occupying first base.

5.12 Dropped/trapped third strike

In legal cases, there can be factual disputes or legal disputes. In the former, the only question is what actually happened. In the latter, the facts are not in dispute, but the question is to how to apply the law to

Game 2 of the 2005 ALCS, White Sox vs. Angels, 1–1 in the bottom of the ninth, two outs and no one on base. With two strikes on Sox catcher A. J. Pierzynski, he swung and missed at a low pitch. Angels catcher Josh Paul either caught the pitch just before it touched the ground or trapped it just after. Home plate umpire Doug Eddings swung his arm out as if to signal strike three but made no verbal signal and no out call. Paul rolled the ball back to the mound. After turning briefly toward the dugout, Pierzynski ran toward and reached first base. Under current rules, is he allowed to stay there? *AP Photo/ Charles Rex Arbogast*

those facts. (Of course, sometimes both are in dispute.) In this book, virtually every quiz falls into the latter category: the facts of what happened are not in dispute, and the question is how to apply "the law" (the *Official Baseball Rules*) to those facts.

One of the most controversial plays in major league postseason history was more analogous to a factual dispute. The question was what the umpire did or didn't do (and what he intended or didn't intend) rather than how to interpret the rules. Nevertheless, once we play with the facts a little, we can raise some interesting questions about how the result might have been different under the rules.

In Game 2 of the 2005 ALCS, the Chicago White Sox were playing the Los Angeles Angels in Chicago. It was 1–1 in the bottom of the ninth, two outs and no one on base. White Sox catcher A. J. Pierzynski was at bat. With two strikes on him, Pierzynski swung and missed at a low pitch from Angels pitcher Kelvim Escobar. Angels catcher Josh Paul either caught the pitch just before it touched the ground or trapped it just after. Home plate umpire Doug Eddings swung his arm out as if to signal strike three, but made no verbal signal and no out call. Paul rolled the ball back to the mound. After turning briefly toward the dugout, Pierzynski ran toward and reached first base. After extensive discussion, he was allowed to stay at first. (Since Paul had rolled the ball away, he could not have attempted to throw Pierzynski out.) This was based on Rule 6.09(b), which provides in part that a batter becomes a runner if the third strike called by the umpire is not caught and first base is unoccupied. A pinch runner, Pablo Ozuna, replaced Pierzynski and stole second base. Third baseman Joe Crede delivered a base hit three pitches later, scoring Ozuna for the winning run.

1: Under current rules, can the batter run to first base in this situation?

No, and due to this play, a Comment was added to Rule 6.09(b). It provides that a batter who does not "realize his situation" on a third strike that is not caught and who is not running to first shall be declared out once he leaves the dirt circle surrounding home plate. In other words, the batter-runner has to head to first base immediately in the good-faith belief that the third strike has not been caught.

2: Part of the reason for the controversy was that Eddings apparently made no verbal signal to go along with his strike-three hand gesture. What if he has loudly yelled "Strike three" as well?

This question raises a point that many fans are unaware of, namely the difference between a third strike call and an out call. The two are not synonymous. In addition, there is the umpire's hand signal and his verbal signal. Craig Burley, who writes a blog called *The Hardball Times*, explains:

"The first thing to note is that the umpire's call and signal are supposed to go together. The signal is a visual aid, and the verbal call is the actual 'call,' but an umpire is supposed to make both together. . . . Umpires are taught that an 'out' call should not be made on a third strike until the umpire is certain that the catcher has held on to the ball—which sometimes isn't until the umpire has sought assistance from a base umpire, who has the better view on trapped balls. 'Strike three, you're out!' is not the proper call. Instead, the umpire should call the strike and then wait to make the out call—and wait as long as necessary. While 'out' has not been called, the play is live."

Many umpires, when they know the ball has not been caught, prefer to alert the players to the fact by calling, "On the ground . . . on the ground," while pointing to the ground. This is not every umpire's standard, however; some just point to the ground and others do nothing. The plate umpire might not make the "out" call or the "on the ground" call because he requires assistance from a base umpire. It seems likely that Eddings was looking for umpire Ed Rapuano to give him assistance (which the base umpire will often do by making an out signal—not a call—or pointing to the ground) but they failed to communicate until later.

Accordingly, in the above play, the problem was not that Eddings did not say "Strike three"; the problem was that he did not verbally call the batter out. This is not to suggest that Eddings necessarily did anything wrong. If Paul did trap the ball, then it was correct for Eddings to signal strike three, just as it was correct for him not to call Pierzynski out.

Bottom of the fifteenth, score tied 3–3. Robin Ventura of the Mets has just hit a bases-loaded grand slam. The runners on second and third scored. Todd Pratt, who was on first, stopped somewhere around third, then ran toward second and embraced Ventura. The rest of the Mets also mobbed Ventura just before he reached second base. He never got there. What's the final score of the game? *Ezra Shaw/Getty Images*

3: Assume a runner was on first with one out when the above play occurred. All other facts are the same. Would the result be different?

Yes. Under Rule 6.09(b), the batter becomes a runner only if the third strike is not called *and* either (1) first base is unoccupied or (2) first base is occupied with two out. However, if the batter-runner runs to first with that base occupied and there are less than two outs, the ball remains in play and the other runners can advance.

5.13 Whether all bases are touched on a home run

On October 17, 1999, the Braves were playing the Mets in Game 5 of the NLCS. In the bottom of the fifteenth(!) with one out and the score tied 3–3, Robin Ventura of the Mets came to bat with the bases loaded. Ventura hit a long drive over the 371-foot sign in right-center field. While Roger Cedeño and John Olerud ran home from third and second base respectively, Todd Pratt, who was on first, stopped somewhere around third base. Pratt then ran toward second and embraced Ventura. The rest of the Mets also mobbed Ventura just before he reached second base. He never got there. After a while, the players (including Ventura) and the umpires left the field and workers began picking up the bases.

1: What is the final score of the game?

It's 4–3. This situation involves the confluence of several rules, including some scoring rules. We start with Rule 6.09(d), which provides in part that a hit over the fence or into the stands "entitles the batter to a home run when he shall have touched all bases legally." In this play, however, Ventura didn't touch all the bases, legally or otherwise.

The scoring rules that apply are 10.06(f) and (g). Rule 10.06(f) provides, "Subject to the provisions of 10.07(g), when the batter ends a game with a safe hit which drives in as many runs as are necessary to put his team in the lead, he shall be credited with only as many bases on his hit as are advanced by the runner who scores the winning run, and then only if the batter runs out his hit for as many bases as are advanced by the runner who scores the winning run." Rule 10.07(g) then states that when the game ends on a homer hit out of the playing field, the batter and any runners on base are entitled to score.

In the above play, since both Cedeño and Olerud had scored before Ventura was frozen in his tracks by his teammates, it would seem—at least by the exact wording of Rule 10.06(g)—that both of their runs should count and that 5–3 should have been the correct score. Nevertheless, in those instances where not all runners do actually score, the situation is scored as if it were a Rule 10.06(f) play. "The game ends in sudden death when the winning run scores," said Elias spokesman Steve Hirdt, who made the official ruling in conjunction with official scorekeeper Red Foley. "The only exception is on a home run, assuming the player rounds all the bases. [Ventura] never rounded the bases."

Since the game was tied when Ventura hit the ball out of the park, Roger Cedeño only had to advance one base to score the winning run. Ventura should only have been entitled to a single. And that was the ruling on the field, meaning that 4–3 was the final score. Ventura's hit is now and will forever be known as the "grand slam single."

One final point. Crew chief Ed Montague told the Associated Press that home plate umpire Jerry Layne watched Cedeño touch home plate, then turned and walked away because he was only looking for the winning run to score. This seems odd. Had Ventura rounded the bases, the final score would have been 7–3. Perhaps Layne concluded that the game was over, and that whether any additional runs scored was an issue for the scorekeeper and not the umpire.

2: What would the result have been if there were two outs and Ventura never made it as far as first base before his teammates mobbed him?

No runs at all would have scored because he never reached first base. This would then have been a "time play" under Rule 4.09(a). As we saw from Rule 6.09(d), a hit over the fence or into the stands entitles the batter to a home run only after he has touched all the bases. Until that happens, he can be put out, and if he doesn't make it to first base, he can be called out for abandoning the base path. So if Ventura never made it to first, with two outs on the play, it would be no different from being thrown out at first on a ground ball—three outs, no runs scored.

3: Say that Ventura's shot had landed right on top of the outfield fence in fair territory. Which of the following statements is true?

A. It's a home run no matter where it lands.

B. It's a home run only if it goes over the fence; otherwise it's a live ball.

C. It's a book-rule double no matter where the ball lands.

D. The rules don't address this situation.

Based on major league custom and practice among umpires, the correct answer is B. Based on the rules, the correct answer is D. Note that Rule 6.09(d) provides that a fair ball is a home run if a ball "passes over a fence." However, hitting the top of the fence is not the same as "passing over" the fence, which suggests no contact at all. Choice A is not correct because if the ball lands back on the field, it will not be called a home run. This happened in the ninth inning of a July 3, 2010, game between the Nationals and the Mets. With the bases loaded, Adam Dunn of the Nationals hit a long drive to center field that hit the top of the fence, just above Ángel Pagán's outstretched glove, and bounced back onto the field. Dunn ended up with the double and knocked in two of the three base runners.

5.14 Ball getting caught in ivy or bouncing over fence

On June 14, 1995, the Cubs were playing the Giants at Wrigley Field. In the bottom of the twelfth inning and the score tied 3–3, Brian

McRae of the Cubs smashed a hit off the right-center-field wall with Todd Pratt on the go from first base. The ball, though, never reappeared from the ivy that Bill Veeck had planted in 1937. Pratt scored on the play for the apparent winning run.

1: Which of the following statements is true as to Pratt?

A. Pratt scores; Cubs win.

B. Pratt has to go back to third base no matter what.

C. Pratt scores if the umpires determine that the ball was visible and could have been retrieved by the outfielders.

D. It depends whether or not the ball bounced first or hit the wall on the fly.

Under Rule 6.09(f), the correct answer is B. This is a ground-rule double at Wrigley Field, and all runners are awarded two bases from their position at the time the pitch was delivered. Choice C is not correct because it makes no difference whether the ball is visible as long as it's stuck. D is not correct either.

Being aware of the rules, Giants outfielders Darren Lewis and Rikkert Faneyte knew exactly what to do next. Nothing. This became a particularly frustrating result for the Cubs. Pratt was waved back to third base on the ground-rule double and never did score. He was out trying for home on an apparent wild pitch, and the Giants won 4–3 in the thirteenth. A noteworthy aspect of the game was that the game-winning hit came off the bat of little-used Mike Benjamin of the Giants. He went 6 for 7 on the day and was in the middle of setting a major league record with 14 hits in 3 games.

"Those Giant outfielders did good," McRae said. "They knew better than to reach in and try to grab it. I remember when we started the season and [coach] Billy Williams told us, 'The ivy's not growing yet, but when it does, the ball will disappear in there. Don't touch it!' That's what happened today."

2: Would the result in the above play have changed if the ball had touched one of the Giants outfielders before getting caught in the ivy?

Yes. The ball would then be alive and in play.

3: True or false? In major league play, when a player hits a ball that lands in fair territory beyond first or third base and bounces over the outfield fence, that is deemed a ground-rule double.

False. Even though everyone refers to this kind of hit as such, it is not actually a ground-rule double. The term "ground-rule double" does not appear anywhere in the rules (other than one Comment), and with reason. The phrase "ground rule" refers to the rules in effect *at a given ballpark*, which are specific to that ballpark. In other words, it is a hit that may be ruled a double at that park but not elsewhere. A ball that lands in fair territory and bounces over the fence is a double in every major league park and is therefore not based on a "ground rule." To be technical about it, it would be a "book-rule double" under Rules 6.09(e) through 6.09(h).

5.15 Designated hitter

On July 15, 1993, the Red Sox were playing Seattle. With two outs in the eighth inning, Seattle was ahead by one run. The Red Sox had Mike Greenwell at the plate and Billy Hatcher at first, representing the tying run. Mariners manager Lou Piniella put pitcher Dave Nelson in left field and brought in Dennis Powell to pitch to Greenwell. At the time, Marc Newfeld was batting sixth for the Mariners as the designated hitter.

1: What consequences, if any, would result from Piniella's move in terms of Seattle's lineup in the top of the ninth inning?

Under Rule 6.10, Newfeld would be out of the game. Once a pitcher is switched to a defensive position, the designated hitter is gone.

2: Could Piniella use a different designated hitter instead of Newfeld?

No. The role of the designated hitter is gone for the rest of the game.

3: On May 19, 2008, the Twins played the Rangers in Minnesota. In the top of the tenth inning, with the score tied 6–6, the Twins shifted Brendan Harris from the DH slot into the infield. Could the team then use a new designated hitter in his place?

No, per Rule 6.10(b)(5). Because of this the Twins lost the use of the DH for the remainder of the game. This forced pitcher Bobby Korecky to bat, and he got a hit in the eleventh inning. Korecky pitched a scoreless twelfth and was credited with the win after Minnesota scored in the bottom of the inning. Korecky became the first Twins pitcher to record a hit in an American League game since the DH rule went into effect in 1973.

4: On August 16, 1988, the Red Sox were playing the Mariners. Sox manager Joe Morgan turned in an incorrect lineup that included two left fielders, Jim Rice and Mike Greenwell, and no designated hitter. Does the umpire have to bring this up on his own or does he have to wait until the other team points it out?

If the designated hitter is not designated prior to the game, one can't be used for that game. The umpire is supposed to enforce this whether the other team brings it up or not. Interestingly, however, in the above case, the snafu wasn't detected by plate umpire Dave Phillips or Mariners manager Jim Snyder until after Seattle's 7–0 victory was in the books. If the umpire notices an obvious error on the lineup card, he can bring it to the attention of the manager of that team anytime before the game starts.

Phillips apparently misunderstood that he was supposed to raise the issue. "I checked the names and saw who was batting," said Phillips. "I just assumed Rice was the designated hitter. Funny that it never came up. But that's usually done by the other team. In my opinion, you have to use common sense as a guide. Before Rice batted, had the Mariners said anything, I would have told the Sox to let their pitcher [Wes Gardner] bat. But when they didn't, and Rice was in the game, he was the designated hitter. Even if I'd known, I'd have waited until they said something." However, the other umpires correctly noted that the umpires are supposed to enforce this rule themselves.

In the game, Greenwell played left field and Rice hit as the designated hitter.

5: On July 22, 1999, the Indians hosted the Blue Jays. Indians manager Mike Hargrove listed cleanup hitter Manny Ramírez as the designated hitter and number 7 hitter Alex Ramírez as the right fielder. However, the wrong Ramírez—Manny—played right field in the first inning instead of Alex. What happens in terms of the designated hitter?

The Indians inadvertently used the designated hitter (Manny) defensively. Therefore they lost the designated hitter for the game. The rules provide that in this instance, Manny stays in the game and keeps his spot in the batting order, but that the pitcher (in this case Charles Nagy) has to hit in place of Alex in the number 7 spot. Nagy went 0 for 2.

6: Would the answer to quiz number 5 change if a relief pitcher was brought in for Nagy?

No, because once a pitcher hits for the designated hitter, that move terminates the use of the designated hitter for the rest of the game, even if another pitcher is brought in.

7: **On October 2, 1974, Rangers manager Billy Martin elected to have pitcher Ferguson Jenkins hit for himself. Could he still use a designated hitter?**

No. A designated hitter can only be used in place of the pitcher.

8: **On July 27, 1986, the Red Sox were playing the Angels. In the top of the fourth inning, designated hitter Don Baylor and right fielder Dwight Evans were called out on strikes by home plate umpire Tim McClelland. Red Sox manager John McNamara was upset about McClelland's calls, as was Baylor, and they both yelled at McClelland from the dugout to make their views known. McClelland ejected them both. Angels manager Gene Mauch then wanted Red Sox substitute manager Rene Lachemann to immediately name a replacement for Baylor as the designated hitter, but Lachemann refused to do so. Mauch protested. Did he have a legitimate gripe?**

No. Under the rules, a substitute designated hitter need not be announced until it is his time to bat.

9: **On September 10, 1980, the Orioles were playing the Tigers. Orioles manager Earl Weaver put pitcher Steve Stone in the designated hitter spot. This took some imagination because Stone was in Toronto awaiting the Orioles' next series. When it came time for Stone to bat, Weaver (who obviously had no intention of using Stone anyway) used left-handed hitter Terry Crowley to hit against right-handed Tigers pitcher Jack Morris. Crowley hit a home run in his second at bat. Did Weaver do anything wrong?**

At the time, no, but if this happened today, yes. Rule 6.10 provides that a designated hitter named in the starting lineup must come to bat at least once, unless the opposing team changes pitchers.

10: If no designated hitter is named in the starting lineup, can one be inserted during the game?

No. On May 17, 2009, Tampa Bay manager Joe Maddon committed a faux pas in the Rays game with the Indians when he failed to list a DH on his lineup card. After Cleveland batted in the top of the first inning, Indians' manager Eric Wedge brought the problem to the attention of plate umpire Ted Barrett, who'd missed it when checking the lineup cards before the game. As a result, the Rays were forced to play without a DH for the duration of the contest. Pitcher Andy Sonnanstine batted in Evan Longoria's number 3 spot and went 1 for 3, hitting a double, in the Rays 7–5 win.

Chapter 6

The Runner

6.1 Running the bases in order

In 1963, Jimmy Piersall of the Mets hit his 100th career home run. To celebrate, he circled the bases in correct order but facing backward. The umps ruled it a legal home run.

1: Did the umps get the call right?

Yes. Under Rule 7.02, a runner has to run the bases in order, but that doesn't prevent him from facing or running backward.

6.2 Two runners on a base/abandoning the base path

On July 18, 2001, the Mets were playing the Marlins. The Mets had Rey Ordóñez on second and Todd Zeile on third with one out when Kevin Appier hit a ground ball to shortstop Alex González. González threw home to catcher Charles Johnson, who ran Zeile back to third. According to official scorer Howie Karpin, "Johnson appeared to have tagged Zeile out before he ever got back to the bag, but third-base umpire Kerwin Danley made no call." Meanwhile Ordóñez had run from second to third, thus leaving both him and Zeile at third base. Johnson then tagged Ordóñez.

While it was unclear whether Zeile had been tagged by Johnson, Zeile nevertheless walked off the field, thinking he was out, and headed toward the dugout. Bill Shannon, one of the official scorers, said, "At that point no call had been made by any of the umpires."

The umps initially decided that both runners would be out. Mets manager Bobby Valentine argued that Zeile left the base because he thought he was out. The umps huddled and agreed, allowing Zeile to go back to third. Obviously this didn't sit well with Marlins manager Tony Pérez. He believed that both runners should have been out. But the umps stood firm on Ordóñez only. Tony went ballistic and was banished for the evening.

1: Did the umps get the call right?

The whole problem was caused by the apparent noncall as to whether Zeile had been tagged out by Johnson before arriving back at third base. Since bases are designed for single occupancy only, the lead or preceding runner, in this case Zeile, had the right to the bag since he wasn't forced to advance. Johnson therefore did the right thing by tagging Ordóñez, an unwanted guest. Rule 7.03(a) says,

"Two runners may not occupy a base, but if, while the ball is alive, two runners are touching a base, the following runner shall be out when tagged and the preceding runner is entitled to the base."

So, if we stop the action at that moment, Ordóñez is out and Zeile is safe. However, the Comment to Rule 7.08 suggests that Zeile would be out as well once he left the base path because he had abandoned his efforts to run the bases. Indeed, the Comment addresses this very situation: "Runner believing he is called out on a tag at first or third base starts for the dugout and progresses a reasonable distance still indicating by his actions that he is out, shall be declared out for abandoning the bases."

Though the umpires didn't handle the play cleanly, Zeile should have been called out since, historically, the onus is on the players both offensively and defensively to know the situation and the rule that applies. Zeile should not have left the base path without being certain of the call. If the umpires confer, they can resolve the situation by using common sense. If an umpire's action or inaction might jeopardize a runner, umpires can correct the situation in a reasonable manner. Since the umpire did not initially rule that Zeile was tagged, he should have remained at third base. However, when he left the base, he should have been ruled out for abandonment.

In the above play, it appears that Zeile headed for the dugout after both he and Ordóñez were standing on third. What if, instead, he had headed for the dugout sooner, believing that he had been tagged by Johnson, i.e., before Ordóñez had reached third? In this case, Ordóñez would be safe at third, since he and Zeile were never occupying the base at the same time.

2: In the above situation, assume that Zeile had never abandoned the base path, but instead made it back to third without being tagged, just when Ordóñez arrived there as well. We saw above that Zeile would be safe and Ordóñez out. Are there any circumstances under which the result would be reversed?

Yes. Ordóñez was out under the above situation because he was not forced to run to third, and Rule 7.03(a) states that the lead runner gets to occupy the base in that situation. If Ordóñez was forced to run, however—say a runner was on first as well when Appier hit his grounder—then, under Rule 7.03(b), the trailing runner is entitled to the base, meaning that Ordóñez could stay at third and Zeile would be out.

6.3 Moving beyond a protected base

On April 28, 2002, the Yankees were playing the Mariners. Seattle's Luis Ugueto, on first base, was stealing on a 3-1 pitch to Mark McLemore. The pitch was called ball four—entitling Ugueto to second base—but Ugueto overslid the bag, unaware that McLemore had received a free pass. Yankees shortstop Derek Jeter tagged Ugueto while he was off the base.

1: Given that McLemore had walked anyway, is Ugueto entitled to stay at second base?

No, he's out. Jeter made a wise play. The comment to Rule 7.04(b) states, "A runner forced to advance without liability to be put out may advance past the base to which he is entitled only at his peril." In other words, the moment Ugueto reached second base safely and left the bag, he was fair game to be put out. Similarly, on April 20, 2007, in a home game against the St. Louis Cardinals, the Cubs' Ronny Cedeño, a runner at first base, was called out at second advancing on a walk to Jacque Jones. With the count 3-2 on Jones, Cedeño ran on the next pitch, drawing a throw from catcher Yadier Molina as the batter took ball four. Cedeño, running on the pitch, slid past the second-base bag and was tagged by shortstop David Eckstein. Cedeño thought the ball was dead because of the walk, but Eckstein and Cardinals manager Tony La Russa knew better. So did the umpires after a brief conference inspired by La Russa's protest when it appeared they would permit Cedeño to stay at second.

2: In Game 3 of the 1997 National League Championship Series between Florida and Atlanta, the Braves' Kenny Lofton was on first and ran on a 3-2 pitch to Jeff Blauser. Ball four was called, but Lofton, unaware of the call, slid headfirst into second and was called out by second-base umpire Eric Gregg. Lofton got up, shaking his head, and walked off the bag. Marlins second baseman Craig Counsell then tagged Lofton again, and Gregg signaled out. The umps huddled and decided to let Lofton stay at second base. Did the umpires make the right call?

Yes. First of all, on a walk, a runner may advance one base if forced to do so, without liability to be put out. Therefore, Gregg had no right to call Lofton out. By doing so, he confused Lofton, who then left second base. How does this situation differ from that in the question above? In the first situation, Ugueto was tagged out after he had already reached second base. In the second situation, Lofton had not yet reached second base but was entitled to it because of the walk to Blauser.

Note that the second-base umpire could have a difficult job in this situation. The lapse in time between the ball-four call and the runner's arriving at second is likely to be brief indeed. Thus, the umpire has to first determine what the home plate umpire called and then act accordingly, which does not leave much time. Things can become even more complicated on 3-2 counts when there is a checked swing. That could hang up a second-base umpire because the plate ump often has to appeal to the first- or third-base ump, which can cause a delay. See *Tip for players* below on how to handle this problem.

3: If the batter swings and misses for strike three and the ball gets by the catcher, how far can the batter advance—first base only or as far as he can reach on the play?

He is entitled to advance to any base at his own risk. As stated earlier, if first base is occupied with less than two outs, the batter is out. The batter would only be entitled to first base if the pitched ball went into dead-ball territory. However, in the above situation, the ball would remain alive and in play.

4: What if, in the Lofton play above, he was on second rather than first, there was no runner on first, and he was tagged out trying to steal third on a ball-four call?

He would be out because he wasn't forced to run to an awarded base.

Tip for players: If you are trying to steal second base with three balls on the hitter when the pitch is thrown, do not vacate second base, even if the umpire has called you out, until it is certain that the pitch was *not* called ball four.

6.4 Ball hitting runner

In a 1957 game between the Milwaukee Braves and Cincinnati Reds, the Reds were batting with Don Hoak on second and Gus Bell on first when Wally Post hit a grounder toward Braves shortstop Johnny Logan. To avoid an apparent double play, Hoak fielded the ball himself with his bare hands. Rule 7.08(f) provides that the runner is out when he is touched by a fair ball in fair territory before the ball has touched or passed an infielder.

1: If you were the umpire, how would you rule this play?

Hoak was smart because, under Rule 7.08(f), although he was out, he was able to avoid the double play. But the punishment did not fit the crime since Hoak's breach of baseball etiquette was to circumvent the rules and keep Post from hitting into a double play. National League president Warren Giles and American League umpire in chief Cal Hubbard were appalled at Hoak's stunt. They put their heads together, and Rule 7.09(g) was born. The rule now gives umpires the authority to call the batter, as well as the runner, out when a runner intentionally interferes for the purpose of breaking up a double play. So, if Hoak tried the same thing today, both he and the base runner would be out.

2: Under the current rules, would it make any difference if the ball hit Hoak by accident?

Yes. Hoak would still be out, but the batter-runner would now be safe at first because Hoak did nothing "willful or deliberate."

6.5 Passing runner on base paths

On April 16, 2006, the Orioles hosted the Angels. In the bottom of the second inning, Javy López came up with one out and Miguel Tejada on first. López drilled the ball toward the farthest reaches of left-center field. Darin Erstad tracked the ball back to the wall and jumped at the last second. When he came down, it was unclear whether he'd made the catch. He hadn't, and the ball left the park. With no immediate call from any of the umpires, Tejada drifted back to first base just in case he needed to tag up. López then passed Tejada.

1: What is the consequence of the play?

López is out. Under Rule 7.08(h), a runner is out if he passes a preceding runner on the base path before that runner is out.

2: On July 3, 2010, the Dodgers were playing the Diamondbacks. In the second inning, with the bases loaded and one out, and the Dodg-

ers' Clayton Kershaw on first, Rafael Furcal hit a fly to deep center, where Chris Young dropped the ball at the wall. Kershaw had rounded second base when he decided to return to first because he thought the ball was caught by Young. Kershaw retouched second base and seconds later crossed paths with Furcal, who was unaware that Kershaw was retreating. What is the consequence of the play?

Even though Kershaw initiated the baserunning error, Furcal was called out because the preceding runner (Kershaw) has the right of way under Rule 7.08(h). However, Xavier Paul and Blake DeWitt, the runners ahead of Kershaw on the bases, were allowed to score since the ball remains alive when a runner passes another runner unless the violation is the third out. In that case, the possibility of a "time play" would exist.

In an unusual play in a minor league game, on June 26, 2007, the Dubuque Golden Eagles played the Cascade Cougars. In the first inning, with Alex Boll on first and one out, Tyler Willman blasted a pitch through the thick, humid air and out of the park. But Cascade right fielder Tony Turnis lost the ball almost immediately, and his confusion crossed up Boll, who never left first, thinking Turnis might still catch the ball. Into his home-run trot, Willman ran past Boll on the bases—an automatic out. After about fifteen minutes the umpires decided that no rule stated Boll had to go back to his base, so he was awarded the run scored. Willman, unfortunately, went from a 2-run homer to an RBI single and out on the base path.

6.6 Overrunning first and then heading elsewhere

On September 6, 2011, the Orioles were playing the Yankees. In the bottom of the seventh, Yankees DH Jorge Posada hit a slow dribbler toward third. Orioles pitcher Tommy Hunter picked up the ball and threw wildly past first baseman Mark Reynolds. The throw was backed up by second baseman Robert Andino. As Posada passed first base on the errant throw, while running in foul territory, he briefly turned his body toward second base. As he casually sauntered back toward first, Andino flipped the ball back to Reynolds, who just as casually tagged Posada just before he retouched first base. First-base umpire Gary Darling called him out. However, Posada argued that he should not have been called out because he stayed in foul territory at all times.

1: Is Posada correct?

No. Rule 7.08(j) provides that while a batter-runner can overrun first base, "if he attempts to run to second, he is out when tagged." The issue is not whether the batter-runner steps into fair territory but merely whether the attempt is made. Even when the attempt is almost negligible, as it was in Posada's case, that is still sufficient to call him out. A video of the play can be seen at http://mlb.mlb.com/video/play.jsp?content_id=18928863.

Similarly, on April 24, 2012, the Braves played the Dodgers. In the bottom of the sixth inning, the Dodgers had Dee Gordon on second and Mark Ellis on first with no outs. Matt Kemp hit a grounder to shortstop Tyler Pastornicky, who threw to second baseman Dan Uggla to start a 6-4-3 double play. But Uggla's throw to Braves first baseman Freddie Freeman bounced off his glove, and Kemp was safe. Kemp, apparently thinking the throw was wild, made a quick step toward second. Freeman noticed it and tagged Kemp on the way back to first base. Umpire Alan Porter ruled Kemp safe. After Braves manager Fredi González argued the call, the umpires huddled and Kemp was ruled out because he violated Rule 7.08(j).

2: Assume that in the above situation with Posada, there were two outs and a runner was on third who scored before Posada was tagged out. Would the run count?

It would. So says the Comment to Rule 7.08(j).

3: Say that Posada headed toward the dugout, but the umpire had in fact called him safe. Could the Orioles put him out by stepping on first before Posada returned to the base?

Yes. This would be considered a runner abandonment play, and he could be called out even without an appeal. It is the same as if a catcher drops a third strike and the batter-runner heads to the dugout rather than toward first base.

4: Say that Reynolds tried to tag Posada before he reached first. What if, in an attempt to avoid the tag, Posada slid under Reynolds's tag, but inadvertently overslid the bag? Could he be tagged out before he got back to first?

No. When it comes to first base, the rules do not distinguish between overruning and oversliding as long as the batter-runner touches the bag. If the batter-runner crosses first base before the throw arrives but fails to touch first base, the first-base umpire is supposed to make the safe signal. However, this is an appeal play, and the batter-runner can be called out on appeal by either touching the base or tagging the batter-runner.

6.7 Leaving the base without tagging/fourth-out appeal

On July 1, 1989, the Yankees were playing the Brewers and leading 4–1. With one out in the last of the eighth, the Yankees had Mike Pagliarulo on third, Bob Geren at first, and Wayne Tolleson at bat. On a suicide squeeze, Tolleson's bunt was caught by pitcher Jay Aldrich. Realizing he had an easy double play, Aldrich took his time and tossed to first to get Geren. Before Geren was doubled off first for the third out of the inning, Pagliarulo crossed home plate and ran toward the dugout to get his glove. The Brewers trotted off the field.

Because of the suicide squeeze, there was no question that Pagliarulo left third base early and that he did not retouch third after Aldrich caught the pop-up bunt.

1: Does Pagliarulo's run count?

Surprisingly, the answer is yes, even though Paglairulo never tagged up, because the Brewers never appealed. Rule 7.10(a) provides that "any runner shall be called out, *on appeal*, when, after a fly ball is caught, he fails to retouch his original base before he or his original base is tagged." "It's a 'fourth-out' situation," umpire Larry Barnett later explained. "Milwaukee had to throw the ball to third base for what would be the fourth out. Then they can choose to make that one the final out and prevent the run from scoring. But Milwaukee didn't do that." Obviously the Brewers should select the out that nullifies any runs.

Another play that involved a "nonappealed fourth out" occurred on April 12, 2009, when the Diamondbacks hosted the Dodgers. In the top of the second inning with one out, the Dodgers had Andre Ethier on third base and Juan Pierre on second. Randy Wolf then lined out to pitcher Dan Haren for the second out. Ethier broke for home on contact. Haren threw to second baseman Felipe López, who tagged out Pierre off second base for the third out of the inning. But Ethier crossed the plate before Pierre was tagged for the third out. Since Pierre was not forced to go to third on the play and Wolf, the batter-runner, made the second out of the inning, not the third, the inning ended in a "time play." Because Ethier scored before Pierre was tagged, Ethier's run counts, unless appealed.

The D'backs could have appealed by throwing to third or tagging Ethier for the fourth out, but they left the field without appealing. If they successfully appealed the fourth out, Ethier's run would have been nullified.

When is it too late to appeal? After all infielders and the pitcher have crossed the foul lines. As long as one infielder, or the pitcher, is in fair territory, the defensive team can still make the appeal. Interestingly, in the above situation, the umpires did not score the run the moment the D'backs' infielders and Haren crossed the foul line and left fair territory. Why? Because there was some question as to whether López (the second baseman) had stepped on second base before tagging Pierre. If he had, chances are the third out would have been recorded before Ethier crossed the plate, and the run would not score. However, it was ruled that he hadn't.

Part of Rule 7.10(d) provides that "appeal plays may require an umpire to recognize an apparent 'fourth out.'" If the third out is made during a play in which an appeal play is sustained on another runner, the appeal-play decision takes precedence in determining the out. If more than one appeal occurs during a play that ends a half-inning, the defense may elect to take the out that gives it the advantage.

2: Let's change the actual facts a little. Assume that instead of a bunt, Tolleson hits a medium fly ball. Because Pagliarulo isn't sure if it is deep enough for him to tag and score, he takes a few steps down the left-field foul line while the fly ball is in the air so he can get a running start. He is on third base when the center fielder catches the ball (i.e., he hasn't left early) and beats the throw home. Does his run count?

No. The comment to Rule 7.10(a) specifically prohibits "flying starts."

3: Say the bases are loaded with two outs. The batter hits a clean single to the outfield. The runner on third scores but the runner on second is thrown out at home. However, the runner on first missed second on his way to third. The second baseman immediately calls for the ball and holds it on second. The umpire sustains his appeal. How many runs score on the play? Or, do we first need to know whether the runner on third crossed home plate before the runner on first missed second?

No runs score. The Comment to Rule 7.10 provides that if the third out is made during a play in which an appeal play is sustained on another runner, the appeal-play decision takes precedence in determining the out. The same result would be reached by Rule 4.09(a), discussed below, which relates to time plays.

4: Many plays involve application of multiple rules. For example, the following play involves failure to retouch a base and the concept of a time play. On May 16, 2009, the Yankees were playing the Twins. In the top of the second inning the Twins had Justin Morneau on third and Michael Cuddyer on first with one out when Brian Buscher flied to Brett Gardner in center. Morneau tagged up and scored easily from third. Cuddyer, who was running with the pitch, slid into second with a pop-up slide and returned to first. The Yankees appealed that Cuddyer never retouched second on his way back to first. Based on Rule 7.10(b), the Twins' outfielder was ruled out by umpire John Hirschbeck. Does Morneau's run count?

Yes, because the third out occurred after Morneau crossed the plate and was not the result of a force-out or the batter-runner's making the third out before reaching first base.

6.8 Appeals of running violations

On May 22, 1992, the Yankees were playing Milwaukee. In the top of the eighth inning, with less than two outs, the Brewers had Dante Bichette on third and Dave Nilsson on first when Scott Fletcher lofted a sacrifice fly to Mel Hall in left field. Bichette tagged from third, but the Yankees appealed that he left too soon. In carrying out the appeal, Hall overthrew third baseman Charlie Hayes, and the ball landed in the seats behind third base. Hall then appealed again by throwing to Hayes, who stepped on third.

1: Assuming that Bichette in fact left third too early, is he now out?

No. Hall's second toss over to Hayes would be considered a successive appeal. Rule 7.10 addresses this issue directly: "Successive appeals may not be made on a runner at the same base. If the defensive team on its first appeal errs, a request for a second appeal on the same runner at the same base shall not be allowed by the umpire. (Intended meaning of the word 'err' is that the defensive team in making an appeal threw the ball out of play. For example, if the pitcher threw to first base to appeal and threw the ball into the stands, no second appeal would be allowed.)" In this case, Hall erred on the appeal since the ball went into dead-ball territory. The Yanks could not appeal again. If Hall's first appeal throw did not go into dead-ball territory, he would have had the right to appeal again.

2: On August 30, 1989, the Padres were playing the Expos. With one out, the Padres had Bip Roberts on third and Roberto Alomar at second when the batter hit a fly to right for the second out. Both runners advanced as the ball was thrown in. After all action had stopped, the Expos contended that Roberts had left third too soon and decided to appeal. The ball was thrown to Expos third baseman Tim Wallach. Before he stepped on third, however, Alomar broke for the plate. Wallach then immediately threw the ball to the catcher, which started a rundown, resulting in Alomar's being tagged out for the third out. Assuming that Roberts had in fact left third too early, would his run count once Wallach stepped on third to complete the appeal?

It would count because of a provision in Rule 7.10 that provides that any appeal must be made "before the next pitch or any play or attempted play." Putting Alomar in a rundown constituted such a play, which nullified the Expos' right to appeal whether Roberts left early. (In fact, Alomar's actions were cleverly arranged by his father, Sandy, who was the third-base coach at the time.)

Some feel that this rule is unfair because it deprives the fielding team of the right to appeal simply because they are trying to retire another batter. In addition, unlike the above play involving two offensive players, the same player subject to the appeal could try to take advantage of this rule. AL umpire Rich Garcia commented, "If a runner knows that he missed a base or left too soon, he could force the defense to make a play on him and possibly be safe. You are giving the offensive player a chance to redeem himself after he made a mistake." Thus, if you have a runner on the bases in this kind of situation, you can have him head to the next base, which might then force the defensive team to make a play right then and there, thereby causing the defensive team to lose its right to appeal. Of course, had Wallach simply stepped on third immediately, rather than getting "suckered" into the rundown play on Alomar, the run would not have counted had Roberts left too soon.

In the above situation, the Padres traded an out for a run. As a general matter, the defensive team should not wait for time before making an appeal.

Questions often arise as to what constitutes a play, and when does continuous action end? Examples of a "play" include (1) throwing to another fielder in an attempt to retire a runner not being appealed; (2) tagging or attempting to tag a runner or base not being appealed; (3) a fielder's running toward a base to retire a runner not being appealed; (4) a fielder's running toward a runner not being appealed for the purpose of tagging him; (5) a pitcher's balk; or (6) if the defensive team errs on the appeal by throwing the ball into dead-ball territory. If the appeal throw is errant but remains in the field of play, the defensive team can still make the intended appeal.

3: In the Padres-Expos situation above, assume that Roberts did not leave third too early, but Alomar did leave second too early, and that the outfielder threw the ball to the cutoff man, Wallach, who immediately tried to throw out Roberts, but failed. The Expos then threw the ball to second to appeal Alomar's action. Given Rule 7.10, quoted above, would the appeal be successful?

Yes. In this case, unlike the actual play described above, everything that occurred is part of one continuous play. The effort to throw out Alomar was all part of the same play as the fly ball, so the right to appeal is not lost.

4: Assume that a batter hits a triple but doesn't touch first base. As the pitcher comes set and is about to throw to first to appeal, the man on third breaks for home. The pitcher becomes distracted and balks. Can he complete the appeal?

No. When a pitcher balks, he can no longer carry out an appeal, and any runners are awarded one base.

6.9 Missing or retouching a base

On April 24, 2002, the Mets were playing the Cardinals at Shea Stadium. In the second inning the Mets had Jay Payton on first base with one out, when Vance Wilson looped a fly ball to right field. Payton took off, but realized on rounding second he had to get back to first when he saw that Eli Marrero was about to catch the ball. Payton retreated directly to first base from where he had been between second and third.

1: Was Payton permitted to run directly back to first?

No.

2: Say that Payton had run back over second base but did not actually touch it. Would that make any difference?

No.

3: Say that Payton had reached second but then, fearing that the fly ball might be caught, started back to first base. Instead, the ball landed in the field and then hopped over the fence for a book-rule double, which would automatically have entitled Payton to third base. Could he run directly from his position between first and second to third (without touching second), based on the book-rule double?

Rule 7.10(b) requires runners to touch each base, whether advancing or returning to a prior base. Based on this rule, Payton would have been out under all three scenarios. The third situation is interesting because it points out that the rule applies whether the runner is advancing or retreating. This situation arose in a July 25, 1982, game between the Orioles and Oakland A's. In the fifth inning, an Oakland batter singled. The next hitter, Dwayne Murphy, sliced a high fly into the left-field corner on a hit-and-run play. The ball landed safely and then bounced into the seats for a double. The runner on first, who was off with the pitch, dove into second base. But then, figuring the ball might be caught, he retreated slightly toward first base. Finally, seeing the baseball drop in, he ran to third. But he didn't touch second base a second time. The Orioles appealed, and umpire Nick Bremigan called the runner out for failing to retouch second base while advancing. A's manager Billy Martin argued that the runner could go to third via any route he chose since the ball hit by Murphy was dead when it bounced into the seats. But Bremigan insisted that the ball's bouncing into dead territory did not free the runner from his customary path. Even when a base runner is entitled to advance, he must touch the bases he passes.

It should also be noted that the manner in which a baserunning error is appealed can make a difference. On April 17, 2012, the Cubs and Marlins played in Miami. In the bottom of the fourth inning, the Marlins had Omar Infante on second and one out when Giancarlo Stanton hit a fly ball to Alfonso Soriano in left field. Apparently getting a bad read on the ball, Infante took off and had rounded third base when he realized he had to return to second because he did not tag up. However, in doing so he cut across the infield instead of retouching third base and was called out on appeal. The Cubs wisely made a continuous-action appeal instead of getting the ball back to the pitcher and appealing off the rubber. Even though the pitcher steps back off the rubber, it is a dangerous way to execute the appeal, because four things can happen and three are bad. The one positive is that the appeal is successfully completed. The three negatives are (1) if the pitcher balks while making the appeal, the appeal is nullified and any runner/runners on base each advance one base; (2) if the pitcher throws the ball into dead-ball territory and "errs" on the appeal, the defensive team loses the right to appeal the runner; and (3) if the pitcher makes a play on another runner, the defensive team loses the right to appeal.

6.10 Return to a missed base after following runner has scored

On April 21, 2009, the Giants were playing the Padres. In the top of the fourth inning the Padres had Adrián González on second and Chase Headley on first with no outs when Kevin Kouzmanoff doubled to right field. González and Headley sprinted to the plate and arrived there at almost the same time. González slid before the tag but missed the plate, and umpire Jeff Nelson properly made no call. Then Headley tried to leap over catcher Benjie Molina but was tagged out. A moment after the tag took place, González returned and touched the plate and was called safe.

1: Does González's run count?

Yes. There were less than two outs on the play, and that González missed home plate the first time does not prevent him from scoring just because Headley was tagged out in the interim.

2: Would González's run have counted if Headley had been safe?

No, because of the seldom-used Approved Ruling to Rule 7.10(b), which reads, "No runner may return to touch a missed base after a following runner has scored." Therefore, once Headley had scored, it was too late for González to retouch the missed base, in this case home plate.

3: Would the answer to quiz number 2 be any different if González had missed third base rather than home plate? Would he be able to retouch third base?

No, since the language refers to any "missed base." So, for example, say González had missed third base on Kouzmanoff's double and the ball scooted far away from the catcher. After Headley's score, González could not run back and retouch third, just as he can't retouch home.

4: Can a runner retouch a missed base if he advances to the next base when the ball is in dead-ball territory?

No. Say that a runner is going from first to third on a hit-and-run. The batter hits a looping fly ball that bounces into the seats for a book-rule double. The runner misses second base and is heading to third. If he reaches third when the ball is in dead-ball territory, he cannot return to touch second base. If he tries to, he can be put out on appeal. If he hadn't reached third when the ball went into dead-ball territory, then he would have the right to touch second and then third.

6.11 Effect of failing to touch a base

On August 30, 2007, the Reds were playing the Pirates. In the fourth inning, Cincinnati had the based loaded with two outs. Edwin Encarnación hit a line-drive single to left field. Ken Griffey scored from third on the hit, and Adam Dunn scored from second. However, the Pirates appealed that Dunn had not touched third on his way home. The umpires agreed.

1: Does Griffey's run count?

A. Yes, because he scored independently of Dunn's miscue.

B. Yes, but only if he crossed home plate before Dunn missed third.

C. No, because the bases were loaded on the play, thus creating a force-out situation.

D. No, regardless of whether the bases were loaded.

The correct answer is C. Rule 7.12 provides that if the third out is the successful appeal of a failure to touch a base and is a force play, the preceding runner does not score. In the above play, because the bases were loaded, Dunn's out would be considered a force play. However, if the bases were not loaded (say runners on second and third only), then Griffey's run would count. The rule states, "If upon appeal the preceding runner is the third out, no runners following him shall score. If such third out is the result of a force play, neither preceding nor following runners shall score."

2: If there was only one out when the play began and Encarnación's hit cleared the bases, would the run scored by the runner on first count?

Yes. If there are less than two outs, the runs that score following Dunn's mistake would count.

6.12 Ball hitting runner or umpire

On June 13, 2008, the Cubs were playing the Blue Jays in an interleague game. In the fifth inning, Kosuke Fukudome of the Cubs singled and Geovany Soto walked. The next hitter, Jim Edmonds, hit a grounder that was headed toward the outfield, but the ball hit second-base umpire Jeff Nelson in the infield. Fukudome came around to score.

1: Which of the following statements is true?

A. If Nelson was positioned in front of the second baseman, all runners advance one base only, meaning that Fukudome gets sent back to third.

B. If Nelson was positioned behind the second baseman, all runners advance one base only, meaning that Fukudome gets sent back to third.

C. It makes no difference where Nelson was positioned—the ball is in play and the run scores.

D. It makes no difference where Nelson is positioned—all runners advance one base only, meaning that Fukudome gets sent back to third.

The correct answer is A. Under Rule 6.08(d), if the ball touches the umpire after having passed a fielder (i.e., the umpire is positioned behind the fielder), then the ball is in play. Otherwise, the runners advance one base only, if forced.

2: What would be the result if Edmonds's grounder had hit Fukudome instead?

Fukudome would be out. Soto would be at second and Edmonds on first.

3: What if the ball had hit Fukudome after touching the pitcher?

The ball remains alive and in play.

4: What if Fukudome was on third and Soto was on first when Edmonds hits a ball that strikes Nelson, positioned in front of second base, and umpire's interference is called? Where would you place the runners?

In the 2006 playoffs, A's center fielder Mark Kotsay hit a foul pop heading into the stands near third base. Tigers third baseman Brandon Inge left his feet, caught the ball in midair while most of his body was in the fan area and landed in the stands. Was this unbelievable catch legal? *AP Photo/Michael Conroy*

Fukudome remains at third base, Soto is awarded second base, and Edmonds is credited with a base hit and is awarded first base. Fukudome stays at third because he was not forced to advance on the play.

Chapter 7

The Fielder

7.1 Jumping into dugout or stands to catch ball

On October 14, 2006, the Tigers were playing the A's in Game 3 of the ALCS. In the first inning, A's center fielder Mark Kotsay hit a foul pop heading into the stands near third base. Tigers third baseman Brandon Inge left his feet, caught the ball in midair while most of his body was in the fan area, and landed in the stands.

1: Is Kotsay out?

Yes, although this is one of those situations where a literal interpretation of the rules could lead to an incorrect answer. The Comment to Rule 6.05(a) provides that if a player is attempting to make a catch in an out-of-play area (such as the stands), he must have at least one foot on the playing surface. This would suggest that headlong dives into the stands would not be permitted. However, it is interpreted such that what is prohibited is standing in an out-of-play area or having one foot in an out-of-play area before making the catch. So long as the fielder has both feet on the playing surface before making his leap and then catches the ball in midair, as Inge did, the catch is legal.

In a 2012 game, the White Sox had Brent Lillibridge on third with one out. Orioles left fielder Nolan Reimold made a sensational diving catch of a foul fly ball. Can Lillibridge try to tag up? If so, does he risk being thrown out? *AP Photo/John Smierciak*

2: Would the answer change of Inge had simply walked down the dugout steps and then made the catch?

Yes. This is prohibited.

3: Would it be a legal catch if Inge simply had one foot in the dugout and one foot on the playing surface?

No. The Comment provides that "neither foot" can be in the dugout or any other out-of-play area. The only way that a catch is legal in this situation is if both feet are on the lip of the dugout (which is considered part of the playing surface) or if one foot is on the lip of the dugout and one foot is in midair.

7.2 Fielder falling into the stands

On April 16, 2012, the White Sox were playing the Orioles in Chicago. With the Sox ahead 3–1 and at bat in the seventh, Brent Lillibridge was on third with one out. Alejandro De Aza hit a foul fly down the left-field line. Orioles left fielder Nolan Reimold made a sensational diving catch and fell into the stands. As soon as Reimold fell into the stands, the ball was dead immediately.

1: Which of the following statements is accurate as to Lillibridge:

A. He stays at third because the ball is dead.

B. He can try to tag and score at his peril.

C. He can tag and score without liability to be put out.

Somewhat surprisingly, the correct answer is C. Under Rule 7.04(c), all runners may advance one base in this situation. Whether it was the right move for Reimold to make the catch depends on the circumstances, such as the inning and the score. However, one wonders how many players are even aware of the automatic base award should they tumble into any dead ball area after making a catch. A fielder might make a great catch but pay a stiff price since a run might score on the play.

2: Would the result have changed in the above situation if the fielder flipped the ball to a teammate while still in midair? On September 15, 1997, the Yankees were playing the Red Sox. In the bottom of the sixth inning with the Red Sox ahead 6–5, the Yankees had Jorge Posada on second and Derek Jeter on third with one out. Tim Raines hit a pop fly toward the box seats off third base. Red Sox third baseman John Valentin dove headfirst, caught the ball by flopping into the seats, and then, with his feet still in the air, flipped the ball back to Nomar

Garciaparra in fair territory. Jeter tagged and scored from third on the play. Garciaparra quickly flipped the ball to Jeff Frye, who was on his way to cover third. Frye tagged Jorge Posada trying to advance to third. Is Posada out on the play?

No. Umpires refer to this type of play as "catch and carry." Let's dissect the play. Valentin made a legal catch because he snared the ball while in the air before landing in the seats. And because he had control of the ball and was able to transfer the ball or show it to the umpire, he was credited with making a legal catch. However, because of 7.04(c), the ball became dead the moment Valentin fell into the stands, and all runners (Jeter and Posada) were awarded one base because there was less than two outs when Raines flied out.

The question is, should a fielder aggressively go after a fly ball near the stands or near any area designated as dead-ball territory late in a close game with the risk of giving up a run? What if this happened in the eighth or ninth inning with the Sox ahead 6–5? Is it worth trading a run for an out? This is a subject that managers and coaches need to address with their players because this type of play can occur on any part of the field.

Outfielders know that with a runner on third base, if they make a catch with less than two outs in foul territory deep in the outfield, the runner on third will tag up and score. If it's late in a close game, they will usually drop the ball intentionally, or let the ball fall to the ground or into the stands untouched. But many players are not aware that Rule 7.04(c) exists, which can carry a severe penalty because it allows a runner or runners to advance a base without the possibility of making a play on the runner.

3: Would it make any difference in the previous example if Valentin had leaned into the stands as far as he could to make the catch but kept his footing?

Yes. The rule refers specifically to "falling" into the stands, so if the fielder keeps his feet, the rule would not apply.

4: What would have happened if Valentin had dropped the ball? Could the runners advance?

No. Under Rule 5.09(e), when a foul ball is not caught, the ball is dead and the runners return. It makes no difference if the ball makes contact with the fielder's glove.

7.3 Touching pitched ball with cap or mask

On July 25, 2010, the Yankees were playing the Royals. With the Royals' Rick Ankiel on third, Yankees catcher Jorge Posada flung his mask after blocking a Chan Ho Park pitch in the dirt to Brayan Peña. The ball rolled a few feet to the right and amazingly ended up under Posada's mask.

1: What is the result of the play?

Ankiel scores. Rule 7.04(e) allows runners to advance one base if a fielder "deliberately" touches a pitched ball with his cap, mask, or any part of his uniform detached from its proper place or person. The ball remains alive and the award is made from where the runner is at the time the ball is touched. Therefore, even though it appeared that Posada had no intent to cover the ball with his mask, his throwing of the mask was nevertheless deliberate. Note that the word "deliberate" is not defined in the rules and may be open to interpretation. For example, it could refer to whether the action itself is deliberate, regardless of whether the result is intended, which was the interpretation made by the umpires in the above situation. Alternatively, it could mean intent, which is Rich Marazzi's view: "If a batter leaves his bat a few feet from home plate and the ball makes contact with the lying bat, it is not deemed interference. I see the Posada play as something similar, although not every umpire may have the same interpretation."

7.4 Glove or equipment leaves hand or body on batted or thrown fair ball/ Equipment leaves hand or body on pitched ball

In the second game of the 2004 NLCS playoff series, the Cardinals were playing the Astros. In the fifth inning, Craig Biggio of the Astros opened with a single and moved up on a balk by Cardinals pitcher Matt Morris. After Jeff Bagwell walked with one out, Lance Berkman lined a single over Albert Pujols's leap. Biggio scored and Bagwell wound up at second. However, Pujols's glove flew off when he jumped, and the mitt missed the ball.

1: Do any of the base runners get extra bases on the play?

No.

2: Would it be relevant if Pujols's glove left his hand intentionally (i.e., he threw the glove at the ball in an effort to stop it) but it missed the ball?

No, it would not be relevant. So long as the glove misses the ball, it is irrelevant whether the action is intentional. The Comment to Rules 7.05(b)–(e) provides that there is no penalty if the ball is not touched. Thus, the runners would remain at the bases they reached.

3: What if Pujols's glove had touched the ball after it unintentionally left his hand? Where would the runners be placed?

Because the touching was unintentional, runners would be allowed to remain at any base they reached safely.

4: Would it be relevant if Pujols's glove left his hand intentionally and it touched the ball? What would be the base award?

If the umpire judges the act intentional and the glove touches the ball, and it's a fair ball, then under Rule 7.05(c), each runner, including the batter-runner, may advance three bases. However, the comment provides, "This penalty shall not be invoked against a fielder whose glove is carried off his hand by the force of a batted or thrown ball, or when his glove flies off his hand as he makes an obvious effort to make a legitimate catch." Accordingly, if the umpire deems the act unintentional, there is no penalty; otherwise there is a three-base penalty, meaning that in the above play, Biggio and Bagwell would score and Berkman would wind up at third. The three-base award is also given under Rule 7.05(b) if the fielder deliberately touches a fair batted ball with his cap, mask, or any part of his uniform detached from its proper place on his person.

In this situation—or any situation where a batter-runner or runner is given an award of one or more bases—the ball is not dead but remains in play. Therefore, if the batter-runner wants to advance farther than the number of bases he is awarded under the rules, he may attempt to do so at his own risk. In effect, this means an attempted advance from third to home, with all preceding runners scoring anyway as a result of the three-base award. Note also that Rules 7.05(a)–(c) apply to fair balls only, whereas Rule 7.04(e) applies to pitched balls, which would include foul balls.

5: As in question 4, assume that Pujols intentionally threw his glove at the ball and hit it. Because of the crazy carom, the ball ricochets away from everyone and Berkman decides to try for an inside-the-park homer. Does he risk being thrown out?

Yes. Under Rule 7.05(c), the batter-runner gets three bases for free but advances to home at his peril. On April 29, 1997, Salt Lake Buzz center fielder Darrin Jackson flung his glove at a ball hit by Tacoma's Raúl Ibañez. Jackson knocked the ball down and Ibañez was credited with his first triple of the season. Tacoma manager Dave Myers later lauded Jackson for his heads-up play (assuming that's what it was) because Myers felt that Ibañez would have had an easy inside-the-park home run otherwise.

Speaking of Rule 7.05(c), in a Bugs Bunny cartoon from 1946, the umpire was clearly unaware of this rule. Then again maybe he figured that the *Official Baseball Rules* did not apply. The situation was this: The Tee Totalers were playing the Gas House Gorillas. In the bottom of the fourth, the Gorillas were winning 94–0. Then Bugs appears and says that he can beat the Gorillas all by himself. The Gorillas take him up on the offer and Bugs plays every position (simultaneously). Eventually Bugs takes a 96–95 lead going into the bottom of the ninth. With one man on and two outs, one of the Gorillas (using a tree for a bat) hits a tremendous drive. To catch it, Bugs takes a "Mellow Cab" and then hops on a bus to get to the "Umpire State Building." He takes an elevator to the top of the building, then climbs the flagpole and throws his glove at the ball. The ball lands in the glove and then Bugs retrieves the glove out of midair. The umpire called the Gorilla batter out. However, based on Rule 7.05(c), this was a wrong call, and the Gorilla seemed to know this. "Out?" he asked incredulously. The Statue of Liberty responds, "That's what the man said, you heard what he said, he said that." There the cartoon ends. Under Rule 7.05(c), the base runner would have scored and tied the game no matter which base he was on. Even the batter-runner may have scored as well. We'll never know. . . .

6: Is there any situation in which Pujols's actions could have led to Berkman's being automatically allowed to completely circle the bases after his hit?

Yes. If Berkman's hit would have flown out of the park in the umpire's judgment if not deflected by a fielder's throwing his glove, cap, or any article of his apparel, Berkman would have been awarded all four bases. Presumably Pujols would have been playing outfield for this to occur. Rule 7.05(a).

7: On August 13, 1995, the Dodgers were playing the Pirates. The Dodgers had Roberto Kelly on third and Tim Wallach on second. Mitch Webster swung at a 1-0 pitch in the dirt. As it started bouncing away, Pirates catcher Angelo Encarnación scooped up the ball with his mask. Where should the umpires place the runners?

In this case, all runners are awarded one base under Rule 7.05(j), which was added to the *Official Baseball Rules* in 2006 (i.e., "if a fielder deliberately touches a pitched ball with his cap, mask or any part of his uniform detached from its proper place on his person"). Thus Kelly would score and Wallach would get third. Note that the three-base award given under Rules 7.05(b) and (c) applies to *batted* balls, while Rule 7.05(j) applies to *pitched* balls.

8: Say that, in quiz number 7, Webster hit a ball to the shortstop, who threw wildly to Encarnación. As he did before, Encarnación then used his mask to get the ball in an attempt to prevent Wallach from scoring as well. We saw above that Encarnación's maneuver would entitle all runners to one base. Same result here?

No. The award would be two bases. Rule 7.05 covers three different situations where players are throwing their gloves or various pieces of equipment at the ball. First is the batted ball (four bases or three bases, depending on the situation, as discussed above). Second is the pitched ball (one base). Finally, we have the "thrown ball" situation, which is two bases "if a fielder deliberately touches a thrown ball with his cap, mask or any part of his uniform detached from its proper place on his person," Rule 7.05(d); or "if a fielder deliberately throws his glove at and touches a thrown ball," Rule 7.05(e). The situation described in quiz number 8 would be an example of Rule 7.05(d). Therefore, Kelly and Wallach would score.

7.5 Ball becomes lodged under fence

On April 21, 2004, the Phillies were playing the Marlins. In the ninth inning of a tie game, the Phillies Plácido Polanco hit a ball to left field. The ball became lodged between the padding at the base of the wall and the warning track. Marlins left fielder Jeff Conine raised his hand to signify that the ball was lodged, and umpire Ed Rapuano ruled the ball dead. The Phillies claimed that Conine should have played the ball as if it were live. Polanco treated the ball as if it were live and circled the bases before being called back to second. Phillies general manager Ed Wade filed an official protest with Major League Baseball.

1: Is there merit to Wade's protest?

No. Under Rule 7.05(f), runners are awarded two bases "if a fair ball . . . goes through or under a field fence, or through or under a scoreboard, or through or under shrubbery or vines on the fence; or if it sticks in such fence, scoreboard, shrubbery or vines." Polanco's ball would be considered to have stuck in the fence.

7.6 Thrown ball becomes stuck

On August 4, 2009, the Boston Red Sox were playing the Tampa Rays. With the game tied in the eighth and Ben Zobrist on first, Tampa's Willy Aybar dropped a well-placed sacrifice bunt that Red Sox pitcher Daniel Bard fielded coming off the mound. He hurried the throw, whirling and firing one of his high-90s fastballs in the general direction of first base. The very general direction of first base (i.e., the throw was poor).

The ball whizzed past everyone and into the Rays' bullpen down the right-field line, where relievers and coaches scattered in an effort to avoid getting hit. Right fielder J. D. Drew hurried over into the corner as Zobrist headed for home with the go-ahead run. As Drew reached the bullpen area, he saw that the ball had become lodged between two bags of baseballs placed along the wall. He threw up his hands. Aybar continued his tour around the bases and eventually crossed the plate.

1: How many runs should score on the play? Where would you place the runners?

No runs score on the play. Put Zobrist at third and Aybar at second (which is just what the umps did). Under Rule 7.05(g), runners are awarded two bases when "a thrown ball goes into the stands, or into a bench, or over or under or through a field fence, or on a slanting part of the screen above the backstop, or remains in the meshes of a wire screen protecting spectators." Whether a ball's getting stuck between two bags of baseballs fits exactly within this laundry list is not clear, but it's close enough. The above play touched off a heated discussion in the blogosphere, with many fans first believing that the umps blew the call, then realizing that they got it right, but then concluding that the rule is a bad one. It certainly looked that way from Tampa's perspective since they wound up scoring no runs in the inning. (They did, however, eventually win the game in the thirteenth on a walk-off homer by Evan Longoria.)

2: Assume that in the above play, Zobrist was stealing and had already reached second base and that Aybar had already reached first when Bard's throw went astray. Would that have made a difference in the result?

Yes. An Approved Ruling to the rule provides that if the runners have advanced at least one base when an infielder makes a wild throw on the first play after the pitch, the award shall be governed by the position of the runners when the wild throw was made. For purposes of the above play, Bard is of course an infielder and Zobrist would be allowed to score since he had legally acquired second base before the throw. Aybar would be awarded third base since he had reached first before the throw.

Rule 7.05(g) is identical to Rule 7.05(f) in the sense that both rules apply to a situation where a ball, loosely speaking, gets stuck or goes into the stands. In both cases, runners are awarded two bases. The only difference is that Rule 7.05(f) relates to batted balls, while 7.05(g) relates to thrown balls (such as Bard's throw in the above situation). However the list of triggering events is not identical. Recall from the previous quiz that Rule 7.05(f) applies to situations where the ball "goes through or under a field fence, or through or under a scoreboard, or through or under shrubbery or vines on the fence; or if it sticks in such fence, scoreboard, shrubbery or vines." Rule 7.05(g) applies in part where the ball goes "over or under or through a field fence, or on a slanting part of the screen above the backstop, or remains in the meshes of a wire screen protecting spectators."

3: Let's assume that, in quiz number 2 above, Zobrist had reached second but Aybar had not yet reached first when Bard made his wild throw. Where would we put everyone?

A. Zobrist at third, Aybar at second.

B. Zobrist scores, Aybar at second.

C. Zobrist at third, Aybar at first.

D. Zobrist scores, Aybar at third.

The answer is A. As discussed in the Approved Ruling, the key factor in determining where to place the runners is whether Aybar and Zobrist had each advanced one base before the wild throw was made. Here, because Aybar had not yet reached first base, that Zobrist had already reached second is irrelevant. Therefore they each are awarded two bases from their position or last legally touched base at the time the pitch was delivered. Zobrist does not get two bases from second, but rather from first. This situation is much more probable than the previous situation because a fielder would be unlikely to uncork a throw once the batter-runner has already reached first base. It can happen though, such as when a fielder has turned his entire body away from the play and lost track of where the batter-runner is. For example, an infielder might chase a deflected ball. By the time the ball is recovered and thrown, the batter-runner has reached first base.

7.7 Thrown ball into stands

On August 12, 2000, the Mets were playing the Giants. Down 1–0 in the fourth inning, the Giants loaded the bases with one out when Bobby Estalella hit a lazy fly to left field. Benny Agbayani ran toward the line to make the catch. With Jeff Kent tagging and scoring, Agbayani jogged toward the seats and handed the ball to a youngster named Jake Burns, who broke into a big smile. "He was eating a hot dog, and then all of a sudden he had a ball in his other hand," said his father, Jim. As soon as Agbayani gave the ball away, another fan shouted that there were only two outs, not three. Agbayani, realizing his mistake, grabbed the ball back from the fan and threw it to the infield.

1: What happens to the base runners?

Agbayani's act of handing the ball to the boy has the same effect as overthrowing it into dead-ball territory. Under Rule 7.05(g), when outfielders make overthrows that go out of play, all runners are awarded two bases from their positions on the base paths at the time the ball was released. Even though Agbayani's action was intentional rather than unintentional, the result is the same. Therefore, the runners on second and third would score, the runner on first would wind up on third, and the batter-runner would be awarded second base.

A similar embarrassing play happened to Milton Bradley of the Cubs. On June 12, 2009, the Cubs and Twins hooked up in an interleague battle. In the top of the eighth inning the Twins had runners on first and third and one out when Joe Mauer hit a sacrifice fly to Bradley in right field. Bradley caught the ball for the second out, then posed like a statue for two–three seconds. He then tossed the ball into the stands, thinking there were three outs. Nick Punto scored from third, and Brendan Harris, the runner on first, was awarded two bases and was sent to third base. As noted, such plays are treated the same as overthrows by an outfielder into dead-ball territory.

2: Would the answer to the previous question change if Agbayani had handed the ball to a ball girl on the field as opposed to a fan in the stands?

Yes. This has happened on a number of occasions. On July 26, 2011, the Arizona Diamondbacks were playing the San Diego Padres and were batting in the top of the sixth inning with Miguel Montero on first and Chris Young on second and one out. Ryan Roberts of the D'Backs hit a pop fly. Padres second baseman Orlando Hudson made the catch in fair territory as he was running toward the foul line. Thinking it was the third out, Hudson flipped the ball to the ball girl stationed along the right-field line. She in turn tossed the ball to a fan in the stands. Several Padres players realized Hudson's catch was only the second out. Padres first baseman Jesús Guzmán begged the fan for the ball. The fan obliged and threw the ball to him.

Even though the ball was thrown into the stands by the ball girl, this play is actually governed by Rule 3.15 instead of 7.05(g). That rule (which we will consider again later) discusses what happens if there is interference with the play by any authorized personnel on the field, including contact with the ball. If the contact is unintentional, the ball remains alive. But in this play, the ball girl committed an intentional act of interference, even though in a passive way, since she was simply catching the ball, which Hudson had flipped to her. Even though the fan eventually threw the ball back to Guzmán, the damage was already done because the ball became dead the moment the ball girl intentionally touched it by catching Hudson's toss. What she did with it thereafter is irrelevant.

When intentional interference occurs under Rule 3.15, umpires treat the play as they would spectator interference. The ball becomes dead immediately, and runners are awarded the bases they would have made had the interference not occurred. This is umpire judgment. In the above play, Young, the runner on second, was allowed to score and Montero, the runner on first, was sent to third base.

3: On September 9, 1983, the Yankees were playing the Orioles. Dave Winfield was batting in the bottom of the fifth inning for the Yanks with Willie Randolph on first base. Winfield hit a Scott McGregor pitch down the right-field line. Orioles right fielder Ken Singleton fielded the ball off the wall and threw to his cutoff man, Rich Dauer, who in turn fired the ball home. The ball got by catcher Rick Dempsey and went into dead-ball territory. When Dauer made his throw, Winfield had not yet reached second base, but when the ball went into dead-ball territory, he was between second and third. Do we place Winfield at third or does he score?

Third base. Rule 7.05(g) provides that the point of determination is when the ball leaves the thrower's hand, not the time when it winds up in dead-ball territory. Therefore, since Winfield hadn't reached second when Dempsey threw, Winfield would only get third base.

4: Say that Winfield's shot went to the shortstop instead, who then threw the ball into the stands in trying to throw out Winfield. When he threw the ball, Randolph had just arrived at second base. Where do we put Randolph and Winfield?

The rules are slightly different when the wild throw is the first throw by an infielder. The governing time is the position of the runners when the ball was delivered by the pitcher. Accordingly, the fact that Randolph had reached second when the throw was made is irrelevant. He was still at first when the ball was pitched. Put them at third and second respectively.

5: Would the result to quiz number 3 be different if the shortstop first threw to second to attempt a double play, but his throw was late, and it was the second baseman's throw to first that went into the stands?

Yes. When a fielder fields a ground ball, if he throws to second, that is the "first" play. The "second" play is the throw to first. In this situation, the runner on second would score and the batter would wind up at second *if* he hadn't gotten to first yet.

It is important to know what constitutes a "play" for these purposes: it is a throw, an attempt to tag a base, or an attempt to tag a runner. A fake is not a play. For example, if the shortstop had only made a fake throw to second, then the throw to first is the first and only play, and runners would be awarded second and third. In both instances, the batter-runner is awarded second.

In this situation, the wild throw was not the first throw ("play") by an infielder but rather the second. Therefore, it again becomes the time that the second baseman threw the ball that is relevant. Since the throw to second was late, Randolph would score. As for Winfield, he would get third base if he had reached first when the throw was made. If not, he would only get second.

6: On August 20, 2009, the Red Sox were playing the Blue Jays. In the fourth inning, Brett Cecil was pitching for the Blue Jays. Jason Bay drew a leadoff walk. After ball four was called, Toronto catcher

Rod Barajas weakly threw the ball back to Cecil, who missed the catch. Cecil then walked over to the ball, looked at it quickly, and threw it into the Blue Jays dugout. Is there any consequence to Cecil's action?

Yes, it's a two-base error under Rule 7.05(g). Bay was awarded third base. If time had been called, it would have been a different matter; here it was a live ball. Bay was awarded third base because he legally occupied first base at the time of the throw.

7.8 Catcher's balk

1: Here's a tough one: Is there any way, besides a balk by a pitcher or a stolen base, that base runners can advance a base while the ball is still in the pitcher's hand? Hint: it has to do with the catcher.

Yes. There is a form of balk caused by the catcher, although since a balk is by definition an act by a pitcher, the balk is charged to the pitcher. (Thus, though one sometimes hears the term "catcher's balk," this is a misnomer.) It occurs when the catcher sets up with one or both feet outside the catcher's box, which violates Rule 4.03, which requires a catcher to station himself directly behind home plate. It is rarely called, but not never. For example, on June 24, 2000, the Braves were playing the Brewers. In the top of the first, with Greg Maddux pitching, the Brewers had a runner on first with one out and Marquis Grissom at bat. Braves catcher Fernando Lunar was straddling the catcher's box while waiting for the pitch. Umpire John Shulock called a balk (on Maddux) which sent the Brewers' runner to second base. That runner eventually scored, and that run was the difference in a 2–1 Milwaukee victory. Braves manager Bobby Cox argued the call and was ejected from the game. Shulock's call was atypical, however, in that a catcher's balk is ordinarily called only on intentional walks, at which it is primarily targeted. As to these walks, the rule provides that the catcher must stand with both feet within the catcher's box until the ball leaves the pitcher's hand.

7.9 Positioning a fielder

1: Can a first baseman straddle the baseline to help prevent an extra-base hit or because he feels he would be better positioned to hold a base runner close or perhaps pick him off?

No. Rule 4.03(c) requires him to be in fair territory. However, unlike the situation with catchers under Rule 4.03(a), for which the penalty is a balk, no penalty is stated for this situation. The umpire can simply advise the player to station himself in fair territory. However, if he continues to ignore the directive, he can be ejected.

Chapter 8

The Pitcher

8.1 Pitching out of the windup

On March 23, 2002, the Mets and the Expos played a spring training game in Florida. After New York's Satoru Komiyama pitched, umpire Joe West told Mets manager Bobby Valentine that Komiyama's delivery was in violation of the rules. Komiyama was hesitating after starting his delivery in the windup position. Valentine was upset because Komiyama had pitched this way throughout spring training without a warning from the men in blue.

1: Was West correct?

Yes. Rule 8.01(a) says that once a pitcher starts his windup, he must continue "without interruption or alteration." However, the knock on the balk provisions of the rules is that they are too subjective, leading to inconsistent interpretations by umpires (as evidenced by the fact that no umpires had previously warned about Komiyama's delivery). Frequently, a particular pitcher's move will be permitted by one umpire, and the exact same move will be called a balk by another. As Ellis Clary, a former major league infielder and later a scout for the Twins, stated, "Beauty is in the eyes of the beholder. So is a balk."

In 1988, after the first couple of months of the season, a report was made public identifying each four-man umpiring crew and the number of balks each called. In the American League, the crew of Don Denkinger, Drew Coble, Tim McClelland, and Larry McCoy called a league-high 60 balks, as did Rich Garcia, Nick Bremigan, John Hirschbeck, and Rick Reed. The low number in the league was 20, called by the team of Jim Evans, Al Clark, Dale Ford, and Ted Hendry. In the NL, Doug Harvey's crew, which included Jerry Crawford, Bob Davidson, and Frank Pulli, led the majors with 65 balks called, while the crew of Bob Engel, Paul Runge, Joe West, and Charlie Williams came up with a low of 11 balks. These large discrepancies must stem from inconsistencies in interpretation rather than the possibility that one crew was constantly drawing more balking pitchers than another.

8.2 Pitching from the set position

The following play occurred in a college game, but the rule involved is comparable to the major league rule.

In June 2005, Arizona State was playing Cal State–Fullerton in the NCAA Super Regionals. In the bottom of the ninth, with the score tied 2–2 and runners on second and third, Arizona State closer Zech Zinicola was attempting to intentionally walk Fullerton's Joey

Andrews to load the bases. On ball four, umpire Jack Cox called a balk because he felt that Zinicola did not come to a complete stop while pitching from the set position.

1: Can a balk be called in an intentional-walk situation?

Yes.

2: What was the consequence of the balk call?

The runners advance one base and the count remains 3-0 on Andrews.

3: In determining whether a balk has occurred, is the pitcher's intent relevant?

Intent is normally not relevant. A pitcher's dropping the ball is a balk, for example. This question is governed by Rule 8.01(b), which discusses pitching from the set position, and 8.05, which discusses the thirteen no-no's that constitute a balk. Rule 8.01 says there are two legal pitching positions, the windup, discussed in Rule 8.01(a), and the set position, discussed in Rule 8.01(b). The set position is indicated by the pitcher "when he stands facing the batter with his pivot foot in contact with, and his other foot in front of, the pitcher's plate, holding the ball in both hands in front of his body and coming to a complete stop." Rule 8.05(m) advises that one of the thirteen kinds of balks is when "the pitcher delivers the pitch from Set Position without coming to a stop." In addressing balks, the rules do not distinguish between any kinds of pitches, including intentional walks.

Based on the foregoing, by the letter of the rules, Cox had the authority to call the balk and did not have to consider the pitcher's intent if he felt that the balk was clear enough based on the pitcher's movements.

The next question deals with the issue of intent, including relevance of intent and answering the question "Intent to do what?" The answer to that question is, intent to deceive the base runners, so as to fool them regarding whether the pitcher is actually going to make a pitch. Without limitations on a pitcher's actions, he could simply stop his delivery halfway through (or do a number of other things as discussed below) and pick off a runner trying to steal a base. This would make the stolen base virtually extinct.

The Comment to Rule 8.05 notes, "The purpose of the balk rule is to prevent the pitcher from deliberately deceiving the base runner. If there is doubt in the umpire's mind, the 'intent' of the pitcher should govern." The phrase "doubt in the umpire's mind" presumably refers to whether the physical act of a balk was committed as opposed to whether there was deliberate deception. Even without intent to deceive, one can envision situations in which the runner *is* nevertheless deceived by the pitcher's movements and thus is (1) thrown out trying to steal, (2) picked off, or (3) frozen in place. Perhaps it is appropriate to call a balk in those instances because the fact of the deception should be considered more important than the pitcher's intent. In short, intent is not relevant in the first instance *unless* there is doubt in the umpire's mind, judging solely from the pitcher's physical movements, as to whether the pitcher has committed a balk.

8.3 Stepping toward bag on pickoff move

In Game 1 of the 2008 World Series between the Phillies and the Rays, Tampa was trailing 3–2 in the sixth inning when the Rays' Carlos Peña reached first on an error. However, he was caught stealing second after left-hander Cole Hamels used a pickoff move to start a 1-3-6 putout, with Phils shortstop Jimmy Rollins applying the tag to Peña. The Rays dugout immediately argued that Hamels balked, which, if called, would have put Peña at second with no outs. The TV broadcasters also immediately commented that Hamels may have balked. However, first-base umpire Kerwin Danley ruled that no balk had occurred.

1: Assuming that Hamels did everything in one continuous motion between the start of his pitching motion and his throw over to first baseman Ryan Howard—i.e., no feints, no pauses, no herky-jerky motions—what would be the basis of the Rays' argument? Hint: it has to do with where Hamels stepped when his foot came down after delivering the ball.

Umpires use an imaginary line from the pitcher's rubber to the first-base line. If they believe that the pitcher stepped on the wrong side of that line—i.e., closer to home than to first—they'll call a balk. Hamels's free foot must come down on the left side of that line if he is throwing to first. Conversely, if his free foot comes toward the batter, he is committed to pitch. The Rays argued that Hamels had stepped toward home rather than first base. If he had, this would have been in violation of Rule 8.01(c), which requires a pitcher to step directly toward a given base before making a throw to that base. Replays of the Hamels play were inconclusive.

2: What if Hamels had made a snap throw to first base to try to pick off Peña and then clearly stepped toward first immediately after?

This would be a balk. As noted in the above rule, the step has to precede the throw, even if the step is directly toward the base.

8.4 Balks

On September 18, 2009, as the Reds hosted the Marlins at Great American Ball Park, Marlins pitcher Brendan Donnelly did something that most umpires had never seen. He delivered a pitch while standing back off the rubber, which is considered an illegal pitch. The Reds were batting in the bottom of the eighth inning with no outs and leading 2–0 with Joey Votto on first base and Brandon Phillips at bat with a full count. Donnelly stepped back off the rubber, but instead of throwing to first or holding the ball, he delivered a pitch to Phillips, who lined out to Brett Carroll in right field. The umps called a balk on Donnelly, sent Votto to second, and allowed Phillips to go to first. The Reds failed to score that inning, and the Marlins rallied to win, 4–3.

1: Did the umps get the call right?

No. If a play follows a balk and all runners, including the batter-runner, advance at least one base, the balk is ignored. If that is not the case, then all runners advance one base. Here since Phillips lined out, he did not wind up on first. As soon as Carroll caught the ball, it became a dead ball and the balk rule should have been enforced by sending Votto to second and having Phillips remain at bat with a full count. But the umps got a bit confused and overpenalized the Marlins.

8.5 Visits to the mound

On August 23, 2006, the Padres were hosting the Dodgers. In the bottom of the fifth inning, after Brian Giles's leadoff single, Brad Penny walked Adrián González with his 101st pitch, prompting manager Grady Little to pay his pitcher a visit. Little was joined at the mound by second baseman Jeff Kent and catcher Russell Martin. When plate umpire Rick Reed headed to the mound to keep the game moving, he overheard Kent complaining loudly to Martin about the umpire's strike zone. Reed reportedly said he "reacted to it." Penny stated Reed "said something derogatory" to Kent.

At that point Little came off the dirt of the mound and met Reed on the grass so as to get between him and Little's players. Little then walked back to the mound to complete his visit with Penny before returning to the dugout. Based on the foregoing, Penny got tossed from the game.

1: Why was Penny tossed from the game?

He was tossed because Little, by leaving the mound and then returning in the same inning, violated Rule 8.06(b), which provides that the pitcher must leave the game if the manager makes a second trip to the mound to the same pitcher in one inning. Little technically violated that rule.

One could argue, given the specifics above, that the umpire should have used a little "judicial discretion" and allowed Penny to remain in the game because Little, while perhaps violating the letter of the rule, did not violate its intent or spirit. Clearly Little only left the mound to prevent any further altercation between his players and the umpire. Moreover, his "return trip" to the mound was only to complete his discussion with Penny.

Two of the issues raised in this situation are, when exactly does the trip to the mound start, and when does it end? Section 7.12 in the *Major League Baseball Umpire Manual* provides that a trip to the mound begins not when the manager or coach first crosses onto the dirt of the mound, but when he crosses the foul line. Under Rule 8.06, it ends when the manager or coach leaves the eighteen-foot circle surrounding the pitcher's rubber.

Interestingly, the Comment to Rule 8.06 provides, "In a case where a manager has made his first trip to the mound and then returns the second time to the mound in the same inning with the same pitcher in the game and the same batter at bat, *after being warned by the umpire that he cannot return to the mound*, the manager shall be removed from the game and the pitcher required to pitch to the batter until he is retired or gets on base." In the above case, the umpires ignored the warning requirement.

A similar situation to the above play occurred in a June 24, 2006, game between the Mets and the Blue Jays, where Mets manager

Willie Randolph was charged with an unconventional visit to the mound in Toronto. In the second inning, Mets right hander Orlando Hernández plunked two batters, allowed a flare base hit, and also served up a three-run homer to Vernon Wells to give the Jays a 6–0 lead. El Duque then threw inside to Troy Glaus, prompting plate umpire C. B. Bucknor to issue a warning to both teams. This inflamed El Duque. Both managers entered the infield. Randolph came out to calm down his pitcher and act as a peacemaker. The problem was, this was considered a visit to the mound. Since pitching coach Rick Peterson had gone out earlier in the inning to talk to El Duque, this constituted a second visit to the mound. Because of the second visit in the same inning, crew chief John Hirschbeck informed Randolph that El Duque would have to leave the game.

2: What if (1) Penny was lifted from the game by his manager after the manager's first visit to the mound and a new pitcher was brought in, and (2) a pinch hitter was brought in as well. Could the manager make a return visit under those circumstances?

Yes. Talking to the new pitcher does not constitute a visit. It is not a first trip to the mound with the new pitcher. The manager's visit is for the pitcher he is removing. Under Rule 8.06(c) and (d), a manager or coach is prohibited from making a second trip to the mound while the same hitter is at bat *unless* a pinch hitter is substituted for the batter. In that case a second visit to the mound is permitted, *but* the pitcher must be removed from the game. (Little had technically violated Rule 8.06(c) as well.)

3: What if Little had not returned to the mound a second time, but instead immediately conferred with his catcher (away from the mound), and then the catcher went to the mound to speak with Penny (or Penny went off the mound to speak with the catcher). Would this constitute a visit by Little?

Yes. The Comment to Rule 8.06 provides, "If the manager or coach goes to the catcher or infielder and that player then goes to the mound or the pitcher comes to him at his position before there is an intervening play (a pitch or other play) that will be the same as the manager or coach going to the mound."

4: What if the "return visit" had been made by a coach as opposed to the manager? What if by another player?

If it was the coach, it would have made no difference. The manager and the coach are considered one and the same for purposes of the rule. However, the rules do not cover players, so that would presumably be permissible. Players can go to the mound unless they are getting instructions from the manager.

Tip for rules compliance: If the manager or coach has any question of another visit's being charged, he should ask the umpire before crossing the foul line. Losing your pitcher is a stiff penalty.

8.6 Damaging or defacing a baseball

On June 14, 2005, the Angels were playing an interleague game against the Washington Nationals. Angels reliever Brendan Donnelly was found to have pine tar on his glove after Washington manager Frank Robinson asked the umpires to check Donnelly's glove. Donnelly never threw a single pitch.

1: Since Donnelly never threw a pitch, did he violate any rules?

Yes, although the backstory was somewhat unusual. Bob Watson, who oversaw discipline for Major League Baseball at the time, suspended Donnelly, citing a violation of Rule 3.02. When this game was played, Rule 3.02 stated in part that if the pitcher threw a discolored or damaged ball, he had to be removed from the game and suspended for ten days. It also provided then (and now) that a player couldn't intentionally discolor or damage the ball by rubbing it with a foreign substance.

Donnelly argued that because he never threw a pitch, Rule 3.02 would not apply. In addition, the "foreign substance" was in the glove, and there was no evidence that he had defaced the ball. However, Rule 8.02(b) prohibits a pitcher from having on his person, or in his possession, any foreign substance, so Donnelly violated that rule anyway. The fact that he did not throw the ball is irrelevant.

Some (including Donnelly) argue that distinction should be made between applying a substance to the ball that merely makes it more tacky (thereby improving the grip), and actually defacing the ball (which adds unpredictability to its flight).

Robinson's actions caused an on-field screaming match between him and Angels manager Mike Scioscia, leading to a one-game suspension for each.

In another situation, after cameras caught a suspicious-looking substance on the glove of Padres ace hurler Jake Peavy, his manager, Bud Black (himself a former pitcher), stated, "I think it's a way different scenario than a guy using a thumbtack, emery board [or] Vaseline [or] the catcher throwing it purposely in the dirt in between innings when they throw the ball down [to second base]. There, you're intending to actually deface the ball. Using anything tacky, like pine tar or rosin, you're just trying to get a feel for the ball to execute pitches." Black also recalled Donnelly as saying that if he didn't use something tacky on the ball, he would be putting the hitter's life at risk because he wouldn't know where the ball was going.

2: What is the only item that may be eaten, drunk, smoked, or injected that is specifically prohibited by the major league rules and for what reason?

The answer is licorice! Rule 3.02 prohibits the use of licorice to discolor a baseball.

8.7 Substitute pitcher facing a batter and visits to the mound

On July 15, 1989, the Twins were playing the Red Sox. In the sixth inning, Red Sox reliever Joe Price entered the game for Eric Hetzel with none out and runners on first and second. He threw one pitch to Jim Dwyer of the Twins. Dwyer started to bunt and checked his swing, but plate umpire Greg Kosc called a strike anyway. Dwyer stepped away from the plate, muttering. It all looked pretty harmless until Kosc, in a sweeping and garish gesture, ejected him.

"I thought the ball was outside," said Dwyer. "I said, 'Oh, Greg.' And he goes, 'The ball was right down the middle.'

"I said, 'The ball was outside.'

"He said, 'Get the expletive out of here.'

"I said, 'Expletive you.' So he throws me out of the game."

Dwyer argued vehemently, twice placing his hand against the umpire. Twins manager Tom Kelly rushed to Dwyer's defense, then replaced him with right-handed hitter Carmelo Castillo. Red Sox manager Joe Morgan responded by going to the mound and bringing in new reliever Mike Smithson. Price, having thrown only one pitch, looking dazed by the development, handed over the ball to the incoming pitcher and disappeared into the Red Sox dugout. However, after much confusion, the umpires ordered Smithson to the dugout and Price back into the game to continue pitching. Morgan was incensed and the Red Sox appealed the ruling.

1: Were the umpires correct in forcing Price to stay in the game?

Yes. Rule 3.05(b) states, "If the pitcher is replaced, the substitute pitcher shall pitch to the batter then at bat, or any substitute batter, until such batter is out or reaches first base, or until the offensive team is put out." Under the above facts, Price was the substitute pitcher. The rule requires that he pitch a full at bat to Dwyer "or any substitute batter," in this case Castillo. Therefore, he could not leave the game in the middle of the combined Dwyer/Castillo at bat.

"I had never even seen the play before," said umpire Larry Barnett, a twenty-two-year veteran. "I just waved the guy Smithson in instinctively. I'm not trying to BS you, I've never seen it before. Then [umpire John Hirschbeck] pointed out the rule."

2: Morgan argued that another rule was inconsistent with the one relied on by the umpires that supported leaving Smithson in the game, at least under these facts. Rule 8.06(d), which addresses visits to the mound, states, "If a pinch hitter is substituted for this batter, the manager or coach may make a second visit to the mound, but must remove the pitcher." Therefore, Morgan's argument is that when he made the second visit to the mound to replace Price, he was obligated to pull him. Is Morgan right?

No. A manager's visit to the mound to replace pitchers is not considered a "visit to the mound" for this purpose. The visit would be charged to Hetzel, not Price. Therefore, Morgan was not correct.

8.8 Ball thrown by pitcher into dead-ball territory

In Game 2 of the 1992 American League Championship Series between Toronto and Oakland, the A's had Willie Wilson on second and Mike Bordick on first. Walt Weiss was at the plate. As Wilson and Bordick were in the midst of a double steal, Blue Jays pitcher David Cone uncorked a wild pitch that got by catcher Pat Borders and started slowly rolling toward the dugout. Wilson and Bordick were flying around the bases, with their head start based on the double steal, and as the ball continued rolling, the speedy Wilson was halfway between third and home and Bordick was well on his way to third. However, Borders might have had a chance to throw out Wilson by hurling the ball to Cone, who was by now covering home, although the ball was still rolling toward the dugout.

1: What's the smart play by Borders?

Let the ball roll into the dugout. Rule 7.05(h) provides that if a wild pitch or passed ball goes into the dugout, the runners are only awarded one base. That's exactly what happened in the above case, in part because Borders's teammates, having knowledge of the rule, were screaming at him to let the ball roll into the dugout. Therefore Wilson, who had easily crossed home plate on the play, was ordered back to third and Bordick was returned to second.

2: Would the result have been the same if Borders had attempted to pick the ball up to throw out Wilson, but instead accidentally kicked it into the dugout?

No, because the rule provides that the runners automatically get two bases in this instance, whether Borders's move was intentional or not.

3: Is there any situation in which Borders might want to ignore all of the foregoing and take his chances on throwing out one of the runners?

In quiz number 1 above, Borders is taking the risk that the ball might come to a dead stop and never reach the dugout, in which case it would still be a live ball. Therefore, if that appears likely to happen, he may as well pick up the ball and take his chances with moving base runners.

8.9 Other situations

On July 3, 2007, the Indians were playing the Tigers. Star reliever Rafael Betancourt was on the mound for the Indians. In the eighth inning, with the score tied 4–4 and the bases empty and one out, Betancourt was facing Carlos Guillén, ahead in the count, 0-2. Suddenly the count was 1-2, yet Betancourt never threw a pitch.

1: How is that possible?

A 2007 rule addition requires the pitcher to deliver the ball within twelve seconds after he receives it. The clock starts when the pitcher is in possession of the ball and the batter is in the box, alert to the pitcher, and stops when the pitcher delivers the ball. The penalty for violation of this rule is an automatic ball, which was called here by second-base umpire Doug Eddings. The rule was enforced on Betancourt again in the ninth, turning a 2-2 count on Brandon Inge into a full count. However both Guillén and Inge were retired by Betancourt.

2: Would Betancourt have been "on the clock" if runners were on base?

No. The rule only applies when there are no base runners.

Chapter 9

The Umpire

9.1 Ejections

The following play occurred in a minor league game, but the interpretation would be the same in a major league game. On June 12, 2008, Mike Hessman of the Toledo Mud Hens hit a long shot that was called foul. A brief argument ensued between Hessman and the umpires. Hessman stepped back into the batter's box and hit another long drive out of the ballpark almost in the same spot, which was ruled fair. While circling the bases, Hessman made a comment to the first-base umpire that was not appreciated, and he was immediately ejected.

1: Does the home run count?

Yes, if he finishes his home run trot. When a player is ejected in the middle of a play, the play proceeds until there is no further action per Rule 9.01(d).

2: What if Hessman, upon hearing that he was ejected, simply ran back to the dugout? Would the home run count?

This presents a more interesting situation, but the answer is no. To be given credit for the home run, Hessman would have to touch all the bases (Rule 7.02). Therefore, his failure to do so means he would have been out, regardless of the home run. The fact that he didn't continue running would have been his own fault since Rule 9.01(d) specifically provides that a disqualification does not take effect until no further action is possible. In this case, he abandoned his rights as a runner once he entered the dugout. The onus is on him to know that ejection does not take place in the middle of the play. The ejection can't begin until continuous action has stopped. Whether runner abandonment has occurred is an umpire-discretion issue.

3: Can a player be ejected after the game is over?

Yes. On June 23, 2010, the Angels-Dodgers game in Anaheim saw Dodgers catcher Russell Martin ejected after the game ended. When this happens, the ejected player is eligible to play in the next game but is subject to a fine. With the Angels leading 2–1 in the top of the ninth, Reed Johnson was on second and Martin was on first with two outs. Pinch hitter Jamey Carroll hit a single to left field. Martin was called out at second base when Angels left fielder Juan Rivera threw behind him after he had rounded the base. Martin was ruled tagged out before Reed Johnson had scored the apparent tying run. Since Martin's was the third out, the game was over. Martin was nevertheless ejected for arguing the call. Two nights later, Dodgers first baseman James Loney was ejected after the game ended when he argued a Mariano Rivera third-strike call by umpire Phil Cuzzi in the Dodgers' 2–1 loss to the Yankees.

The discretion of umpires to eject players, coaches, or managers for unsportsmanlike conduct or language is broad. In another incident involving Russell Martin, on September 26, 2011, home plate umpire Paul Schrieber tossed Martin (who now was a Yankees catcher) from the game in the fifth inning because he made a joke following back-to-back walks by pitcher Phil Hughes. Or at least Martin claims his comments were a joke, telling reporters afterward that he asked, "Did you stretch before the game tonight?" and then added, "I feel like you're kind of tight tonight." Given the situation, it's not hard to see how Schrieber may have missed the humor, especially since Martin admitted afterward that he was being critical of the strike zone. However, as Martin put it afterward, "What, we can't talk anymore? It's a game, man, we're supposed to be having fun. I was just trying to get him to laugh. I didn't say he sucked. I didn't say he was the worst umpire in the league. I didn't cuss at him. I didn't say any of that stuff. And I got thrown out. That's tough to do.

9.2 Umpires' calls and appeals of those calls

On June 22, 1990, the Reds were playing the Dodgers. In the bottom of the ninth, with the score tied 5–5, umpire Terry Tata called Eric Davis of the Reds safe on a play at home, which would have won the game for the Reds. However, a moment later he reversed himself and called Davis out. The Dodgers went on to win 7–6 in eleven innings.

1: Was Tata permitted to reverse himself?

Although Rule 9.02(a) provides that an umpire's decision on judgment calls is final, the rules do not specifically address if or when an umpire can change his mind on a judgment call. As we will see below in the section on time plays, there was a play where an umpire was permitted to change a call several innings later, but (1) that play involved a misinterpretation of the rules rather than a judgment call, and (2) the league indicated that such a situation would not be permitted to recur. It would seem, though, that if an umpire reverses himself on a judgment call before another play has occurred, it would be a case of no harm, no foul. Of course, an intervening action between the initial call and the reversed call would complicate matters.

According to Rule 9.02(a), calls that involve an umpire's judgment—such as safe vs. out, balls and strikes, etc.—are final. Moreover, not only are such calls final, but according to the rule, no player, manager, or coach is even permitted to object to such judgment decisions. This is obviously one of baseball's routinely ignored rules. One wonders why managers and coaches so routinely challenge exactly these kinds of calls, often getting thrown out in the process. Umpires cannot reverse these calls whether they are wrong or right. One also wonders why the umpires tolerate any of these disputes at all, especially when managers storm onto the field to argue for a few minutes. The possible benefit of "working the ump" has to be weighed against getting thrown out. (In no other major sports league are coaches allowed to enter the field and interrupt play to dispute calls.)

Notwithstanding Rule 9.02(a), some calls that are judgment calls can be appealed and reversed, especially those not enumerated in Rule 9.02(c). For example, on April 21, 2010, the Reds were playing the Dodgers. With the bases loaded and two outs, Aaron Harang of the Reds hit a soft liner to right, and Dodgers right fielder Andre Ethier appeared to make a sliding catch to end the inning. First-base umpire, and crew chief, Tim McClelland called it a catch for the apparent third out. Replays, however, showed that the ball clearly hit the ground first. After both teams left the field, Reds manager Dusty Baker came out to argue and appeal the call.

The umpires conferred and McClelland's ruling was overruled. The rule cited was 9.02(c), which reads, "If a decision is appealed, the umpire making the decision may ask another umpire for information before making a final decision. No umpire shall criticize, seek to reverse or interfere with another umpire's decision unless asked to do so by the umpire making it."

"I called him out. We got together; through consultation we determined that he didn't catch the ball," McClelland told a pool reporter. "We got a directive that says we can place runners where we thought they would have been had the call been called accurately the first time. We put the runners at the bases."

2: Did the umpires do the right thing in reversing the call?

Yes. To analyze this play, we have to consider the interaction of Rules 9.02(a), (b), and (c). As discussed above, Rule 9.02(a) provides essentially that judgment calls are final. However, Rule 9.02(b) provides, "If there is reasonable doubt that any umpire's decision may be in conflict with the rules, the manager may appeal the decision and ask that a correct ruling be made." Rule 9.02(c) provides, "If a decision is appealed, the umpire making the decision may ask another umpire for information before making a final decision." The above play fell into this category.

Some have commented that Rules 9.02(a) and 9.02(b) are "seemingly contradictory." However, this is not the case. The distinction between them is analogous to the distinction between the facts of a legal case and the law of a legal case. When a judge's decision is appealed based on the facts of a case, that decision is entitled to great deference. By contrast, when a judge's decision is appealed based on the law as he or she perceived it, then the higher court gives the decision much less deference and indeed reviews it as if it were a new case. Rules 9.02(a) and (b) operate in a similar fashion. Rule 9.02(a) is referring to certain judgment calls, as we saw above (safe vs. out, ball or strike, etc.). On the other hand, Rule 9.02(b) is referring to an umpire's decision that is in conflict with the rules, which are really the laws of baseball. If this occurs, Rule 9.02(c) refers to the mechanics by which this process takes place.

Managers as well as umpires need to be aware of Rule 9.02(c), which allows managers to request crew consultation if an umpire's decision is in conflict with the rules. That rule, which came into being in 2010, goes beyond that, however, since some judgment calls by umpires not in conflict with the rules are routinely reversed after the umps huddle. The manager must appeal only to the umpire who made the protested decision and let the umps take care of the rest.

If an umpire's signal confuses the players on the field, this can be cause for reversal if the actions of the umpire jeopardize the runners. This is what should have happened in the Dodgers-Padres game on April 15, 2012. With the game tied 4–4 in the ninth, the Padres had Chase Headley and Yonder Alonso on first and second with Jesús Guzmán at bat. Guzmán attempted to avoid a Javy Guerra pitch that was high and inside. He pulled his bat back, but the ball struck the bat and trickled into fair territory in front of the plate. Plate umpire Dale Scott raised both arms as if he were calling "time" or "foul." He then pointed to the ball, indicating it was fair. At no time did he verbalize a foul call.

The runners, as well as Guzmán, did not run, thinking the ball was dead based on Scott's initial signal of raising his arms. Dodgers catcher A. J. Ellis picked up the ball and fired to third baseman Juan Uribe to start an easy 2-5-6-3 triple play. Padres manager Bud Black argued the play and was ejected. However, he did not request a crew consultation and there was none. Since Scott's actions clearly confused the Padre runners, this would have been an ideal situation for a crew consultation. The *Major League Baseball Umpire Manual* states, "Umpire dignity is important but never as important as getting the play right."

3: In one specified instance in the rules, a manager (or catcher) may appeal an umpire's judgment call that would otherwise be covered by Rule 9.02(a). What is it?

Whether the batter went around on his swing or checked it. While the manager can't directly complain that the home plate umpire made the wrong call, he can request that the umpire ask another umpire for assistance. This comes from the Comment to Rule 9.02(c). Obviously, this only applies to a called ball.

On August 24, 1998, the Mets were playing the Diamondbacks. In the bottom of the eighth, the Mets had John Olerud on first and Jermaine Allensworth on second. On a 3-2 pitch to Brian McRae, with both runners on the move, home plate umpire Greg Bonin initially ruled that McRae had checked his swing on Willie Banks's curveball for ball four. That should have loaded the bases. However, catcher Kelly Stinnett instinctively threw to second in an effort to catch Olerud stealing. Stinnett then appealed to umpire Bill Hohn at third base, who immediately ruled that McRae had not checked his swing and had therefore struck out. Making matters worse for the Mets, Olerud was thrown out at second, making the old "strike 'em out, throw 'em out" double play. Replays showed that Hohn's call was correct, that McRae did go around for strike three.

4: Mets manager Bobby Valentine nevertheless complained about the play. On what basis?

First, although Rule 9.02(c) did not exist in 1998, it has always been the case that a catcher could appeal a case like this. Rather, Valentine argued that Bonin, who had held up four fingers for a walk, had to ask for help from another umpire to change his call, and that help could not be volunteered and could not be offered in response to an appeal by a player. When umpires place a runner in jeopardy, they can reverse a call under Rule 9.02(c). It does not appear in this play that the umpires put Olerud in jeopardy.

The Comment to Rule 9.02(c) provides helpful "advice" to base runners in this situation, and it specifically contemplates the situation that occurred above: "Base runners must be alert to the possibility that the base umpire on appeal from the plate umpire may reverse the call of a ball to the call of a strike, in which event the runner is in jeopardy of being out by the catcher's throw." On the above play, it is not clear whether Olerud's attempt to steal second was affected by Bonin's initial ball-four call or whether he even knew about it. If he did, the natural inclination would be to slow down in the belief that McRae had walked.

5: On July 3, 2006, the Mets hosted the Pirates. In the top of the sixth inning, Jason Bay of the Pirates hit a grounder to third baseman

David Wright, who threw wide to first baseman Carlos Delgado. Bay ran past Delgado and did not touch first base as he went by the bag. On his return to first, Delgado tagged Bay and he was called out by umpire Ángel Hernández. Would Hernández have been able to call Bay safe at that moment?

Yes. Even though this is an unwritten rule of umpire mechanics, many umpires will call a batter runner "safe" at first if he is not tagged or the fielder misses the base. This is not to say, however, that the batter-runner cannot be called out on appeal. However, some umpires will simply make no call at all in this situation until the batter-runner either touches first or is called out on appeal. This is similar to how such plays are handled at home plate: "no touch, no tag, no call."

6: Whether or not Hernández called Bay safe at the moment he passed the bag untagged, what determines whether Bay will ultimately be safe or out?

He will be out either by appeal or by being tagged before he gets back to first base. Note, however, that the way Bay acts after he passes first can be relevant. Say, for example, that he runs fifteen feet past the bag and is casually strolling back to first. In this type of "relaxed action," the Mets can either tag him or make an appeal. However, if Bay were to immediately realize his error and run hard back to first, then he would have to be tagged first and the Mets could not immediately yell for an appeal, the same way that basketball players sometimes immediately ask for a timeout when about to get tied up after chasing a loose ball.

9.3 Conflicting calls by umpires

Look at the photo below, where one umpire is signaling out at the same moment as another is signaling safe. How did it happen? On May 12, 1969, the Dodgers' Bill Sudakis tried to take second on a looper into short center that the Cardinals' shortstop and second baseman both chased. However, center fielder Curt Flood fired the ball into second, where third baseman Mike Shannon was covering. John Kibler, the second-base umpire, had initially gone out toward center field. Seeing that, first-base umpire Ed Vargo hustled into second just in time for the play . . . and the arrival of Kibler back to the second-base area. Kibler, on the left, is calling Sudakis out, while Vargo is adamant with a safe call. Home plate umpire Al Barlick told the bewildered Dodgers manager that the call was Kibler's and the runner was out.

The Dodgers' Bill Sudakis tried to take second on a looper into short center. Cards center fielder Curt Flood fired the ball into second. John Kibler, the second-base umpire, had initially gone out toward center field. Seeing that, first-base umpire Ed Vargo hustled into second just in time for the play . . . and the arrival of Kibler back to the second-base area. Kibler, on the left, is calling Sudakis out, while Vargo is adamant with a safe call. What happens now? *© Bettmann/Corbis*

1: How would this be handled today?

They would huddle and decide which was the correct call. Under Rule 9.04(c), "if different decisions should be made on one play by different umpires, the umpire-in-chief shall call all the umpires into consultation [and] shall determine which decision shall prevail."

9.4 Bench players protesting an umpire decision

1: Which of the following statements is true:

A. An umpire can without warning order players on the bench to the clubhouse for arguing an umpire's decision.

B. Players on the bench have less leeway to argue balls and strikes than other kinds of umpire's decisions.

C. A player on the bench who has been ordered to the clubhouse for arguing can play in the game afterward anyway if needed.

D. An umpire cannot order anyone to the clubhouse for arguing decisions if he doesn't know who is arguing.

Choice A is not correct because the umpire is supposed to give a warning first. Choice D is not correct because the umpire has the right to clear the bench of all substitute players if he can't detect the offending player or players. Choice C is correct, although the language of the rule is somewhat ambiguous. Rule 4.08 provides that the manager of the offending team shall have the privilege of recalling to the field those players needed for substitution.

Note that this rule is distinct from Rule 9.01(d), which addresses actually ejecting players from games—this rule involves simply removing players (or anyone else on the bench) from the bench to the clubhouse. Therefore, while the umpire's sanctioning tools under this rule are rather weak, he always has the outright ejectment option in his back pocket.

There is precedent for clearing an entire bench. On September 27, 1951, the Brooklyn Dodgers were playing the Boston Braves. In the bottom of the eighth inning, with the score tied 3–3, the Braves had Bob Addis on third and one out. The batter hit a grounder to second baseman Jackie Robinson, who fired to catcher Roy Campanella in an attempt to throw out Addis. Although it looked as if Addis was out, home plate umpire Frank Dascoli called him safe. First Campanella was ejected and so, too, was coach Cookie Lavagetto. Then the Dodgers bench got into it, and eventually Dascoli ordered them all to the clubhouse.

In an interesting side note to this story, sitting on the bench for the Dodgers that day was Bill Sharman, who had been called up from the minors earlier in the day. Sharman was among the players removed. He never did get into a major league game, but he did win several NBA titles with Bill Russell and the Boston Celtics and is now in the pro basketball Hall of Fame. So, Sharman became the answer to two trivia questions: (1) Who is the only NBA Hall of Famer to earn a spot on a major league roster even though he never played? (2) Who is the only baseball player to have been removed from the dugout to the clubhouse who never played a major league game?

Chapter 10

Other Situations

10.1 Announcement of substitutions

On August 6, 2008, the Dodgers were playing the Cardinals. In the top of the eighth, with the Dodgers trailing 9–4 and a man on second, the Dodgers Mark Sweeney left the on-deck circle and went toward home plate to pinch-hit for second baseman Pablo Ozuna.

When home plate umpire Chris Guccione saw Sweeney coming up to bat, he looked to the Dodgers dugout for manager Joe Torre, who was supposed to point to Sweeney to officially signal that he had entered the game. However, while Guccione was looking for Torre with his back turned to home plate, Sweeney stepped into the batter's box.

Torre then decided that he wanted to send Jeff Kent to the plate instead of Sweeney, so he could use Sweeney as a pinch hitter for another batter later in the inning or game. Torre asked Guccione if Sweeney was in the game. Because Torre hadn't pointed at Sweeney (and because Guccione hadn't noticed Sweeney digging into the box), Guccione said no.

"That was when I pointed at Kent," Torre said. Torre's pointing at Kent meant Kent had officially entered the game. No pitches were made to Sweeney.

1: Was Guccione's answer to Torre correct?

No. Under Rule 3.08(a)(2), even if no announcement of a batter substitution is made, the batter is considered to have entered the game once he takes his place in the batter's box. Therefore, Sweeney *was* in the game, regardless of what Guccione told Torre.

2: Torre argued that he had a right to rely on what Guccione told him and that he should be able to use Sweeney later in the game, especially because Sweeney never even saw a pitch. Torre said, "When an umpire tells me something, I think if I can't believe an umpire, how can I go about my business?" Was he right?

No. When Torre pointed at Kent, Sweeney was out of the game, without ever having seen a pitch. That Guccione gave Torre incorrect information, and that Torre relied on that information, was simply unfortunate for Torre.

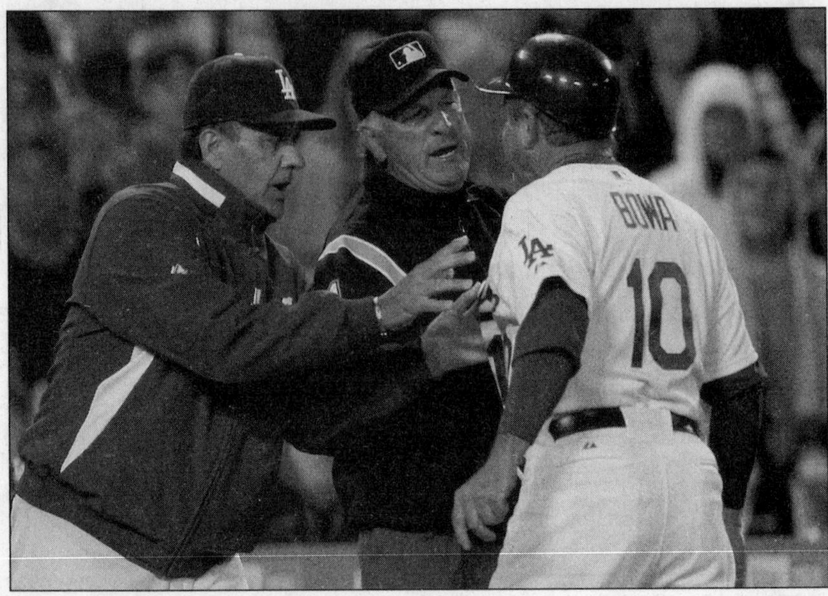

Los Angeles Dodgers manager Joe Torre, left, attempted to separate irate third-base coach Larry Bowa, right, from third-base umpire Ed Montague after Bowa was thrown out of the game by Montague for standing outside his coaching box. Does Bowa have a beef? *AP Photo/Kevork Djansezian*

10.2 Positioning of base coaches

1: True or false? The *Official Baseball Rules* prohibits the first- or third-base coach from standing outside his respective coach's box, and he can be ejected if he does.

Believe it or not, though there is a caveat, the answer is true. Rule 4.05(b)(2) provides that base coaches have to remain within the coach's box at all times. In terms of actual enforcement, this rule ranks right up there with Rule 3.09, which prohibits fraternizing between players while on the field.

Is the rule ever enforced? Rarely (for reasons discussed below) but not never. The Comment for Rule 4.05 notes that it has long been common practice for coaches to stand "slightly outside" the coaching-box lines. (Now there's an understatement if ever there was one.) In 2008, new language was added to the Comment after this sentence that provides that, until the ball passes by, a coach cannot position himself closer to home plate or fair territory than the coach's box.

On April 1, 2008, just after this provision was added to the Comment, the Dodgers were playing the Giants. In the sixth inning, umpire Ed Montague felt that Dodgers third-base coach Larry Bowa was standing closer to home plate than permitted by the rule and told him to move back. Bowa refused and was ejected by Montague.

In commenting on the rule, writer Tim Brown stated, "In many situations, third-base coaches position themselves closer to the plate and further into foul ground, both to broaden their sightline and lessen the chance of being struck by a foul ball. . . . Third-base coaches often are the most active bodies on the field, vying for angles and insights, buying time and prodding runners, often more than one at a time."

Former third-base coach Rich Donnelly estimated that in a three-hour game he would spend maybe twenty seconds in the required area and added, "For him to do his job, he has to operate at different places. The box is one hundred percent useless. They must be awfully bored in those offices. We third-base coaches, we know what to do out there. We don't need to be told where to go. We know what the risks are. The boxes, the helmets, the whole thing is absurd. The suits are making all the rules. It's ridiculous."

The Comment to the rule adds that, with one exception, the rule is only to be enforced when the opposing manager complains. For example, if the manager thinks that one of the opposing base coaches is stealing signs by positioning himself outside the box, he can bring this to the attention of the umpire. The exception, however, is that the requirement of not being closer to home plate or fair territory exists whether the opposing manager complains or not. Indeed, in the Bowa situation, the Giants had not complained, but there he was too close to home plate.

Finally, given the proximity of base coaches to the batter, one would think that this would be an extremely hazardous line of work—and it can be. While there have been no fatalities in major league games, on July 23, 2007, first-base coach Mike Coolbaugh, coaching for the Tulsa Drillers, a Double-A affiliate of the Colorado Rockies, died after being hit by a line drive off the bat of Tino Sanchez of the Arkansas Travelers. Coolbaugh, a former major league player, had only been coaching at first for a few weeks.

10.3 Inciting fans

On October 4, 2003, the Red Sox were playing the Athletics at Fenway Park. Ted Lilly was pitching for the A's. Standing on the top step of the Red Sox dugout in the bottom of the fifth inning, in an attempt to urge the crowd to mockingly chant Lilly's name, three Red Sox reserves each had white letters taped to the backs of their jackets that spelled out "LI-L-LY."

A few thousand fans chanted the name "Lilly" during the inning, but the motivational jackets were not an overwhelming success. Lilly for the most part was. He allowed only 2 hits in 7 innings, even though the Red Sox won 3–1.

1: Did the players' conduct raise any issue regarding the rules? (No issue was raised by the A's or the umpires.)

Yes. Under Rule 4.06(a), no member of a team can incite a demonstration by spectators.

2: What if, instead, the same players simply held up a large placard in the dugout that said "LILLY," but which the fans could not see? Any issues there?

This is probably off-limits as well. Rule 4.06(a)(2) prohibits players from using language that reflects on opposing players, umpires, or spectators. Whether the use of a sign constitutes "language" may be open to debate because it is not spoken, but I say that it certainly does.

10.4 Distracting a hitter

On August 12, 1950, the New York Giants were playing the Phillies. With the Phils' Andy Seminick at bat, the Giants second baseman Eddie Stanky started waving his arms up and down in an effort to distract Seminick.

1: Was Stanky violating any specific baseball rule?

At the time, no, although Stanky was nevertheless ejected under the umpires' catchall power to oversee the game. After Stanky pulled this stunt, however, it became illegal. Rule 4.06(b)—which could perhaps be called "the Stanky Rule"—now provides that fielders cannot deliberately distract the batter. The penalty is removal from the game, although normally a warning is given first.

10.5 Conduct after ejectment

On May 31, 2000, the Red Sox were playing the Kansas City Royals in Fenway Park. In the second inning, with Royals runners on first and third, Johnny Damon hit a liner into the right-field corner. The ball came to a quick stop, as if a fan had touched it. (If the ball had been touched, then, under Rule 3.16, the umpires would have had discretion as to where to place the runners.) However, first-base umpire Jerry Crawford ruled that the ball was not touched by a fan, meaning that the Royals runner on first scored on the play. Red Sox manager Jimy Williams ran out of the dugout to argue the play with Crawford. Things got heated and Williams was ejected from the game. Bench coach Buddy Bailey assumed managerial duties after Williams's ejection. After the Sox had fallen behind 9–2, Red Sox stars Nomar Garciaparra and Carl Everett were taken out of the game in the seventh inning. In the eighth, however, the Red Sox rallied to score 5 runs to make the score 9–7. Because Garciaparra and Everett had been removed from the game, though, they were not available to contribute to the rally. The Sox lost 9–7.

After the game, there was controversy not only about the wisdom of removing the two Sox stars from the game, but who made the decision to do so. At first, Williams said that he had made the decision. "I accept the responsibility even though the kids we put in there had production," Williams said. "My reasoning, to be honest, is legs. I'm looking at it from the long run—a 9–2 game in the eighth." Shortstop Garciaparra also supported the decision: "You've got to understand what he's thinking. I just got off the DL and we're going on the road for fourteen days."

Bailey, however, later contradicted Williams, while defending him: "It was my decision. It was a situation where he was trying to protect the coaches just like he protects the players. You know how [Williams] is. As a manager, he's not going to let anybody take the rap—not his players and not his coaches."

When Williams was apprised of Bailey's remarks, he appeared to support them and thus reverse his previous claim (and those of his players) that he had made the decision to take Garciaparra and Everett out of the game: "I'll back my coaches all the way. . . . Basically what I meant [on Wednesday] was that I accept the responsibility of our coaches making those decisions and I'll stand by them."

1: Why was there any discussion at all as to who made the decision to take out Garciaparra and Everett?

Because Rule 4.07 clearly provides that an ejected manager shall leave the field immediately and take no further part in the game. The rule does not specify the penalty for violating its terms. However, after claiming responsibility for the on-field moves, Williams learned that American League vice president of operations Frank Robinson was planning to review the matter, meaning Williams might be subject to disciplinary action. He may therefore have become concerned, which could have led to Bailey's claiming that the responsibility lay with him, followed by Williams's volte-face.

According to one Sox player, it is common knowledge throughout the major leagues that most ejected managers simply run the game from the dugout runway, out of plain sight. Williams acknowledged, however, that Major League Baseball had recently issued a directive warning managers from that practice.

2: On September 10, 2010, the Yankees were playing the Rangers. In the bottom of the tenth inning, Rangers second baseman Ian Kinsler was ejected from the game by home plate umpire Dale Scott for arguing a third-strike call. Three innings later, with the scored tied 5–5, Nelson Cruz of the Rangers hit a walk-off home run. As Cruz was rounding the bases, Kinsler came out with the rest of his teammates to welcome Cruz at home plate. Was he permitted to do that in view of the walk-off homer?

No, and he was suspended for one game for his actions. The reasoning was that, because Cruz had not yet touched home plate when Kinsler came out onto the field, the game was not over yet, and therefore Kinsler had no right to be on the field.

10.6 Participating in a game

On April 6, 2005, the Dodgers were playing the Giants. In the fifth inning, Dodgers closer Eric Gagne, who was on the disabled list with a sprained elbow ligament, started arguing ball and strike calls from the dugout with home plate umpire Bill Hohn. He was suspended for two games.

1: Why?

The Comment to Rule 3.17 specifically provides that while players on the disabled list may sit in the dugout during the game, they cannot participate in any activity during the game, including "bench-jockeying." Gagne's conduct was considered bench-jockeying, and he thus received the suspension (even though neither the rule nor the Comment specifies the penalty for a violation). Players not on the disabled list (and managers) are not prohibited from bench-jockeying, but they can be ejected if they go over the line.

In 2010, both Chipper Jones of the Braves and Ross Gload of the Phillies were ejected from games while on the disabled list. Also, prior to 1976, the opposing manager had to give his consent for a player on the disabled list to sit on the bench.

2: Say that instead of Gagne, Dodgers catcher Jason Phillips was on the DL. Between innings, while the substitute catcher was putting on his gear, Phillips went out to warm up a pitcher. Is that permitted?

No. Disabled players are prohibited from entering the playing surface at all during the game for any purpose. However, on August 15, 2010, the Cincinnati Reds used shortstop Orlando Cabrera, who was on the disabled list, as their batboy. He not only performed all the functions of a batboy—retrieving foul balls hit off the screen, bringing extra balls and water to the home plate umpire—he even wore a jersey with "BB" on the back.

3: We know now that while players on the disabled list may sit in the dugout during the game, they are pretty much confined to sitting there quietly. What about other players in the dugout, however, who are not playing in the game? For example, can a reserve outfielder go out between innings to warm up one of the outfielders in the game?

Yes. Although Rule 3.17 requires players and substitutes of both teams to confine themselves to the bench unless actually participating in the play or preparing to enter the game, this is confined to live-ball situations and not what takes place between innings. As noted above, players on the disabled list (other than perhaps Orlando Cabrera!) cannot enter the playing surface at all.

10.7 "Play" vs. "time" on foul ball

On July 3, 2003, the Oakland A's hosted the Seattle Mariners. The A's were batting in the fourth inning when Eric Byrnes grounded out harmlessly to first baseman Greg Colbruun. However first-base umpire Greg Gibson called a foul ball immediately after Byrnes made contact. Gibson thought Byrnes had hit the ball off his front foot, thus making it foul.[1] Thinking the ball was in play, Byrnes took off for first on the crack of the bat, apparently not aware at first that Gibson had ruled the play a foul ball. It is not clear whether Byrnes later heard Gibson repeat the call and then slowed down.

Seattle skipper Bob Melvin argued the ball never hit Byrnes's foot. Three of the four umpires agreed. The crew met near the pitcher's mound for a couple of minutes and decided to call Byrnes out, but first called upon Oakland manager Ken Macha, who, after a heated discussion, protested the game.

1: Did the umps make the right call by calling Byrnes out, or to answer do we first have to know whether the ball actually touched Byrnes?

1. *If the ball had in fact hit Byrnes, it would clearly be a foul ball. Rule 2.02 defines a foul ball as "a batted ball that . . . while on or over foul territory, touches the person of an umpire or player." The batter's box is foul territory.*

The Red Sox had Gabe Kapler on first when Tony Graffanino homered. While rounding second, Kapler ruptured his Achilles tendon. He fell to the ground but couldn't continue. Graffanino stood about ten feet away from his fallen teammate. After a five-minute delay, Boston manager Terry Francona put in a substitute runner to round the bases for Kapler. Was Francona's move legal? What if Graffanino had instead hit a ball off the fence? ***AP Photo/CP, Frank Gunn***

According to the rulebook, they probably made the wrong call, whether the ball actually touched Byrnes or not. Macha cited Rule 5.02 as the basis for his protest. The rule reads, "After the umpire calls 'Play' the ball is alive and in play and remains alive and in play until for legal cause, or at the umpire's call of 'Time' suspending play, the ball becomes dead. While the ball is dead no player may be put out, no bases may be run and no runs may be scored." The point of Macha's argument is that once Gibson called "foul" it was the same as if he had called "time." Gibson killed the play. In addition, Rule 5.09(e) provides that the ball is dead when a foul ball is not caught.

A former umpire said that he has seen plays where a foul ball was called and the call was ignored if it did not affect the runner or runners. He thought the umpires were justified in reversing Gibson's call only if the mistaken call did not affect the outcome of the play. Some umpires divert from the actual terms of the rulebook and adopt a "no harm, no foul" policy (in this case literally so). The current philosophy is to get the call right.

2: What if the situation were reversed and Byrnes believed that he did bat the ball off his foot and thus didn't move out of the batter's box, but the umpire didn't call a foul ball? He is then out at first base. Would the umps be making the right call in calling him out even if Byrnes was correct that the ball touched him?

In this situation, even if the umps were wrong (i.e., they missed that the ball hit Byrnes's foot), they would be right in that the ball is always alive and in play until they call "time" or a foul ball. As is implicit from Rule 5.02, until the umpire actually calls the ball foul, then the players must assume that it is not foul.

In 2010, Rule 9.02(c) was expanded to give the umpires far greater leeway to consult with one another after an appeal and to reverse many types of calls after such consultation.

10.8 Incapacitated player

On September 14, 2005, the Red Sox were playing Toronto. In the top of the fifth inning, the Red Sox had Gabe Kapler on first when Tony Graffanino followed with a homer to left that gave the Sox a 3–2 lead. While rounding second base, Kapler ruptured his Achilles tendon. He fell to the ground, got up on one knee, but couldn't continue. Graffanino stood about ten feet away from his fallen teammate. After a five-minute delay, Boston manager Terry Francona put in a substitute runner, Alejandro Machado, to round the bases for Kapler and complete his run.

1: Was Francona's move valid?

Yes. Under Rule 5.10(c)(1), when an accident incapacitates a player or an umpire so as to prevent him "from proceeding to a base to which he is entitled, as on a home run hit out of the playing field, or an award of one or more bases, a substitute runner shall be permitted to complete the play." Interestingly, this was the first run that Machado ever scored in the major leagues.

2: What if Graffanino had not hit a home run, but instead hit a line drive that bounced off the fence and then Kapler's injury occurred? Is a substitute runner allowed?

No, because it's a live ball and in play.

3: Could Graffanino have picked Kapler up and carried him around the bases?

Yes.

4: Could Graffanino have pulled Kapler around the bases?

No, because if Graffanino were pulling Kapler, that means that he would have passed him, and Rule 7.08(h) specifically prohibits a runner from passing a preceding runner.

5: If Kapler's injury had occurred when he was rounding third, and Graffanino had hit a home run, could the third-base coach have assisted him on the final portion of the circuit?

No. Rule 7.09(h) prohibits the first- or third-base coach from touching or holding the runner, or physically assisting him in returning to or leaving third base or first base.

Sometimes a play occurs that makes one wonder whether teams are aware of Rule 5.10(c)(1). For example, on May 9, 2012, Matt Joyce of the Rays hit a two-out, 3-run homer in the top of the ninth inning to give the Rays a 4–1 lead over the Yanks. The moment Joyce hit the ball, he crumpled to the ground in the batter's box after rolling his left ankle. He got up and jogged around the bases in "Kirk Gibson" fashion after the ball sailed over the right-field wall. He was not offered any assistance. Either the Rays were not aware that a rule offers protection in this situation, or perhaps they felt that he could gut it out and didn't want to take him out of the game. Joyce got taped and played the bottom of the ninth on defense.

10.9 Calling "time"

On April 14, 2002, the Yankees were playing the Red Sox at Fenway Park. Yankees third baseman Robin Ventura led off the eighth inning. With a 3-2 count, Sox pitcher Sunny Kim threw a called third strike. However, unbeknownst to anyone else, first-base ump Larry Young had called "time" just before the pitch was thrown because a beach ball had rolled onto the field.

1: Did the first-base umpire have the authority to call "time" and does it undo what happened next, even if no one else was aware of the call?

Yes. The first-base umpire did have the authority to call "time" (whether anyone else knew about it or not) and the strikeout pitch was nullified. Under Rule 9.04(b)(2), field umpires, as well as the plate umpire, have the authority to call "time" whenever they deem it necessary. Ventura, given new life, turned an apparent strikeout into a run when he hit a home run into the center-field bleachers. This rule can cause heartbreak to either side.

2: On July 19, 2006, the Yankees were playing the Mariners. In the bottom of the seventh inning, the Yankees had Alex Rodríguez on first and no outs when Andy Phillips hit a shot to deep right center. On a play at the plate, A-Rod was called safe. Mariners catcher René Rivera turned his back on Phillips and argued with plate ump Mike Reilly. Phillips saw this and took off for third. Meanwhile Seattle manager Mike Hargrove came out to argue the play before "time" was called. Third-base umpire Andy Fletcher then called "time," and sent Phillips back to second. Yankees manager Joe Torre argued that Fletcher should not have called "time." Did Torre have a beef?

Yes. Rule 5.10(h) prohibits an umpire from calling "time" *while a play is in progress*, unless there is light failure or if a runner becomes incapacitated while the ball is dead. In this case, the play was still in progress.

A similar situation arose earlier that year in a game between the Braves and the Mets. On May 7, the Braves had Brian McCann on third and Ryan Langerhans on first when John Smoltz hit a dribbler that just cleared the batter's box. Mets catcher Paul Lo Duca barehanded the ball and appeared to tag the charging McCann on the rear end. Umpire Ángel Hernández ruled McCann safe, which gave the Braves a 1–0 lead. In protest of the call, Lo Duca went ballistic, displaying his "touchdown dance," and spiked the ball in front of Hernández, which earned the Mets backstop a trip to the showers. While Lo Duca was carrying on, Langerhans waltzed to third base, and Smoltz, who had hesitated between first and second, took off for second base. Hernández, for some reason, called "time" after Lo Duca picked up a still-live ball during his protest and before Smoltz had reached second. Smoltz was ordered to return to first, which upset Braves skipper Bobby Cox, who was subsequently ejected.

10.10 Base coach acting to draw a throw

In a game way back in 1914, Cardinals manager Miller Huggins was coaching third base (as was common practice at the time) in a game against the Brooklyn Dodgers. In the seventh inning, with a Cards runner on third, Huggins reportedly yelled at the Brooklyn pitcher, "Hey, Bub, let me see that ball!" The startled young pitcher threw it over to Huggins, who then stepped aside and let the ball roll away while the runner on third scored. The umpires ruled that because "time" had not been called, the run counted.

1: Would the result be the same today?

No. Rule 7.09(j), which did not exist in 1914, provides that it is interference by a coach when "with a runner on third base, the base coach leaves his box and acts in any manner to draw a throw by a fielder." The second part of this rule is just what Huggins did (though it is not known where he was standing nor would it have mattered at the time). Therefore, he would have committed interference and the ball would be dead.

10.11 Effect of reversed calls

On April 6, 2006, the Reds were playing the Pirates. With the score tied 5–5 in the bottom of the eighth inning, the Reds had runners on first and second with two outs when Adam Dunn hit a sinking liner off Mike González that diving center fielder Chris Duffy trapped on a short hop. Duffy held his glove for the umpires to see, and third-base umpire Bruce Dreckman raised his arm to signal out. Duffy knew all along he had trapped it. "I just decided to play it up as a catch," Duffy said. "And then I saw the ump giving the out call."

The jubilant Pirates left the field while the Reds fumed, led by manager Jerry Narron. The four umps huddled and reversed the call. The question the umps then had to decide was where to place the runners. They decided to allow Felipe López, the runner on second, to score, and to place Chris Denorfia, the runner on first, on third. Dunn remained at first. The reversed call gave the Reds a 6–5 lead, which proved to be the final score.

1: Did the umpires handle the situation correctly?

They did not, not because of the *Official Baseball Rules*, but because of Section 4.12 of the *Major League Baseball Umpire Manual*, which provides, "Some judgment calls are not subject to reversal. An example is a catch/no catch situation with multiple runners." An equivalent situation would be a pass-interference call in football. Thus, in the above play, by getting it right (correctly ruling that Duffy had not caught the ball), the umps got it wrong (impermissibly reversing a judgment call).

Why the prohibition on reversing the catch/no-catch call with runners on base? Because the umpire's original call will signal the runners to advance or return. The original call will also determine which base a fielder will throw to. If a call is reversed, the umpires must then arbitrarily place the runners, as they did in the play above. This can incite further problems.

2: Would it have made any difference if the bases were empty when the play happened?

It would have made a difference and the umps' reversal would have been appropriate. With no base runners, no one is taking action (advance or return) based on the umpire's original call. Here, the only goal is to get the call right.

10.12 Plays not addressed by the rules

Compare the following two plays.

Play No. 1: On August 8, 2001, the A's were playing the Red Sox. In the third inning, Johnny Damon, then of the A's, lined a one-out shot down the right-field line that skidded along the grass and into a plastic beer cup that had been dropped out of the stands just in front of the foul pole. The speedy Oakland outfielder raced around the bases and appeared to have a sure triple, but Trot Nixon, the right fielder, threw up his hands to call the umpires' attention to the circumstances. While the umps jogged out to the corner, Damon walked home with an apparent inside-the-park home run. Crew chief Dana Demuth, however, conferred with Greg Gibson and Charlie Reliford and ruled the hit to be a double. Oakland manager Art Howe protested, but Damon was sent back to second.

Play No. 2: On May 9, 1997, the Yankees were playing the Royals. In the sixth inning, the bases were loaded for Kansas City with one out. José Offerman was on second and Jay Bell was on first. Jeff King of the Royals hit a hard grounder to third. Charlie Hayes stepped on third to force Offerman, but his throw skipped to the left of Tino Martinez at first. As a result of the bad throw, Bell hustled from first to third and then took a wide turn around third. Martinez retrieved the ball in short right field and threw quickly to pitcher Kenny Rogers, who was acting as a cutoff man. When Rogers threw to Hayes at third, Bell appeared to be caught in a rundown. However, before Bell was tagged, he was called out anyway by third-base umpire Dale Ford, who mistakenly believed that Bell had passed Offerman on the base paths even though Offerman was already out. With the Yankees back in the dugout (believing there were now three outs), the umpires huddled on the infield grass. They overruled Ford's decision, waved the Yankees back onto the field, and returned Bell to third and King to second. The Yankees protested the decision, but the protest was not upheld.

1: What do the above two plays have in common?

Both these situations are not governed by any of the rules and, in each case, the umpires used their discretion under Rule 9.01(c) to handle them. That rule gives umpires the authority to rule on any point "not specifically covered by these Rules." It's a nice catchall for umps in these kinds of situations. The first play above is similar to spectator interference in that the umpires can award whatever base they feel the runner would otherwise have reached.

PART TWO: SPECIALIZED ON-THE-FIELD SITUATIONS

Certain situations merit a separate discussion either because they are widely misunderstood, happen frequently, have many nuances, or because of all of the foregoing. The following situations fall under the general headings of interference, obstruction, time plays, defining a legal catch, the infield fly rule, and batting orders.

Chapter 11

Interference

11.1 Batter interference

11.1A Batter-runner interference on throw to first base

In the 2001 American League Division Series, the A's were playing the Yankees. In the bottom of the fifth inning, Yankee outfielder David Justice tapped a grounder in front of the plate. A's catcher Ramón Hernández fielded the ball and flipped it underhand to Jason Giambi at first base as Justice was about to reach the bag. The ball struck Justice, who was running just inside the foul line.

1: Which of the following statements is correct?

A. Justice is out if the umpire feels that he interfered with Giambi's ability to take the throw.

B. Justice is safe because Hernández should have taken care to avoid hitting him.

C. It depends on whether the umpire feels Justice was trying to intentionally interfere with the throw.

D. Justice is out if the umpire feels Justice was trying to intentionally interfere with Giambi's ability to take the throw.

The answer is A. Rule 6.05(k) provides that a batter is out when "in running the last half of the distance from home base to first base [i.e., the final forty-five feet] . . . he runs outside (to the right of) the three-foot line, or inside (to the left of) the foul line, and in the umpire's judgment interferes with the fielder taking the throw at first base." Thus Justice would be out if the umpire felt that he interfered with Giambi's ability to take the throw, regardless of Justice's intention (which is why D is wrong). The runner's box has been in baseball since 1881.

2: What if Justice was running inside the foul line but Hernández's throw had hit him while he was not yet halfway to first base?

A. Justice is out if the umpire feels that he interfered with Giambi's ability to take the throw.

B. Justice is safe because Hernández should have taken care to avoid hitting him.

C. It depends on whether the umpire feels Justice was trying to intentionally interfere with the throw.

D. Justice is out if the umpire feels Justice was trying to intentionally interfere with Giambi's ability to take the throw.

In this case, the correct answer is D. If the umpire felt there was intentional interference, then Justice could be called out even though there is no restricted baseline for the first forty-five feet. Choice A is not correct because of the intent requirement on the first forty-five feet to first base.

3: Would the result in the first problem be different if the ball had been hit to the third baseman instead, who then hit Justice while he was running well inside the baseline toward first?

No, as long as the umpire felt that Justice interfered with Giambi's ability to take the throw. It does not matter which fielder is making the throw or that that fielder's ability to make the throw is impaired by the runner. It only matters whether the runner interferes with the receiving fielder's ability to catch the ball.

4: Is it relevant whether the ball hits Justice?

No. If the umpire felt that Justice's running outside the designated area interfered (intentionally or not) with Giambi's ability to catch the ball, and if Justice is more than halfway to first base, it makes no difference whether the ball actually hits Justice.

5: What would be the result if Justice interfered with Giambi's ability to make the catch but Hernández made a poor throw that was uncatchable without Giambi's taking his foot off the base? Would Justice be safe?

Yes. This is analogous to the pass interference rule in football: if the ball is deemed uncatchable or unplayable, then there is no interference.

11.1B Batter interference with the catcher

On May 10, 2006, the Reds were playing the Nationals. In the second inning, with one out and less than two strikes, Nats catcher Brian Schneider attempted to steal second base with Liván Hernández at the plate. The throw from Reds catcher Jason LaRue flew into center field. However, Hernández swung at the pitch and then stepped over home plate and ducked as LaRue made his throw to second. Because of Hernández's actions, LaRue could not follow through on his throw to second.

1: Which of the following is true?

A. Schneider is out.

B. Hernández is out and Schneider goes back to first base.

C. Schneider is awarded the stolen base if the umpire feels that there was no intentional interference by Hernández.

D. Hernández is out if the umpire feels that there was intentional interference.

The correct answer is B, per Rule 6.06(c). The concept of intent has nothing to do with the interference, and the word "intent" does not appear in its definition. Thus C and D are incorrect. A is incorrect because Schneider has to go back to first base rather than being called out.

2: Would it have made any difference if Hernández interfered with the throw, but LaRue still threw out Schneider?

Yes. If the runner is thrown out, the batter will not be called out for interference.

3: What would happen if it was strike three and Schneider was not thrown out?

Then both the batter and the runner would be out.

4: Say that, as Schneider was attempting to steal second, Hernández swung and missed so hard that the bat carried around and struck LaRue before he had a good grip on the ball. Which of the following is true?

A. Hernández is out.

B. Schneider is awarded the stolen base if the umpire feels that Hernández's actions were unintentional.

C. Hernández is not out if the umpire feels that his actions were unintentional.

D. None of the above.

The correct answer is C. This is one of the few instances in which a player's intent can make a difference to the result of the play even if the player's actions fit within the definition of interference. Normally when a batter interferes with the catcher, the batter is called out and the runner is returned to his base. However, if the batter unintentionally interferes on the backswing, the runner is returned to the base, but the batter is not out, per Rule 6.06(c). He remains at bat. In this case, Schneider does not get the stolen base—he has to return to first. Of course, if Schneider had been thrown out, the interference would be ignored.

A play involving possible interference on a backswing occurred on August 16, 2008, when the Yankees and Royals played in New York. Early in the game, Derek Jeter was batting for the Yankees with Johnny Damon on first base. Damon took off on a pitch that Jeter missed. Plate umpire Wally Bell called "time" and sent Damon back to first because Jeter had unintentionally interfered with Royals catcher John Buck on his backswing. If Buck had made a play on Damon and thrown him out, the backswing interference would have been ignored.

5: Here is a variation on the previous problem. On September 2, 2011, the Phillies were playing the Marlins. In the bottom of the second inning, with no outs, the Marlins had Bryan Petersen on first and John Buck at the plate with one strike on him. As Petersen was trying to steal second, Buck swung and missed the pitch. Phils catcher Carlos

One of the most controversial plays in World Series history. With a runner on first, Ed Armbrister of the Reds bunted the ball in front of home plate. Boston catcher Carlton Fisk charged to field it. Fisk got tangled up with Armbrister, causing Fisk to throw wildly into center field. Umpire Larry Barnett ruled no interference. Right call? *AP Photo/Stan Denny*

Ruiz made an errant throw to second base, and the ball skipped away from second baseman Chase Utley. Upon seeing that, Petersen took off for third, but he was thrown out by Utley, with third baseman Plácido Polanco applying the tag. However, home plate umpire Sam Holbrook ruled that Buck had interfered with Ruiz's throw to second. What is the result of the play?

Buck is out for batter interference. Even though Petersen was thrown out at third, he still has to go back to first base. Although the exception to Rule 6.06(c) states that the batter is not out if any runner attempting to advance is put out, that only refers to being put out at the initial base he was trying to reach (here, second base), and not a subsequent base that he attempts to reach as a result of a poor throw by the fielder who was interfered with.

11.1C Batter-runner (or runner) interference with fielder attempting to field batted ball

One of the most controversial—if not *the* most controversial—plays in World Series history took place in Game 3 of the 1975 World Series between the Boston Red Sox and the Cincinnati Reds. With Cincinnati batting in the bottom of the tenth after the Red Sox had rallied from a 5–1 deficit to knot the score 5–5, César Gerónimo was on first with an opening single. Ed Armbrister then pinch-hit for pitcher Rawly Eastwick. Armbrister bunted the ball in front of home plate, and Boston catcher Carlton Fisk charged to field it. Armbrister and Fisk came together as Armbrister took two steps toward first, backed up, then started again. A photo of the play shows Fisk directly behind Armbrister, looking up in the air, appearing as if he is about to climb Armbrister's back.

When Fisk picked up the ball, he threw toward second base in an attempt to get the lead runner. However, the throw was wild into center field, and the Reds now had runners on second and third base because of the throwing error. Home plate umpire Larry Barnett made no call on the play. Fisk and Boston manager Darrell Johnson argued vehemently with him, asserting that Armbrister interfered with Fisk and that Armbrister should be out. Barnett later said that it was "simply a collision" and not interference.

1: Did Barnett make the right call or should he have called interference on Armbrister?

Opinions differed right from the start on this and continue to do so to this day. We start with the rather broad definition of offensive interference: "an act by the team at bat which interferes with, obstructs, impedes, hinders or confuses any fielder attempting to make a play." We then turn to Rule 7.09(j) (which was 7.09(l) at the time), which provides that it is interference by a batter-runner when "he fails to avoid a fielder who is attempting to field a batted ball, or intentionally interferes with a thrown ball."

The argument against Barnett's call is that Armbrister did indeed "fail to avoid" Fisk, which would seem to qualify as interference, especially since the question of intent is irrelevant for purposes of the definition. In defense of Barnett, however, umpire Jim Evans said, "Some people think that anytime there is contact, there has to be interference. That's not true. You have to ask yourself the question 'Is it illegal interference?'" According to Evans, three things can happen when a batter and runner collide. It could be interference (on the batter), obstruction (on the catcher), or it can be inadvertent contact, or, as Barnett said, "simply a collision." Barnett obviously felt that the play fell into the last of these categories. Also, as Armbrister explained, "I hit the ball in front of the plate and it bounced high. I started to break for first and Fisk just came from behind and bumped me." Photos of the play seem to support Armbrister's statement.

At the time of the play, the National League had given umpires a list of special instructions as a supplement to the rulebook. It stated that collisions of this type in the area of home plate were not to be called interference. Barnett, despite being an AL umpire, was apparently following these instructions. There now exists a Comment to Rule 7.09(j) that retroactively supports Barnett's call: "When a catcher and batter-runner going to first base have contact when the catcher is fielding the ball, there is generally no violation and nothing should be called."

11.2 Runner interference

11.2A Runner interference with thrown ball or fielder making a play on batted ball

On May 25, 2004, the Royals were playing the Tigers. Trailing 4–3 in the top of the ninth inning, Detroit had Carlos Guillén on first and Alex Sánchez on third with one out. Iván "Pudge" Rodríguez then tapped a slow roller to Royals shortstop Ángel Berroa. In attempting to break up a possible double play, Guillén, who was running like a wild racehorse, slid past the bag and made a rolling block to hinder Relaford's throw to first base. Relaford's throw was in fact too late to double up Rodríguez. It appeared that the Tigers had tied the game. Second-base umpire C. B. Bucknor ruled Guillén out for interference.

1: Assuming for argument that Guillén's actions did not actually prevent the double play, did the umpire make the right call?

Yes. He enforced Rule 6.05(m), which provides, "A batter is out when a preceding runner shall, in the umpire's judgment, intentionally interfere with a fielder who is attempting to catch a thrown ball or to throw a ball in an attempt to complete any play." Thus, since it's a judgment call, it would be impossible for the umpire to have made the "wrong call." Whether the runner's actions were successful is irrelevant. What is relevant is the *attempt* to break up the double play, if done in an illegal fashion. Even if Guillén had beaten the throw to second, he would have been out anyway, by virtue of Rule 7.08(b), which provides that a runner is out when "he intentionally interferes with a thrown ball; or hinders a fielder attempting to make a play on a batted ball."

2: True or false? Guillén's interference means that he is out at second but has no effect on the batter-runner, Rodríguez.

False. Under 6.05(m), the batter-runner is out as well due to Guillén's interference. The game thus ended on this unusual double play.

There are five types of interference that can take place around second base, baseball's combat zone, that are illegal:

1. A runner cannot execute a roll block.
2. A runner is prohibited from throwing his body at the fielder's body by using a sideways motion.
3. A runner cannot hook or trip the pivot man's legs or crash into the pivot man at second base in a double-play situation.
4. A runner is prohibited from sliding in such a way that his entire body is more than three feet outside or inside a direct line between first and second base. (The runner has to be able to reach the base with his arm or leg.)
5. Beginning with the 2004 season, if a runner makes any contact that begins after the bag, on the shortstop side of second base, the batter-runner will also be ruled out. That was precisely Guillén's sin in the play above.

Following the game, Bucknor explained why he enforced the "automatic double play" against the Tigers, ruling both Guillén and Rodríguez out. "He [Guillén] slid way past the bag like a rolling block trying to break up a double play. If he slides and he can touch the bag, he's all right. He was still standing when he went in."

Guillén, obviously not aware of the rule, was shocked by Bucknor's call, as was Tigers skipper Alan Trammell. Guillén complained, "Why do I have to slide before the bag? He had already released the ball out of his hand. He made a good, hard throw and he [Rodríguez] is still safe." The fact that Guillén was standing when he went into the bag didn't help his case. His mistake cost his team at least a 4–4 tie and maybe the ball game. Relaford, the victim on the play, said, "He [Guillén] hit me somewhat. I was just trying to get rid of the ball. He didn't slide. He just came in and tried to roll into me." That was enough for Bucknor to throw the book at Guillén.

The strange game-ending play left the Tigers growling. Trammell

2004 ALCS. Red Sox–Yankees. Alex Rodríguez hit a soft roller toward first. Sox pitcher Bronson Arroyo picked up the spinning squibber, put the ball in his glove, and went to tag A-Rod. Rodríguez gave a chop, knocking the ball out of Arroyo's glove and down the first-base line. Jeter came around to score on the play. Is this interference on A-Rod or obstruction on Arroyo, as argued by Yankees manager Joe Torre? *AP Photo/Amy Sancetta*

said he had never seen an ending like that. "To lose a game like that at the end, I'm not very happy. I just can't believe they called it at that particular time," he lamented.

Interference with a thrown ball or fielder making a play on a batted ball does not always occur at second base. A famous play involving runner interference occurred in Game 6 of the 2004 ALCS between the Red Sox and the Yankees. In the eighth inning, the Yankees were trailing 4–2 and had Derek Jeter on first with one out. Alex Rodríguez hit a soft roller toward first. Sox pitcher Bronson Arroyo and first baseman Doug Mientkiewicz both converged on the ball and soon recognized the obvious: neither was covering first. Arroyo picked up the spinning squibber, put the ball in his glove, and went to tag A-Rod. Rodríguez, seeing what was developing, came

October 11, 2007, NLCS Game 1 between Arizona and Colorado. The D'Backs had Justin Upton on first when Augie Ojeda hit a grounder to third baseman Garrett Atkins. Atkins then threw to second baseman Kaz Matsui for an out. Upton, running from first, slid past second base and then rolled his right shoulder into Matsui's left leg, knocking him to the ground. Is this interference? If so, what is the result of the play? ***AP Photo/ Ross D. Franklin***

down hard with a left-hand chop, knocking the ball out of Arroyo's glove and sending it down the first-base line. Jeter came around to score on the play.

First-base umpire Randy Marsh signaled Rodríguez safe. Almost immediately, Red Sox manager Terry Francona was on his way to first base, pointing out to Marsh that what A-Rod did is not allowable. Mientkiewicz said he thought he blocked Marsh out, and he did. "I did not see Alex wave at him and knock the ball out," Marsh said. "In that situation, [plate umpire] Joe West could see it clearly. He was the man who really helped us out. He had the best shot. He was sure of it." Eventually, all six umpires converged and ruled Rodríguez out because of interference, which meant Jeter, who already was in the Yankee dugout celebrating his run, had to go back to first base. Not second base, where he would have ended up had Rodríguez been out in anything resembling a normal putout. On an interference call, runners must return to their original base, per Rule 7.08(b). Joe Torre tried to argue that there was obstruction, but that would not apply since Arroyo was in possession of the ball.

Rule 7.09(f) is similar to Rule 6.05(m), although it specifically applies to double-play situations. It provides that if a base runner willfully and deliberately interferes with a batted ball, or with a fielder who is fielding a batted ball, with the obvious intent to break up a double play, then the runner and the batter-runner are both out. On October 11, 2007, in Game 1 of the NLCS between Arizona and Colorado, the D'backs had Justin Upton on first when Augie Ojeda hit a grounder to third baseman Garrett Atkins. Atkins then threw to second baseman Kaz Matsui for an out. Upton, running from first, slid past second base and then rolled his right shoulder into Matsui's left leg, knocking him to the ground.

"You had obvious intent on the part of the runner to break up the double play, and that's when it turns into intentional," said second-base umpire Larry Vanover, citing Rule 7.09(f). "Once [Upton] got to the base, I thought he threw his hip into the guy, and his intent at that point is not to get to the base. His intent is to crash the pivot man, so you've got obvious intent there." Rockies manager Clint Hurdle pulled his team off the field after angry fans threw water bottles and other debris onto the field following the call. The game was delayed for about eight minutes.

11.2B Runner (or batter) interference by hindering or impeding following play being made on a runner

On June 25, 1995, the Rangers hosted the A's. In the top of the first inning, Mark McGwire was at bat with Rickey Henderson on second and Stan Javier on first. McGwire rapped a single to left field, where

Rangers outfielder Rusty Greer fielded the ball and fired it to the plate in an attempt to nail Henderson. Rangers catcher Pudge Rodríguez bobbled the ball as Henderson slid home safely. As he sat in the area of home plate, Henderson nudged the ball where it lay on the ground before Rodríguez could get his hands on it. In the process, while Javier was advancing to third. Rodríguez grabbed the ball and hurled it to third in a failed attempt to erase Javier.

1: Which of the following statements is correct?

A. The rules don't address the situation because Henderson has already scored and so is no longer a runner, giving the umpire discretion to act as he sees fit.

B. Javier is out because the rules provide that if a player in Henderson's situation interferes with the play, then the runner (Javier) is out, whether Henderson's actions were intentional or not.

C. Javier is out because the rules provide that if a player in Henderson's situation intentionally interferes with the play, then the runner is out.

D. Henderson is out because of his interference.

Until recently, rather surprisingly, the correct answer was A. Former Rule 7.09(f) provided, "It is interference by a batter or a runner when any batter or runner, who has just been put out, hinders or impedes any following play being made on a runner. Such runner shall be declared out for the interference of his teammate." Note, however, that Henderson had *not* been put out; he had legally scored. Now, however, the rule has been amended. The new rule 7.09(e) provides, "It is interference by a batter or runner when . . . any batter or runner who has just been put out, *or any runner who has just scored*, hinders or impedes any following play being made on a runner. Such runner shall be declared out for the interference of his teammate." So now the correct answer is B. Whether the actions of the batter or runner are intentional does not appear to be relevant under the rules. Thus C is incorrect. D is incorrect because Henderson had legally scored.

2: On August 8, 2006, the Rangers were playing the A's. In the top of the ninth, the Rangers were at bat, trailing 7–6. With one out, Jerry Hairston was on first and Mark DeRosa at the plate. On a 3-2 count,

In the 2008 playoffs, the Phillies had Ryan Howard on third and Shane Victorino on first with no outs. Pedro Feliz hit into a 5-4-3 double play, and the Phils scored an apparent run when Howard crossed home plate. However, the umpire ruled that Victorino interfered with Brewers second baseman Craig Counsell because he never slid before the bag. What is the result of the play? Does Howard's run count? *AP Photo/Charlie Neibergall*

Hairston took off for second base. DeRosa swung and missed. Hairston was safe. However, home plate umpire Jim Joyce ruled that DeRosa interfered with catcher Jason Kendall's attempt to throw out Hairston. What is the result of the play?

In this case, they would both be out. Rule 7.09(e) provides that it is interference if a batter or a runner who has just been put out hinders or impedes the following play being made on a runner. In that case, the rule states that the runner (Hairston) is declared out due to the interference of his teammate (DeRosa). Similarly, on July 20, 2011, the Red Sox were playing the Orioles. In the top of the sixth inning the Red Sox had Josh Reddick on first base and no outs. With a 3-2 count on Carl Crawford, Reddick took off for second on the pitch. Crawford fanned and interfered with catcher Craig Tatum. Plate umpire Mike Winters ruled both Crawford and Reddick out because Crawford, who was just retired, interfered with Tatum. Normally, an umpire will not call interference when the catcher does not make an attempt to throw to a base. In the above play, however, Crawford's interference virtually did not allow Tatum to make a throw.

3: In Game 3 of the 2008 NLDS, the Phils were playing the Brewers. The Phils had the bases loaded and no outs in the top of the ninth trailing 4–1 when Pedro Feliz hit a ground ball to Bill Hall at third base. Hall threw to Craig Counsell at second to start a 5-4-3 double play. The double play was completed and the Phils scored an apparent run when Ryan Howard, the runner on third, crossed home plate. However, second-base umpire Jim Joyce called interference on Shane Victorino, who was running from first to second. Victorino never slid before the bag on the play. Instead he ducked his head and rammed into Counsell before hitting the ground. What is the result of the play? Does Howard's run count?

In a 2010 game, Willie Harris hit a double to right field, scoring Pudge Rodríguez. Nyjer Morgan was on first. With St. Louis catcher Bryan Anderson standing nearly on top of the plate waiting for the ball, Morgan circled the bases, ran into Anderson, and tripped right past home plate without touching it. Rodríguez gently nudged Morgan back toward home to touch the plate, which Morgan did, for the apparent score. Does the run count? *AP Photo/Susan Walsh*

Because of the interference call, the play was dead immediately. Under Rule 7.09(e), Feliz was out as a result of Victorino's interference, and Howard had to return to third, since no runners can advance when runner interference is called.

4: On August 28, 2010, the Cardinals were playing the Nationals in Washington. In the bottom of the eighth, the Nationals had the bases loaded with Mike Morse on third, Pudge Rodríguez on second, and Nyjer Morgan on first. Willie Harris hit a double to right field, scoring Morse and Rodríguez. With St. Louis catcher Bryan Anderson standing nearly on top of the plate looking at the ball being thrown into the infield, Morgan ran into Anderson and tripped

right past home plate without touching it. Home plate umpire Dan Bellino didn't say anything. Rodríguez was standing just beyond the batter's circle on the grass to the right of home plate. He gently nudged Morgan back toward home to touch the plate, which Morgan did, face-first, for the apparent score. Was Rodríguez's action legal?

No. It is illegal for a batter or a runner who has just scored or has been put out to help runners touch home plate. This would be interference by an offensive teammate, and the runner is out. A video of the play can be seen on MLB.com.

11.2C Runner being hit by ball

On July 4, 2004, the Yankees were playing the Mets. The Yankees had Jorge Posada on first base with one out in the top of the eighth and the score tied 5–5. Miguel Cairo hit a grounder that went underneath diving Mets first baseman Mike Piazza. The ball struck Posada in the leg.

1: Which of the following statements is correct?

A. Posada is out because the runner is always out when hit by a batted ball.

B. Posada is safe because the ball had already passed Piazza when it hit him.

C. It depends on whether the umpire judged Mets second baseman Ty Wigginton could have made a play.

D. It depends on whether the umpire judged that Piazza could have got out of the way of the ball.

The answer is C. Rule 7.09(k) provides, "It is interference by a batter or runner when . . . a fair ball touches him on fair territory before

Cleveland had Jhonny Peralta on third and Víctor Martínez on first. The Tigers' Travis Hafner hit a grounder, and Peralta, trying to score on the play, got caught in a rundown. He was tagged out by catcher Pudge Rodríguez, leaving Martínez on second and Hafner on first. However, home plate umpire Derryl Cousins ruled that Hafner's bat had nicked Rodríguez's mitt on the swing. Here we see Rodríguez's predictable reaction. What is the result of the play? *AP Photo/Paul Sancya*

touching a fielder. If a fair ball goes through, or by, an infielder, and touches a runner immediately back of him, or touches the runner after having been deflected by a fielder, the umpire shall not declare the runner out for being touched by a batted ball. *In making such decision the umpire must be convinced that the ball passed through, or by, the fielder, and that no other infielder had the chance to make a play on the ball.*" If the infield is playing in, it is possible for a runner to be struck by a batted ball and not be called out.

In the above situation, first-base umpire Eric Cooper said that because Mets second baseman Ty Wigginton was close enough to have made a play, Posada's being struck by the ball constituted interference.

2: If Posada had not been immediately behind Piazza and if Wigginton could not have made a play, could Posada have tried to kick the ball away?

No. The remainder of Rule 7.09(k) provides, "If, in the judgment of the umpire, the runner deliberately and intentionally kicks such a batted ball on which the infielder has missed a play, then the runner shall be called out for interference."

11.3 Catcher's interference

11.3A Catcher's interference on batter's swing

On July 3, 2007, the Indians were playing the Tigers. In the third inning, Cleveland had Jhonny Peralta on third and Víctor Martínez on first with none out. Travis Hafner was at the plate. Hafner hit a grounder, and Peralta, trying to score on the play, got caught in a rundown and was tagged out by Tigers catcher Pudge Rodríguez, leaving Martínez on second and Hafner on first. However, home plate umpire

Derryl Cousins ruled that Hafner's bat had nicked Rodríguez's mitt on the swing.

1: What is the result of this play?

A. Hafner is awarded first base and Peralta and Martínez advance.

B. Hafner is awarded first base and only Martínez advances

C. Hafner remains at bat but Peralta and Martínez advance.

D. Hafner is out for interfering with Rodríguez.

The correct answer is B, based on Rule 6.08(c). Peralta does not advance because he is not forced to advance. It should be noted that when the bat makes contact with the catcher's mitt on the swing, the umpire will most likely rule interference on the catcher. As rules expert Rich Marazzi has stated, "From the perspective of catchers, maybe it should be called the 'Rodney Dangerfield Rule' because catchers never get any respect when their mitt gets in the way of a bat. Although history tells us that the batter sometimes may initiate the interference, the catcher is always found guilty in the court of baseball law." In the above play, Rodríguez was indeed called for catcher's interference, meaning Hafner was awarded first base, Martínez second, and Peralta was sent back to third.

2: In what respect is the catcher's interference rule similar to a pro football penalty?

It is similar in that the victimized team is explicitly given the right to decline the infraction, the same way that, in football, a penalty can be accepted or declined. If it is declined, then the results of the play stand as if there were no interference. However, unlike in football, in baseball, the manager of the offensive team must initiate the conference with the umpire when he elects to take the play instead of the penalty. If he doesn't, the umpire will invoke the penalty aspect of the rule.

3: Why might the hitting team want to decline a catcher's interference call?

The batter-runner and all other runners must advance one base for the interference to be ignored or nullified. If both of these conditions are not met, the manager of the offensive team can elect to take the play or the penalty. Say for example a runner is on third with one out. The batter hits a fly ball deep enough to score the run. Catcher's interference is called. The manager may elect to take both the run and the out. The manager of the offensive team also has the right to accept the play or the penalty when the play follows the pitch of a defaced or doctored ball. Here again, the manager of the offensive team has the option of taking a legally scored run off the board.

4: Can there be catcher's or batter's interference on a backswing?

No. Backswing interference ordinarily has no penalty. The Comment provides that the backswing interference must be unintentional, but that is virtually always the case. The Yankees and Royals played in New York on August 16, 2008. Early in the game, Derek Jeter was batting with Johnny Damon on first base. Damon took off on a pitch that Jeter missed. Plate umpire Wally Bell called "time" and sent Damon back to first because Jeter had interfered with Royals catcher John Buck on his backswing. Normally when a batter interferes with the catcher, the batter is called out and the runner is returned to the base. The exception is if the batter unintentionally interferes on the backswing; then the runner is returned to the base, but the batter is not out per Rule 6.06(c). He remains at bat. If Buck made a play on Damon and threw him out, the backswing interference would have been ignored. Similarly, the catcher is not called for interference when his mitt or any part of his body or equipment makes contact with the bat on a backswing.

11.3B Catcher's or fielder's interference on steal attempt

On June 1, 2009, the Padres were playing the Phillies. With Brian Giles at the plate and Adrián González of the Padres on first, Phils pitcher Brad Lidge bounced a pitch and it kicked away from catcher Carlos Ruiz. González was attempting to steal second on the play. Ruiz recovered the ball and fired to Jimmy Rollins covering, but Ádrian González snuck in under the tag. However, Rollins then appeared to push González off the base and tagged him before he could get back.

1: If Rollins had pushed González off the base, would González be safe?

Yes. Rule 7.04(d) provides that a base stealer is entitled to the next base if there is fielder's interference. In this play, second-base umpire Paul Emmel called González out, but that could be because in his judgment Rollins did nothing wrong.

2: If, instead, Ruiz's catcher's mitt had interfered with Giles's swing, what would have been the call?

Giles would get first base and González would get second. However, note that only runners who are forced may advance in this situation. If González had been on second, he would have stayed there.

3: What would be the result if Ruiz's mitt had interfered with Giles's swing, but González, unaware of the catcher's interference, acciden-

tally overslid second base and was tagged by Rollins before he could get back?

Giles would get first base and González would be out. With catcher's interference, if all runners, including the batter-runner, advance at least one base on the play, the interference is nullified. In this play, the batter-runner (Giles) never advanced one base. Therefore the penalty aspect of the rule would be invoked. Giles would be awarded first base and González would be awarded second. However, even though González would get second base for free because of the catcher's interference, he can still be tagged out because of the overslide. With catcher's interference, you get the next base for free but no farther, whether you miss the base altogether or touch it and then slide past.

11.3C Catcher's interference on squeeze or steal of home

On August 3, 1995, the Mets were playing the Reds. With two out in the bottom of the sixth, the Reds had Ron Gant on third and Reggie Sanders on second. With right-handed batter Bret Boone at the plate, Gant took advantage of the rookie battery of Reid Cornelius and Alberto Castillo and dashed for home. Castillo bolted out of the catcher's box to grab the outside pitch slightly in front of home plate, then dove back across the plate to tag Gant before Gant reached home. Nevertheless, home plate umpire Paul Runge said the run should score.

1: Did Runge make the right call?

Yes. Runge called catcher's interference on Castillo under Rule 7.07, which provides in part that if a runner on third tries to score on a squeeze play or a steal, and the catcher steps on or in front of home base without possession of the ball, the pitcher is charged with a balk, the batter is awarded first base on the interference, and the ball is dead. Because of the balk, Gant scores from third, under Rule 8.05. Although Castillo was in possession of the ball when he tagged Gant, Runge felt that because Castillo had stepped in front of home plate before he had caught the pitch, he had interfered with Boone.

"I called catcher's interference and a balk on the pitcher," Runge said. "That rule was put in because the easiest way for a catcher to prevent a steal of home is to interfere with the hitter. Then the ball is dead. Also, it's to the catcher's advantage to jump out over the plate because if he has to sit back, that's at least two more steps for the runner."

2: In view of Runge's call, where would you place Sanders and Boone?

Because of the catcher's interference/balk call, Boone was awarded first base and Sanders was awarded third base, as per Rules 7.07 (the interference creates a balk) and 8.05 (penalty for a balk is that all runners advance one base). The penalty here is more severe than the catcher's interference described in Rule 6.08(c). For the runners on base, it is treated like a balk because the defense is taking unfair advantage of the runner coming in from third base. When catcher's interference is called, if the batter and all runners advance one base, the interference is nullified.

3: On August 1, 1971, the Reds were playing the Dodgers in Los Angeles. In the bottom of the eleventh, with the score tied 4–4, the bases were loaded with two outs. Manny Mota was on third base. Willie Crawford was at bat for the Dodgers. On an 0-1 pitch by Reds reliever Joe Gibbon, Crawford swung and missed as Mota broke for home on a steal attempt. Reds catcher Johnny Bench reached for the ball and tagged Mota before he scored. However, home plate umpire Harry Wendelstedt ruled that Bench had interfered with Crawford's attempt

to swing at the ball—i.e., catcher's interference. Fill in the blanks in the following sentence: On the above play, aside from the catcher's interference, ___________ is charged with ___________.

The pitcher, Joe Gibbon, is charged with a balk, per Rule 7.07.

4: What is the consequence of the play?

Crawford gets to go to first base, and because the bases were loaded, Mota scores even though he had been thrown out at home. Game over.

11.4 Fielder interference—interfering with foul ball

On May 27, 1981, the Mariners hosted the Royals. In the top of the sixth inning, Amos Otis of the Royals tapped a roller toward third. Three Mariners converged on it, but they all realized they could not field it in time to throw out the fleet Otis. Their only hope was that it would trickle foul. Unfortunately for them, it kept rolling straight along the foul line in fair territory. Mariners third baseman Lenny Randle then dropped to the ground and blew the ball into foul territory. Initially, the plate umpire, Larry McCoy, threw up his arms signaling a foul ball. But Royals manager Jim Frey protested, and the call was changed to a hit. Mariners skipper Rene Lachemann squawked, but lost.

1: Did McCoy make the right call?

Yes, since Rule 9.01(c) gives the umpires the authority to rule on anything not specifically covered in the rules, and the rules do not address the situation of "fielder interference." McCoy concluded that altering the course of a ball by blowing on it creates an unfair advantage for the defensive team.

2: Say that there was a runner on third with less than two outs and that Otis's roller went toward first rather than third. If the ball stays fair, the runner on third can score on the play. To make sure that happens, Otis stops running toward first, stoops down, and blows on the ball so that it *doesn't* become foul. He successfully prevents the ball from rolling foul and the runner scores. Is his action legal?

The umpires would make the same call as in the previous problem. Rule 7.09(k) does provide for interference when "a fair ball touches [the batter] on fair territory before touching a fielder," but in the above case, Otis never touched the ball.

3: In a 1957 minor league game, Domingo Carrasquel of Great Falls (Montana) was on third base when, trying to be a nice guy, he picked up a foul grounder off the bat of a teammate and tossed it back to the Idaho Falls pitcher. The umpires made no call. Was Carrasquel's action a violation of the rules or was it "no harm, no foul"?

Carrasquel should have been called out and was later called out by the league president after a protest by Idaho Falls. Rule 7.09(b) provides, "It is interference by a batter or a runner when he intentionally deflects the course of a foul ball in any manner." That's just what Carrasquel did. The penalty for interference is that the runner is out and the ball is dead. This rule only applies if there is a chance that the ball might become fair.

11.5 Verbal interference

On May 30, 2007, the Yankees were playing the Blue Jays. In the top of the ninth inning, the Yanks had Hideki Matsui on second and Alex Rodríguez on first with two outs and were leading 7–5 when Jorge Posada hit a high fly between Blue Jays third baseman Howie Clark and shortstop John McDonald. As A-Rod was running to third, he yelled, "Hah!"—obviously with the intention of distracting the Toronto infielders. Clark, who was playing his first big league game of the season, said, "I heard a 'Mine' call, and so I let it go," deferring to McDonald. The ball fell untouched, and Matsui scored on the play. Posada was credited with an RBI base hit. The Blue Jays complained about A-Rod's actions, but the umpires let the play stand.

1: Could A-Rod have been called out for verbal interference?

While this is a judgment call for the umpire, the answer is yes, but it is rarely called at the major league level because major league fielders are expected not to be distracted by comments, especially from fans. However, by a strict interpretation of the rules, verbal interference can be called. Rule 2.00 defines offensive interference as "an act by the team at bat which interferes with, obstructs, impedes, hinders or confuses any fielder attempting to make a play."

Clearly the interference doesn't have to be physical since "confusing" the fielder is a form of interference. Clearly, also, Clark was in fact confused on the play since he apparently misheard both what was said and who said it. (He said that he thought his own teammate was yelling "Mine" rather than A-Rod yelling "Hah!")

2: Would the result have changed if A-Rod had yelled the same thing, with the same intent, but while sitting in the dugout rather than rounding the bases?

It would have made no difference. The rule refers simply to the team at bat, and thus it would not matter if the player attempting to interfere was on the field or in the dugout. Since fielders often hear remarks from the opposing team when approaching an opponent's dugout, the call would be unlikely on the major league level.

11.6 Team interference—failure to vacate space

In a 1976 game, the Orioles were playing the Oakland A's. Sal Bando was at bat for Oakland, and Larry Haney was in the on-deck circle. Bando hit a pop-up near where Haney was standing. Haney made a good-faith effort to get out of the way of Orioles catcher Rick Dempsey, but failed, and the ball fell to the ground. Baltimore wanted an interference call on Haney, but didn't get it.

1: Did the umpires make the correct call?

Yes, because in this instance the rule is not interpreted exactly as written. Rule 7.11 provides that players, coaches, or any member of the offensive team "shall vacate any space (including both dugouts) needed by a fielder who is attempting to field a batted or thrown ball." However, as interpreted, umpires will not normally call interference when they believe that the person made a good-faith effort to get out of the way, as did Haney. This type of situation can occur on a foul pop when the wind is gusting and the fielder has to adjust accordingly. The interference rule is very subjective, however, and umpires may not all call a given play in the same way.

2: If Haney was called for interference, what is the penalty?

The batter or runner on whom the play is being made is called out (in this case Bando).

3: Would it have made any difference if Haney had been standing in the dugout rather than the on-deck circle and did not vacate his space?

Yes. This is another respect in which Rule 7.11 is often not interpreted exactly as written. We saw above that the umps may not call interference if they believe that the member of the offensive team made a good-faith effort to get out of the way. When a player is in the dugout, however, the umps generally do not even require the player to vacate his space, so long as there is no overt interference.

11.7 Umpire interference

11.7A Home plate umpire interference

Throughout this book, we have considered offensive and defensive interference in various situations. However, there can also be umpire interference. On August 19, 2008, the Phillies were playing the Nationals. In the bottom of the seventh, Shane Victorino of the Phils raced from first to third base when a snap throw from Nationals catcher Jesús Flores to first sailed into right field. During the throw, Flores's arm clipped the chest protector of home plate umpire Joe West.

1: Which of the following statements is accurate?

A. If West calls umpire interference on himself, Victorino has to go back to first base.

B. If West calls umpire interference on himself, Victorino has to go back to second base.

C. An umpire cannot unilaterally call interference on himself. Flores would first have to argue umpire interference, and if the umpire agrees, Victorino would have to go back to first.

D. There is no such thing as umpire interference—the play is just a part of the game. Victorino stays at third.

The answer is A, per Rule 5.09(b). That is what happened on the play.

2: Assume that Victorino was on first and Phils shortstop Jimmy Rollins was on third. Victorino steals second. On the play, the Nationals second baseman, Emilio Bonifacio, covering second on the Victorino steal, notices Rollins heading for home. Bonifacio flings the ball to the catcher, but on the throw, his arm bumps into the second-base umpire, Ed Hickox, who was in the area to make a call on the steal attempt. As a result of that interference, Rollins scores. What is the result of the play?

Rollins scores. Umpires are not considered to interfere with thrown balls by fielders with the exception of the catcher when trying to throw out a runner or when returning a ball to the pitcher.

3: Say that Flores's throw clipped West's chest protector as Flores was merely trying to throw the ball back to the pitcher. As the ball rolled in the infield, Victorino stole second. Would Victorino be credited with a stolen base?

No. An addition to the rule was added for the 2010 season. If a catcher is returning the ball to the pitcher, and he is in some way interfered with by the plate umpire, no runner can advance on the play and all runners must return to their original bases.

11.7B Umpire interference in the field

The most common type of umpire interference is when the second-base umpire, working in front of the infielders during potential stolen-base situations, is touched with the ball. For example, the Pittsburgh Pirates and Milwaukee Brewers played at Miller Park on July 9, 2010. In the top of the eighth inning, the Pirates had Garrett Jones on second and two outs when Lastings Milledge hit a shot that was heading toward center field and would have scored Jones. However, the ball struck second-base umpire Chris Guccione, who was working on the infield side in front of Brewers second baseman Rickie Weeks.

1: Is this umpire interference?

Yes. Umpire interference occurs when a fair ball touches an umpire in fair territory before passing a fielder or when the umpire hinders a catcher's attempt to throw out a base stealer or to retire a runner on a pickoff.

2: What is the result?

Milledge was credited with a base hit and Jones was sent back to second base, per Rule 7.04(b). The canceled run proved to be pivotal as the Brewers won the game 5–4.

3: Why wasn't Jones awarded third base?

Because when this type of umpire's interference occurs, runners advance only if forced.

Umpires, as well as managers, players, and broadcasters, have fallen asleep regarding that aspect of the rule. For example, the Minnesota Twins and New York Yankees played at Yankee Stadium on July 15, 1995. In the top of the eighth inning, the Twins were leading 7–4 and had Pat Meares on third and Chuck Knoblauch on first with no outs. Rich Becker hit a shot up the middle that struck second-base umpire Dale Ford, who was positioned in front of second base. Ford called "time" and correctly placed Knoblauch on second and Becker on first. But Meares was erroneously allowed to score. Because he was not forced to advance on the play, he should have remained at third base following the interference call.

4: What if Guccione had been standing behind Weeks?

Then there would be no umpire interference. The ball would remain in play.

5: What if a throw from Brewers catcher George Kottaras to Weeks hit the umpire as opposed to Milledge's hit?

When the throw is from a fielder, the ball remains alive and in play and hopefully so does the umpire. During the 2001 season, the Cardinals' Albert Pujols hit a ground ball that struck second base.

In the 1996 AL playoffs, Derek Jeter of the Yankees hit a fly ball to right field. Orioles outfielder Tony Tarasco appeared to settle underneath the ball, but as he was waiting, twelve-year-old Yankees fan Jeff Maier reached over the fence, glove in hand, and deflected the ball into the seats. Is this fan interference? *AP Photo/Mark Lennihan*

Diamondbacks second baseman Jay Bell picked up the ball and attempted to throw out Pujols at first, but the ball struck umpire Larry Young above the left eye. Young received stitches and was hospitalized overnight. The ball remained in play and Pujols reached first base.

The Boston Red Sox were victimized by the rule in a game against the Cleveland Indians at Fenway Park on September 22, 2008. In the bottom of the sixth inning with the Indians ahead 4–2, the Sox had Jason Bay on second and Jason Varitek on first with two outs. Jeff Bailey hit a ground ball inside the third-base line. The ball would have rolled into the outfield except that it struck umpire Gerry Davis in fair territory. The ball stopped just beyond the infield dirt while Bay was rounding third. Indians third baseman Jamey Carroll picked it up, and Bay got caught in a rundown between third and home and was tagged out sliding back to third. The Indians won the game 4–3. If Bailey had hit a line drive that remained in the air and struck Davis and was subsequently caught by an Indians player, it would be ruled no catch since batted balls that strike umpires are no longer in flight. Umpires are treated as part of the ground.

Perhaps the most bizarre umpire's interference call involved former umpire Terry Cooney. "It was at Oakland in 1986," recalled Cooney. "I was umpiring in front of second base when the batter hit a line drive that disappeared into my umpire's jacket. I found the ball in the armpit of my jacket."

11.8 Spectator interference

There have been a number of famous (or infamous, depending on your perspective) spectator-interference plays. Some of them have occurred in postseason play. For example, on October 9, 1996, the Orioles were playing the Yankees in Game 1 of the American League Championship Series in New York. In the bottom of the eighth, the Yankees were trailing 4–3, with one out and no base runners. Derek Jeter hit a fly ball off reliever Armando Benítez to right field. Tony Tarasco backed

In the 2003 NL playoffs, Luis Castillo of the Marlins hit a fly ball to left field that was heading foul toward the seats. Cubs left fielder Moises Alou reached over the barrier to catch the ball. Just as he was about to do so, Cubs fan Steve Bartman, who was sitting in the front row, reached up and deflected the ball away. Is this fan interference? *AP Photo/Amy Sancetta*

to the warning track and appeared to settle underneath the ball. But as Tarasco was standing waiting for the ball, twelve-year-old Yankees fan Jeff Maier reached out, glove in hand, and deflected the ball into the seats. Right-field umpire Richie Garcia ruled it a home run, which tied the game 4–4. Bernie Williams led off the bottom of the eleventh with a home run to give the Yankees a 5-4 win.

Another notorious play (from the perspective of Cubs fans) occurred in Game 6 of the 2003 National League Championship Series. The Cubs were ahead of the Marlins three games to two and were leading the Marlins 3–0 in the eighth inning. With one out, Luis Castillo of the Marlins hit a fly ball to left field that was heading foul toward the seats. Cubs left fielder Moises Alou reached over the barrier to catch the ball. Just as he was about to do so, Cubs fan Steve Bartman, who was sitting in the front row, reached up and deflected the ball away. Left-field umpire Mike Everitt ruled no fan interference. Castillo stayed alive. He eventually walked, and the Marlins went on an 8-run tear in that inning and went on to win the game. They also won Game 7 and the series.

1: Assuming that both Tarasco and Alou would have caught their respective fly balls, which of the following statements is true?

A. Both Garcia and Everitt got their calls right.

B. Both Garcia and Everitt got their calls wrong.

C. Everitt was right and Garcia was wrong.

D. Garcia was right and Everitt was wrong.

Spectator interference occurs when a spectator reaches out on the playing-field side of the stands and (1) touches a live ball or (2) touches a player and hinders an attempt to make a play on a live ball. However, there is no spectator interference when a fielder reaches into the stands to catch a ball.

Regarding the above plays, unless Garcia felt that Jeter's fly ball was going into the stands (which replays show it wasn't), the correct answer is C. The difference between the two plays is that, in the Tarasco/Maier play, Maier had to reach over the fence, while in the Alou/Bartman play, Alou was reaching into the stands to try to make the catch. Under Rule 3.16, upon spectator interference with a thrown or batted ball, the ball is dead at the moment of interference, and as with Rule 3.15, the umpire imposes such penalties as he believes will nullify the interference. If the spectator interference clearly prevents a fielder from catching a fly ball, then the umpire should declare the batter out.

Based on this distinction, Bartman's actions did not constitute fan interference because he was not reaching over the wall. However, Maier's actions should have been considered fan interference because he reached over the wall.

After the game, Garcia admitted that he got the call wrong and Jeter should not have been credited with a home run. He had made his call thinking that the ball's trajectory was carrying it into the stands. After reviewing the video replay, however, he did maintain that Tarasco would not have caught the ball, and that Jeter would have been placed on second or third base.

When the 1996 ALCS moved to Baltimore, Orioles fans expressed their displeasure with Garcia for his missed call by holding up signs that said "Garcia 3:16," a takeoff on the John 3:16 sign held up by fans at some sporting events.

Normally when there is spectator interference, all runners, including the batter-runner, are awarded two bases. But umpires have the authority to place the runners at any base they judge the runners would have made had the interference not occurred. In addition, they are not required to give each runner the same number of bases. On April 24, 2010, the White Sox were playing the Mariners in Chicago. With the score tied 2–2 in the top of the ninth, the M's had José López on second, and Jack Wilson on first when Casey Kotchman hit a bounding ball down the first-base line, where a fan interfered with the play. The ball was dead the moment the interference occurred. The umpires awarded both López and Wilson home plate, meaning

Wilson was given three bases on the play, even though Kotchman was only awarded second base.

Regarding the infamous Bartman play, the loose ball was snatched up by a Chicago lawyer and sold at auction for $113,824.16. On February 26, 2004, it was publicly exploded. In the years since the incident, the Bartman seat (aisle 4, row 8, seat 113) has become a tourist attraction at Wrigley Field. Bartman has passed up $25,000 to sign autographs at a memorabilia convention and over $100,000 to appear in a Super Bowl commercial. In fairness to Bartman, many other events occurred both before and after that incident that were far greater contributing factors to the Cubs' losing the series (including an error on Cubs shortstop Alex González later in the same inning on what should have been an inning-ending double play), but often perception is reality, and few people remember those other events.

In April 2008, Moises Alou was quoted by the Associated Press as saying, "You know what the funny thing is? I wouldn't have caught it, anyway." However, Alou later disputed that story. "I don't remember that," he said to a writer from the *Palm Beach Post*. "If I said that, I was probably joking to make [Bartman] feel better. But I don't remember saying that." Alou added, "It's time to forgive the guy and move on." His 2008 quote is also not in keeping with his reaction and comments just after the play occurred. He jumped up and down with his arms outstretched. After the game he said, "I timed it perfectly, I jumped perfectly. I'm almost one hundred percent that I had a clean shot to catch the ball. All of a sudden, there's a hand on my glove."

On April 22, 2012, the Tampa Rays were playing the Twins in Tampa. In the eighth inning, Twins left fielder Josh Willingham hit a high fly ball to foul territory sending first baseman Carlos Peña toward the stands. As he got in position to make the catch, former NBA center Matt Geiger, sitting in the front row, suddenly lunged for the ball and interfered with Peña. The ball went off Geiger and into the hands of another fan behind him, resulting in a mere strike to Willingham. Geiger was escorted from his seat by security. The television announcers, unaware of Geiger's identity at the time, were puzzled as to why the Tampa fans were high-fiving him as he walked up the steps when he had just cost the Rays an out. It turns out that Geiger was not ejected, but merely relocated. Replays are inconclusive as to whether it was Geiger or Peña who reached over the barrier, but if it was Peña, then Geiger was acting within his rights. A video of the play can be seen at http://deadspin.com/matt-geiger.

11.9 Interference by personnel on field

11.9A Base coach assisting a runner

On May 13, 1988, the Yankees hosted the Angels. In the bottom of the first inning, the Yanks had Willie Randolph on second base and Jack Clark on first with two outs when Claudell Washington singled to left field. As Randolph rounded third, he and third-base coach Clete Boyer made contact about fifteen feet down the line. As a result, Randolph had to hustle back to third.

1: Does it matter whether Boyer assisted Randolph back to third?

Yes. Rule 7.09(h) provides that a runner is out when "in the judgment of the umpire, the base coach at third base, or first base, by touching or holding the runner, physically assists him in returning to or leaving third base or first base." Accordingly, it's up to the umpire to decide whether or not there was a physical assist. So it is not necessarily the fact of the collision that is relevant, but what happens afterward.

On May 8, 2009, the Orioles and the Yankees clashed in Baltimore. In the top of the fourth inning, the Bronx Bombers had Nick Swisher on third and one out. Swisher, standing off the bag in foul territory, was conversing with third-base coach Rob Thomson when O's pitcher Jeremy Guthrie threw to third in an attempt to pick off the yakking Yankee. Thomson pushed Swisher back to the bag to beat the throw, but third-base ump Tim Tschida immediately called Swisher out for coach's interference.

Notwithstanding the fact that the rule requires "physical assistance" for there to be interference, it is not always consistently applied, and some umpires have ruled interference based on contact alone even when the contact was inadvertent or minor. On September 5, 2010, the Twins were playing the Rangers. In the top of the ninth the Rangers had the bases loaded with Michael Young on second. Vladimir Guerrero hit an infield single. Young rounded third, then stopped and retreated to third, where he dove back safely. However, third-base umpire Alfonso Márquez ruled that Young and third-base coach Dave Anderson had come into contact and called Young out for Anderson's interference. There was some question as to whether Anderson and Young touched at all. Replays suggest that they may inadvertently have slapped hands right before Young stopped and turned back to third. Crew chief Tim Tschida (the same umpire who was involved in the previous play) said, "The ruling on the play is that a base coach either touching, physically assisting in any way, with the base runner is not allowed and the runner is called out."

11.9B Other personnel on the field

On May 26, 1989, the Red Sox were playing the Angels. In the top of the sixth inning with Dick Schofield of the Angels on first, Claudell Washington hit a hard liner that went just inside the first-base line. The ball appeared to strike the ball boy on his left foot. He apparently thought at first that the ball had gone foul, then was too late getting out of the way when he realized his mistake. The ball ricocheted away, and Schofield scored from first on the play and Washington wound up at second.

1: Should the ball have remained alive and in play?

Yes. Under Rule 3.15, if the interference is by someone authorized to be on the field (aside from members of the offensive team, a coach in the coach's box, or an umpire) and is unintentional, then the ball is alive and in play. Since the interference in this case was unintentional, the run counts and Washington winds up at second base.

2: Would the result have been different if the ballboy had intentionally picked up the ball based on his good-faith belief that it was a foul ball?

Yes. Even though the mistake was made in good faith, the interference would nevertheless be considered intentional. Under Rule 3.15, the ball is considered dead at the moment of interference, and the umpire imposes such penalties as he believes will undo the interference. The umpires decide whether the interference was intentional. This is the same as spectator interference. It is not an automatic two-base award.

3: On August 10, 1991, the Astros were playing the Braves. Houston third baseman Ken Caminiti was chasing a foul ball down the third-base line when he collided with a security guard. The guard, seated along the left-field line in Atlanta–Fulton County Stadium, had picked up his stool and run for daylight to avoid Caminiti, but his efforts were wasted. As a result of the contact, Caminiti was unable to make the catch. Should Caminiti be credited with a putout?

No. As with the first question above, since the interference was unintentional, the ball is alive and in play.

4: Would the result have been different if the hit had been a pop-up that was falling where the third-base coach was (properly) standing and the coach did not intentionally interfere, but also made no effort to move from the coach's box?

Yes. In Rule 3.15, an exception is made for "members of the offensive team participating in the game, or a coach in the coach's box, or an umpire." The Comment to this rule in turn refers to Rule 7.11, which, as we saw before, provides in part coaches "shall vacate" space needed by a fielder trying to field a batted or thrown ball. Thus if the third-base coach made no attempt to vacate the needed space, then interference would be called and the batter would be out.

5: On July 29, 1991, the Yankees hosted the A's. The A's José Canseco was batting with one out when he ripped a shot off the glove of Yankee third baseman Pat Kelly. As the ball reached the left-field tarpaulin, a Yankee ball boy extended his left arm and grabbed the ball. What should be the ruling on the play?

Since the interference was intentional, Canseco should go to the base where he would have wound up if the interference had not occurred. On this play, the umps put him at second base. In these situations, the umpires may have two decisions to make. First they decide whether the interference is intentional. If it is, they have to decide what would have happened on the play had the interference not occurred.

It should be noted that the question of whether the interference is "intentional" has nothing to do with whether the person interfering was trying to aid one team or another. For example, even if a ball girl grabbed a ball because she wrongly believed it was foul, the act was still intentional.

Chapter 12

Obstruction

There are two types of obstruction, which are known as "Type A obstruction" and "Type B obstruction." When a play is being "directly" made on a runner, such as a rundown play or a pitcher obstructing the batter-runner between home and first, this is Type A obstruction and is covered in Rule 7.06(a). Type A obstruction almost always occurs in a rundown when the middle man does not move to the side quickly enough and remains in the lane. Type B obstruction occurs when the ball is in the outfield and the runner is circling the bases. The ball is a good distance away from him.

In the 2003 playoffs Jason Varitek of the Red Sox got caught in a rundown between third and home. After several exchanges, Varitek was tagged, but not before he had made contact with A's third baseman Eric Chávez, who did not have the ball at that moment. At the time of contact, Varitek was headed back to third base. Should Chávez be called for obstruction? *AP Photo/James Rogash*

12.1 Fielder obstruction on a runner while play is directly on the runner—Type A obstruction

In Game 3 of the 2003 American League Division Series between the Boston Red Sox and the Oakland A's, Jason Varitek of the Red Sox got caught in a rundown between third and home. After several exchanges, Varitek was tagged, but not before he had made contact with A's third baseman Eric Chávez, who did not have the ball at that moment. At the time of contact, Varitek was headed back to third base.

1: Should Chávez be called for obstruction?

Yes. The definition of "obstruction" is "the act of a fielder who, while not in possession of the ball and not in the act of fielding the ball, impedes the progress of any runner." Did that occur here? Yes. Chávez did not have the ball when contact was made and wasn't about to make a play.

With Type A obstruction plays, even though it is not always clear whether the fielder has obstructed the runner, as a matter of practice the fielder will normally be called for obstruction. During a rundown, the fielder without the ball must vacate the area so he doesn't hinder or impede the advance of the runner. There is no guideline in feet or inches as to the distance a fielder must vacate.

2: Varitek was on his way back to third on the play. Should he be awarded third or home?

He should be awarded home. Under Type A obstruction, the runner is awarded the next base following the last base he legally touched regardless of the base toward which he was headed.

3: The Comment to Rule 7.06(a) provides that if there is obstruction, the umpire shall signal obstruction and the ball is immediately dead. Assume, however, that Varitek had been caught between second and third and the throw from the second baseman to Chávez sailed over his head and into the dugout and that the umpire had called obstruction after the ball was thrown. Would Varitek score?

Yes. The Comment provides that even though the play is dead, the runners are to be awarded such bases as they would have been awarded had the obstruction not occurred. When a throw is made just before the obstruction is called and the ball is in flight and goes into dead-ball territory, runners are awarded their bases from their position at the time of the throw. Note that, since it is a dead-ball situation, the runner is only entitled to advance as many bases (if any) as the rules allow for the particular overthrow.

4: For there to be obstruction, the fielder without the ball has to "impede the runner." But if the runner goes out of his way to initiate the contact, does that mean that no obstruction would be called?

In theory, yes, but in reality, the fielder is virtually never given the benefit of the doubt. Because players are well aware of this dichotomy between theory and practice, a runner often tries to initiate contact as a way of avoiding being tagged out in the rundown.

For example, on August 24, 2008, the Chicago White Sox hosted the Tampa Bay Rays. The White Sox had A. J. Pierzynski on second base and one out with the score tied 5–5 in the bottom of the tenth inning. Jermaine Dye hit a grounder to shortstop Jason Bartlett, and Pierzynski got caught in a rundown. After several exchanges, Pierzynski was tagged but was awarded third base when second-base umpire Doug Eddings ruled obstruction on Rays third baseman Willy Aybar because Pierzynski and Aybar made contact. However, it appeared that Pierzynski purposely went after Aybar by extending his elbow into him. In postgame remarks, as reported on the Rays Web site, Pierzynski basically admitted that he had an agenda: "I was just looking for somebody to get close enough, and luckily he [Aybar] did."

Michael C. Dorf, a Columbia University law professor, wrote an interesting article discussing both the above play and the fairness—or unfairness—of vesting discretion in the umpires on a play such as this, and its application to the legal process generally: "America's Favorite Pastime Exposes a Necessary Evil in the Legal System: Harmless Error in Baseball, and in Law."

Tip for players: Given that umpires will almost never give fielders the benefit of the doubt, if a runner is caught in a rundown, he should try to get close enough to the fielder without the ball to initiate contact with him, since the fielder will often be helpless to avoid the contact. Of course, if the runner truly believes that he can successfully retreat to the previous base or advance to the next base without being tagged (which normally only occurs if the fielding team makes a physical or mental miscue), then this advice would not apply.

12.2 Fielder obstruction on a runner while play is not on the runner—Type B obstruction

This play comes, amazingly, from the same game as in the previous section, namely Game 3 of the 2003 American League Division Series between the Boston Red Sox and the Oakland A's and again involves Jason Varitek of the Red Sox. In the sixth inning of the game, the A's had the bases loaded. Ramón Hernández bounced a grounder toward short that eluded Nomar Garciaparra and rolled into left field. As Miguel Tejada, the runner on second, rounded third, he collided with third baseman Bill Mueller, who was trying to get in position for a throw from Manny Ramírez in left. Third-base ump Bill Welke ruled Mueller obstructed Tejada. Upon seeing this call, Tejada slowed to a jog, whereupon the ball was thrown to Varitek, who easily tagged him, since Tejada was making no effort to beat a throw. The umpires ruled that Tejada was out.

1: Given the obstruction on Mueller, did the umps make the right decision in calling Tejada out?

Yes. This is a Rule 7.06(b) (Type B) obstruction situation. With this type of obstruction, the runner does not get carte-blanche protection. The umpire must decide if the runner would have made the next base if there had been no obstruction. One may ask why the result on this play would be different from that in the Veritek-Chávez play, given that Tejada was interfered with by Mueller. The difference is that no play was being made directly on Tejada when the interference occurred. He was not caught in a rundown, but was simply trying to round third base. If a runner attempts to advance beyond his protected base, he does so at his own risk.

In the above play, the umpire had to decide whether Tejada would have scored but for the interference. Given his leisurely pace after the interference call (based on his mistaken understanding or lack of understanding of the rules), the umpire thought that Tejada would obviously not have scored had there been no interference. Of course, had Tejada been aware of the rule and kept running at full speed, then the umpire's job would have been tougher because he would have had to decide whether Tejada would have scored but for the obstruction.

After the game, third-base umpire Bill Welke explained the play: "When that happens, we do not call 'time.' We point to the obstruction. We let the play run through until all play has ceased. Then my job is a judgment call. Had Tejada been thrown out by a step or two, I would have called 'time' and protected him and scored the run, because I had the obstruction at third. When Tejada stopped, then he was tagged. Had that obstruction not occurred and a runner stops halfway between home and third and then is tagged, he cannot be protected under the obstruction rule."

2: Does the ball remain alive in the above situation?

Yes. With Type B obstruction, the play is *not* dead at the moment of obstruction, but rather "the play shall proceed until no further action is possible."

3: Say that Tejada was between second and third and the umpire felt that he would have reached third base but for the type B obstruction. Could he have tried for home?

Yes, because as noted, the ball is not dead. If the obstruction had occurred between second and third, Tejada could have been protected at third. The Comment to Rule 7.06(b) provides that this is a judgment call. He can advance farther only at his own risk.

4: If Tejada had been out on a close play at the plate, would umpires have allowed him to score?

They should because one must assume that Mueller's obstruction made the difference between Tejada's being called safe or out.

5: Is it possible for a fielder to be called for obstruction even if he is nowhere near the runner?

Yes. There is such a thing as visual obstruction, though it is not often called. It was called on August 6, 2004, in a game between Seattle and Tampa Bay (on a play that ended the game no less). The Devil Rays (now just the "Rays") had Carl Crawford on third and one out in the bottom of the tenth inning with the score tied. Tino Martinez lofted a fly to short left field that was handled by Raúl Ibañez. On the play, Mariners third baseman Willie Bloomquist went out as a cutoff man and José López covered third.

Crawford, after bluffing a break for home, was trotting back to third as Ibañez's perfect throw reached Mariners catcher Miguel Olivo. It appeared that the game would continue with two outs and runners on first and third. However, while Crawford was trying to pick up the flight of the ball to prepare his tag-up, third-base umpire Paul Emmel believed that López got a little bit too cute by moving back and forth in the line of Crawford's vision to the left fielder. Therefore he ruled visual obstruction on López and sent Crawford home, giving the Devil Rays a 2–1 win. López was nowhere near Crawford on the play.

It is not clear whether Emmel was making his call as Type A or Type B obstruction. Crawford was making his way back to third on the play so one could argue that the play was not on the runner. However, would Ibañez be throwing the ball to home plate at all but for Crawford?

According to Rich Marazzi, since no play was being made "directly" on Crawford, this should have been a Type B obstruction. By allowing Crawford to score, the umpires, led by crew chief Joe West, ruled this play a Type A obstruction since Crawford was awarded home. Marazzi's view is that the umpires misinterpreted Rule 7.06(b) (Type B obstruction) and the game could have been protested by Mariners manager Bob Melvin. According to Melvin, he was told by West that the play could not be protested.

If the throw from Ibañez went to third base and López was blocking the base without the ball and wasn't about to make a play, this would have been Type A obstruction because a play would "directly" have been made on Crawford. By Ibañez's throwing home and Crawford's returning to third base, there obviously was no play being made "directly" on Crawford.

Chapter 13

Time Plays

Because many baseball fans do not understand the nuances of the time-play rule, I will discuss the applicable rule, 4.09(a), first. The rule provides that a run scores if a runner touches all of the bases before there are three outs. However, there are three exceptions to this general rule: the run does not count if the runner touches home plate during a play in which the third out is made (1) by the batter-runner before he touches first base; (2) by any runner being forced out; or (3) by a preceding runner who is declared out because he failed to touch one of the bases.

13.1 Time plays

On April 28, 2007, the Indians were hosting the Orioles. In the top of the third with the Orioles clinging to a 2–1 lead, the Birds had Miguel Tejada on first and Nick Markakis on third and one out when Ramón Hernández lifted a fly ball to center field that Grady Sizemore dove for and caught. Tejada, forgetting how many outs there were, or running at the crack of the bat, had rounded second base and was easily doubled up at first base. But Markakis, the runner on third, tagged up and crossed home plate long before the third out was recorded on Tejada. Since the third out was recorded as part of the same play, home plate umpire Marvin Hudson waved off the run.

1: Did Hudson make the right call?

No, and in a highly unusual development, the umpires conceded the error three innings later and added a run to the Orioles score.

This is a classic time play. As noted above, a run does not count if the third out is made by a runner being forced out. Umpire Hudson may have believed that this exception to the general rule applied to the above play and that it was a force play. However, Markakis crossed the plate before the third out was made. Because the third out was not the result of a force-out, the run should have counted. However, Orioles manager Sam Perlozzo never protested the misinterpretation of Rule 4.09(a) and the game proceeded with the Orioles leading 2–1.

In explaining how the score was changed later in the game, Rich Marazzi opined that many people handled the situation poorly:

> Before the start of the fourth inning Baltimore coach Tom Trebelhorn brought the play to the attention of crew chief Ed Montague disputing Hudson's call. Hudson subsequently discussed the situation with Montague. "We kicked it around, and now I'm having a brain cramp on it," Montague said in a *USA Today* story. "So I sent Bill [umpire Bill Miller] in. I said, "You know what, 'cause we're debating, you go in. Let's make it 100 percent sure.' "
>
> Miller checked the Rule and said the run should have counted. In the sixth inning, after the Indians tied the score, 2–2, Montague called the official scorer and shocked everyone by adding a run to Baltimore's score, realizing that the umpires erred by not allowing Markakis's run to score in the third inning. . . .
>
> From this corner, the situation was handled poorly from the umpires down to Perlozzo. For the sake of baseball, it was unfortunate. To begin with, why didn't Perlozzo argue with Hudson regarding the denial of Markakis's run? His team just lost a run. And why did Trebelhorn wait until the fourth inning to discuss the ruling? He should have known that a protest must be made before the next pitch, play or attempted play. And how could the umpires add a run in the middle of a game even if the Orioles had earned it three innings earlier? Incredibly, both managers played three innings of the game not knowing what the score was. Neither did the fans.
>
> MLB President Bob DuPuy denied the Indians' protest [which claimed that] it was too late (three innings later) for the umpires

to make the correction. He acknowledged that the umpires misapplied Rule 4.09(a) but he cited Rule 9.01(c), which says that umpires can rule on any point that is not specifically covered in the rules, and since the rules don't state when the umps can make a correction, the umpires were justified in doing what they did. . . . However, is there anything from preventing the umps in the future from changing the score after the game ends if they realize they've misinterpreted a Rule? Have we established a dangerous precedent here?

2: Recall the situation in the play above—runners on first and third with one out when Hernández hits a fly ball to Sizemore in center. Assume now that there are two outs and Sizemore misses Hernández's fly ball. Markakis scores, Tejada winds up at third, and Hernández winds up at second. After the play is over, the Indians appeal, arguing that Hernández missed first base while making the turn, and they are correct. Assuming that Markakis crossed home plate before Hernández missed first base, what is the result of the play this time?

The run would not count, even though Markakis scored before Hernández missed first base. Rule 4.09(a) provides that one of the times a run does not score is if that occurs during a play in which the third out is made by the batter-runner before he touches first base. Since Hernández's failure to touch first base was during the play, Markakis's run would not count even though he crossed home plate first.

3: Would the result in the previous question be different if Hernández had instead missed second base while trying to stretch his hit into a triple?

Yes. The rule specifically refers only to the batter-runner's failure to reach first base or to touch it when he becomes the third out as a result of an appeal. So for this reason, the run would count because it was a different base that Hernández did not touch.

The situation of a third out nullifying a run on a similar basis occurred on August 9, 2010. Atlanta Braves pitcher Mike Minor was batting in the second inning with Alex González on third and two outs in a game against the Houston Astros. Minor hit a Bud Norris pitch to right field that bounced in front of Hunter Pence. The Astros right fielder fielded the ball and fired to first baseman Brett Wallace. Minor was ruled out by umpire Fieldin Culbreth (a great first name for an umpire if ever there was one).

After Minor was called out, he immediately pointed to the area of home plate, wondering if González would score. He apparently thought that this was a time play, which it was not. It would have made no difference whether González crossed the plate before or after Minor was called out because a run cannot score when an inning ends with the batter-runner making the third out before reaching first base. If Minor was thrown out at first after a routine grounder to shortstop, even casual fans would realize that the run would not count, but when the ball goes out to the outfield, it's not as obvious.

Because the batter-runner is seldom retired on a 9-3 play, the batter-runner in most cases assumes he will reach base without a play and may not run hard. The batter-runner and first-base coach should pay careful attention to where the defense is playing, especially the right fielder. If he fields a hard line drive that bounces in front of him, the potential for a 9-3 putout exists.

Ironically, this was Minor's first at bat in the major leagues. He probably is the only player in baseball history to be put out 9-3 in his first major league at bat.

4: Let's continue to examine the time play by tinkering with the actual play that occurred in the Indians-Orioles game. Assume again that Tejada is on first, Markakis on third, and Hernández is at bat. There are two outs. This time Hernández hits a clean single to Sizemore in center. Markakis scores and Tejada winds up at third. However, the

Indians appeal the play, successfully arguing that Tejada failed to touch second base. Does the Markakis run count?

No, even though he scored before Tejada missed second base. The reason is that, by failing to touch second base, and being called out on appeal, Tejada was in essence forced out at second base. It would be no different than if Hernández had hit a grounder to the third baseman, who then threw out Tejada at second (a play in which it is more obvious that the run would not count). This is therefore an example of the force-out exception.

5: Assume again that Tejada is on first, Markakis is on third, and Hernández is at bat. There are two outs. This time Hernández hits a home run. The runners and Hernández all circle the bases. However Markakis fails to touch home and on appeal is called out. How many runs score on the play?

No runs score. Rule 4.09(a) provides that a run is not scored in which the third out is made "during the play" by a preceding runner because he failed to touch one of the bases. In this case none of the runs would count because, even though Hernández hit a home run, Markakis—as the "preceding runner"—was called out on the play. This is an example of the third exception above.

6: Say that there are two outs with Tejada on first and Markakis on third. Hernández hits it out of the park. The runners and Hernández all circle the bases. However Tejada fails to touch third and on appeal is called out. How many runs score on the play?

Only Markakis's run scores. Rule 4.09(a) provides that a run is not scored in which the third out is made "during the play" by a preceding runner because he failed to touch one of the bases. In this case Hernández's run would not count (even though he hit a home run) because Tejada—as the "preceding runner"—was called out on the play. Because Markakis precedes Tejada, his run counts.

7: On June 25, 2009, the Phils were playing the Rays. In the top of the sixth inning the Phils had Matt Stairs on third and Pedro Feliz on first with one out. Eric Bruntlett hit a fly ball to B. J. Upton in medium-deep center field. Stairs tagged up and jogged home in a leisurely fashion. While Stairs was trotting to the plate, Upton fired to first to double up Pedro Feliz before Stairs crossed the plate. Does Stairs's run count?

No. Since this was a classic time play (no force-out), the event that governs is the one that occurs first, in this case the out on Feliz.

8: Can a run score when there is a triple play?

Yes. On May 27, 2006, the Twins were playing the Mariners. In the top of the eighth inning the Mariners had the bases loaded—Richie Sexson on third, Carl Everett on second, and Adrián Beltré on first. Twins relief pitcher Juan Rincón then replaced Jesse Crain. Rincón threw one pitch to get out of the inning. The first batter Rincón faced, M's catcher Kenji Johjima, hit a grounder to second baseman Luis Castillo, who tagged Beltré running to second. Castillo fired to Justin Morneau at first to retire Johjima for the second out. Morneau then spotted Everett having rounded third too far and threw over to nail Everett and end the inning. Because Sexson scored before Everett was tagged out, and the inning did not end in a force play or the batter-runner making the third out before reaching first base, Sexson's run counted. It was the first time a run had scored on a triple play since 1977.

A similar inning-ending play where a run counted because there was no force occurred on September 15, 1990, when the Mets were playing the Phillies. In the sixth inning, the Mets had the bases loaded with one out. Keith Miller was on first base and Howard Johnson was on third. Dave Magadan hit a bouncer to Phils second baseman Randy Ready. With Miller on the move from first, Ready intended to tag Miller and throw to first baseman Ricky Jordan for the inning-ending double play. However, Miller sized up the situation and stopped between first and second, where Ready couldn't readily tag him. Ready then immediately threw to first to retire Magadan, and Jordan then threw to shortstop Dickie Thon, who tagged Miller to complete the double play. While all this was going on, Johnson crossed home plate. Because the third out was not from a force play, the run counted.

9: Some plays involve application of multiple rules. On September 12, 1983, the Cardinals played the Pirates. In the sixth inning, the Cardinals had George Hendrick on first when Andy Van Slyke hit a liner to right field for extra bases. Hendrick scored and Van Slyke headed for third. When Pirates catcher Tony Peña attempted—unsuccessfully—to gun him down, third baseman Jim Morrison accidentally fell on Van Slyke as the ball bounced away.

Third-base coach Chuck Hiller, who was shouting for Van Slyke to score, helped the Cardinals runner to his feet. When this happened, umpire Randy Marsh pumped out Van Slyke because of Hiller's interference. If there had been two outs on this play, would Hendricks' run count?

Yes, because the interference took place after Hendrick had crossed the plate. The exception to the time play aspect of the rule occurs when coach's interference involves a batter-runner before he reaches first base. For instance, if a batter-runner popped an attempted suicide-squeeze bunt up the first-base line and the first-base coach hindered the fielder from making a play, the batter-runner would be called out and the runner who crossed the plate would return to third. If, with two outs, an umpire thought the first-base coach intentionally interfered with the batter-runner heading to first for the purpose of aiding the scoring runner, an umpire might call out a runner who is advancing from third.

13.2 Scoring a run—time-play end-of-regulation situations—Merkle's boner

One of the most famous and controversial plays in baseball history involved a Rule 4.09 inning-ending force-out way back in 1908. On September 23 of that year, the Giants and Cubs, tied for first place, played at New York's Polo Grounds. With the score tied 1–1 in the bottom of the ninth, and two outs, the Giants' Fred Merkle singled. Moose McCormick went from first to third on the play. Al Bridwell then singled, scoring McCormick and apparently winning the game. Giants fans ran onto the field, a common practice in those days, to celebrate the victory. To get out of the crowd, Merkle turned right and headed for the clubhouse, which was located behind center field, without touching second base. Amid the chaos, Cubs second baseman Johnny Evers retrieved the ball (although there remains much controversy about that as well) and touched second base. Because Merkle was forced at second on Bridwell's hit, it was a force play. Umpire Hank O'Day called Merkle out on the force, which nullified the run and ended the inning. The game was then called because of darkness and declared a tie. The teams finished the season tied, so the tie game was replayed; the Cubs won 4–2, winning the pennant and then the World Series—their last.

This play was governed at the time by Rule 4.09(a), and thus the run did not count since Merkle was forced out. Today, however, this would be considered a runner abandonment play. If the runner abandons the right to advance, he is deemed out at that point. If a preceding runner crossed the plate before the abandonment occurred, the run would count.

1: Say that the bases were loaded in the above situation, and Bridwell walked, forcing in the run. On his way to first, and upon seeing the runner cross home plate, Bridwell headed for the dugout. Would this have a different result than in the actual play?

No. Even though it was a bases-loaded walk, Rule 4.09(b) still requires the batter-runner to touch first base and the runner on third to touch home plate before the umpire can declare the game over. This situation almost arose in a May 15, 2010, game between the Tigers and the Red Sox in Detroit. With the score tied 6–6 in the bottom of the twelfth, Ramón Santiago drew a bases-loaded, two-out walk from Ramón Ramírez. Magglio Ordóñez, the runner on third, was headed home with the winning run when he noticed Santiago, after taking a few steps toward first base, retreating toward home plate to join the celebration. Ordóñez and Adam Everett, who was in the area of home plate, both shouted to Santiago to keep running to first. Santiago put on the brakes and ran to first base to end the game. If Santiago had never touched first, the game would have continued to the thirteenth inning. If there were less than two outs and Santiago failed to go to first base, Ordóñez's run would have counted, but Santiago would have been declared out under the Rule 4.09(b) penalty.

2: On the issue of abandoning the base paths, assume the following: There are two outs. It's the bottom of the ninth. The game is tied. (Are you excited yet?) The home team has a runner on first. The batter hits a home run. Thinking that the game is over, and in his elation, the runner on first simply heads for the dugout. What's the result? Has the home team won, assuming that the hitter completes his trip around the bases?

In this case, the base runner's boneheaded play actually wipes out the home run. When he "abandoned his efforts to run the bases," per the Comment to Rule 7.08(a), he was out at that moment. Since that became the third out of the inning, the home run would effectively be nullified. If there had been less than two outs, Rule 7.12 provides that the status of a following runner is not affected by a preceding runner's failure to touch or retouch a base.

3: In the play discussed above, Magglio Ordóñez is headed home from third after a bases-loaded "walk-off walk." Even assuming that he touches home plate and that Santiago reaches first, his run might not count (although, in fairness to the reader, this involves one of the rules that is rarely if ever invoked). How is it possible?

The "penalty" section of Rule 4.09(b) requires the runner on third to touch home plate "in a reasonable time." This is baseball's equivalent of the excessive-celebration rule in football, i.e., to prevent the runner on third from engaging in too many shenanigans on his way home. The penalty is that the runner on third is out. The penalty is the same if instead it is the batter-runner who "refuses to advance and touch first base." If, with a runner on third and less than two outs, the batter-runner refuses to advance to and touch first base, then the run counts but the batter-runner is out.

Chapter 14

What Is a Legal Catch?

On July 26, 2004, the Blue Jays were playing the Yankees at the SkyDome. After Toronto first baseman Carlos Delgado reached into the stands and caught a foul ball along the first-base line, a fan snatched it out of his glove.

1: Did Delgado make a legal catch of the ball?

No. The three requirements for a legal catch are (1) the fielder must have secure possession of the ball; (2) the fielder must hold the ball long enough to prove he has complete control of the ball; and (3) the fielder's release (transfer) of the ball must be voluntary and intentional. With regard to the second requirement, the fielder must also have his body under control and not be staggering after having possession. For example, if a fielder staggers and falls to the ground and the ball drops out of the glove, even after having possession, it would be ruled no catch. Unlike in football, the ground can cause a "fumble." Clearly, however, the third requirement is perhaps the least understood and the one that has haunted umpires for decades. It means the fielder (or, in rare cases, another fielder) must take the ball out of his glove. Because of this requirement, Delgado did not make a catch—he did not make a voluntary and intentional release of the ball. Rather, the fan took it out of his glove.

2: What if Delgado had caught the ball with his hat? Would that be a legal catch?

No luck here. A fielder cannot use a cap or any other part of his uniform in getting possession.

3: What if, in the first situation above, the fan was so eager to catch the ball that he actually pushed Delgado away? Would Delgado be entitled to claim interference?

Surprisingly, the answer is no. There can be no interference when a fielder reaches into the stands to catch the ball. One suspects that most fans are unaware of this rule.

4: What if Delgado caught the ball just as he was falling into the dugout. He is held up by his teammates so he doesn't actually fall into the dugout. Would that be a legal catch?

Yes. The Comment to the definition of "catch" provides that this one counts. Players on either team can prevent a fielder from falling.

5: On September 26, 1982, Atlanta was playing the Padres. In the top of the third inning, the Padres' Gene Richards lofted a fly ball to left field. Braves left fielder Terry Harper snared the ball in fair territory after making a long run. He then crossed into foul territory, his momentum carrying him across the line into the bullpen railing. Trying to cushion his landing, he grabbed the railing to brace himself before tumbling into the bullpen area, and he dropped the ball. Assuming for argument that Harper had firm possession and control of the ball prior to falling into the bullpen area, did he make a legal catch of the ball?

No. According to umpire Ed Vargo, regardless of whether Harper had possession and control, like Delgado, he did not make a voluntary and intentional release of the ball since the ball dropped out of his glove. There is no catch if the fielder "simultaneously or immediately" collides with a player or a wall, or falls down, and then drops the ball. Vargo's call ignited a firestorm among Braves fans and in the national media. Some sportswriters noted that Harper took four full strides before dropping the ball, and thus his dropping of it could not be considered "simultaneous or immediate." The play occurred in the middle of a pennant race and cost the Braves a run in a game they wound up losing by a run (although they did eventually win the division).

There have been many other plays where the fielder may have had possession and control but where satisfaction of the voluntary and intentional release requirement has been questionable. On April 28, 2010, the Tigers played the Twins. The Twins were leading 6–5 in the sixth when the Tigers Johnny Damon hit a Ron Mahay pitch to the gap in left center. Twins center fielder Denard Span sprinted from right center to left center and gloved the ball. He then carried it two to three steps. But as Span tried to slow his momentum down to reverse, spin, and transfer the ball to his throwing hand, the ball wound up on the

Rick Ankiel is laid out after catching a fly ball and then crashing into the outfield wall. Just before the crash, he took the ball out of his glove, but upon hitting the wall, he dropped the ball from his throwing hand. Is it a legal catch? *AP Photo/Jeff Roberson*

ground. Third-base umpire Paul Emmel ruled the play "no catch." Twins manager Ron Gardenhire argued the call, but the call stood even after the umpires huddled to discuss it. Gardenhire continued to argue and was ejected by umpire Gary Darling.

Span said, "The ball hit my glove. I tried to slow it down, get momentum to reverse spin and throw the ball. That's when the ball came out." He was charged with an error. In explaining his call to a pool reporter, Emmel said, "It's not how the ball goes in your glove, it's how it comes out." Emmel judged that Span did not intentionally release the ball from his glove to make the exchange. Following the noncatch, the Tigers scored six runs in the inning to take an 11–6 lead, which proved to be the final score.

One of the most extraordinary examples of voluntary and intentional release (transfer) took place in the Phils-Cards game at St. Louis on May 4, 2009. In the top of the eighth inning the Phillies' Pedro Feliz hit a deep line drive to left center. Cards center fielder Rick Ankiel snared the ball on the run. Just before his momentum caused him to crash into the wall headfirst, he took the ball out of his glove. Upon hitting the wall, Ankiel dropped the ball from his throwing hand. But because he removed the ball from his glove before dropping it, he made a proper transfer of the ball and was credited with a legal catch. If he never took the ball out of his glove or attempted to do it before making contact with the wall and dropped the ball, he would not have made a legal catch. Ankiel was hurt on the play and had to be carted off the field.

Game 3, NLDS, Phils-Brewers. Corey Hart tracked down a liner off the bat of Jayson Werth. The ball rested in Hart's glove about the time he crashed into the wall. When he stumbled to the ground, the ball popped out of his glove. Is this a legal catch? *AP Photo/Ben Smidt*

In the top of the sixth inning of Game 3 of the 2008 Phils-Brewers NLDS, Jayson Werth of the Phils drilled a hard liner off Dave Bush to deep right field. Going full speed, Corey Hart made a gallant effort to run down the ball on the warning track. The ball rested in Hart's glove about the time he crashed into the wall. When he stumbled to the ground, the ball popped out of his glove. Hustling all the way, Werth ended up on third with a triple while the right-field umpire ruled no catch. Because Hart made no effort to transfer the ball from his glove, he did not make a legal catch despite the fact that he had brief possession and control of the ball. In judging the validity of a catch, the fielder must begin removing the ball from his glove.

Brewers manager Dale Sveum said, "Corey never did really reach in his glove and pull it out. Once you make contact with an object or another player, you have to get up and grab the ball out of your glove, otherwise it is not a catch. Corey verified it. He said he was just getting ready to go in, and he was trying to get it, and it just trickled out of his glove before he was able to grab it."

The standard for most umpires is that the fielder must begin taking the ball out of his glove to get credit for the transfer. If he drops it after that, the catch will still be legal.

In the 2009 *Major League Baseball Umpire Manual* the standard for making a transfer is not quite as strict when a player falls to the ground with the ball. Section 8.1 reads, "If a fielder gets a hand or hands on the ball and falls down in the attempt, he must come up with the ball to be ruled a catch." The language covering a transfer attempt is noticeably absent from this section.

The problem with the transfer part of the rule as written is that it is subject to interpretation. The same play with a different umpiring crew might have a different result. Over the years, rules expert Rich Marazzi has queried many umpires on their interpretation of what constitutes a valid transfer of the ball. Here are some answers:

TIM McCLELLAND: "It is when a player actually reaches into his glove and is in the act of pulling it out."

JOE BRINKMAN: "It means the player who caught the ball could give it to another player."

BRUCE FROEMMING: "He's got to go in his glove to get the ball. Once he goes in the glove and secures the ball at any point and then drops it, we've got the out."

RICH GARCIA: "It's basically having the ball in your hand. You have to touch the ball with your throwing hand. The rule is interpreted differently among umpires."

JIM EVANS: "You have to see him touch the ball and start out with it. Some umpires are saying the act of flipping the ball [with glove] is a voluntary and intentional release."

6: In Game 4 of the 1999 American League Division Series, Red Sox shortstop Nomar Garciaparra hit a fly ball between Indians second baseman Roberto Alomar and right fielder Manny Ramírez. Alomar caught the ball and fell to the ground with the ball still in his glove. While he lay there, Indians center fielder Kenny Lofton took the ball out of Alomar's glove. Did Alomar make a legal catch of the ball?

Surprisingly, the answer to this question is yes. While it may not seem intuitive that the actions of Alomar and Lofton combined would satisfy the "voluntary and intentional release" requirement, no provision in the rules says that this has to be satisfied by the player who caught the ball. To the contrary, the Comment to the definition of "catch" specifically discusses this situation and provides that it is a catch. Thus, whether he knew it or not, Lofton was making a smart play since the ball could otherwise have rolled out of Alomar's glove.

Chapter 15

The Infield Fly Rule

One may not consider there to be much of a connection between the legal profession and the infield fly rule, but lawyers seem to love writing law-review articles discussing legal principles and the equitable underpinnings of the infield fly rule. They are simultaneously scholarly and yet often semisatirical. The progenitor of all of them was a 1975 article in the *University of Pennsylvania Law Review* by a law student, William Stevens, entitled "Aside: The Common Law Origins of the Infield Fly Rule." This was followed by other light pieces that have appeared in the nation's most prestigious law school journals, such as John J. Flynn, "Further Aside: A Comment on the Common Law Origins of the Infield Fly Rule"; Margaret Berger, "Rethinking the Applicability of Evidentiary Rules at Sentencing: Of Relevant Conduct and Hearsay and the Need for an Infield Fly Rule"; Mark W. Cochran, "The Infield Fly Rule and the Internal Revenue Code: An Even Further Aside"; Charles Yablon, "On the Contribution of Baseball to American Legal Theory"; Neil B. Cohen and Spencer Weber Waller, "Taking Pop-Ups Seriously: The Jurisprudence of the Infield Fly Rule"; and Anthony D'Amato, "The Contribution of the Infield Fly Rule to Western Civilization (and Vice Versa)."

D'Amato's article is typical of the metaphysical yet amusing approach taken by those scholars who long to write about the infield fly rule:

> The intellectual stage had now been set for Aristotle's explication of the Infield fly rule. . . . If there are baserunners and fewer than two outs, an infielder might *feign* to catch the ball and yet let it drop, thus commencing a double play. In that event the baseball would have reached the ground through the *deliberate*

> *and intentional efforts* of the fielder in violation of his immanent obligation to keep the ball in the air. In short, we have arrived at a teleological *hoistus petardis*. . . .
>
> The logic of the rule is impeccable, as seen even today in its extensive employment in the finest legal reasoning. Our Aristotelean sorites stacks up as follows: since the fielder *can* catch the infield fly, it follows that he *should* catch it. But if he *should* catch it, then he *ought to* have caught it. Since he *ought to* have caught it, then he is *deemed* to have caught it. But if he is *deemed* to have caught it, he *might as well* catch it. Since he *might as well* catch it, he catches it. Thus the ball has been prevented from hitting the ground after all. *Quod erat demonstrandum* (i.e., thank you very much, ladies and gentlemen).

Let's now put aside the legal underpinnings to the infield fly rule and consider some actual plays that have involved its interpretation.

On July 2, 2005, the Mets were playing the Marlins. In the bottom of the third inning, the Mets had José Reyes on first base and one out when Carlos Beltrán hit a soft fly ball to Marlins first baseman Carlos Delgado. Beltrán, thinking he would easily be erased, didn't run hard out of the box. Delgado saw this and let the ball drop to the ground. Since Reyes, who can run like a rabbit, was frozen on the fly ball, he had to hold the bag. Reyes thus became an easy out. Delgado picked up the ball and threw to second to start a 3-6-3 double play.

1: Was this play an infield-fly-rule situation?

No. For the infield fly rule to apply, runners must be on first and second or bases loaded with less than two outs.

2: Was it therefore a legitimate double play?

Yes.

3: Would it still have been a double play if Delgado had touched the ball but intentionally let it drop?

No. Rule 6.05(l) provides that the batter is out when an infielder intentionally drops a fair fly ball or line drive, with first, first and second, first and third, or first, second, and third occupied before two players are out. The ball is dead and runner(s) return to their original base(s). However, Delgado took advantage of an Approved Ruling to 6.05(l), which states, "In this situation, the batter is not out if the fielder permits the ball to drop untouched to the ground, except when the infield fly rule applies." The infield fly rule did *not* apply in this situation since there was only a runner on first.

Since Delgado alertly allowed the ball to fall to the ground "untouched," the ball remained in play. Of course, there is a risk that the untouched fly ball could take a bad hop, and you could end up with no outs and runners on first and second.

4: On May 17, 1998, the Rockies were playing the Brewers. In the first inning, Milwaukee had Mark Loretta on second and José Valentín on first. Dave Nilsson popped up toward Rockies second baseman Mike Lansing. The infield fly rule was called by the umpire. However, Lansing lost the ball in the sun and Loretta ran to third. Is this permissible?

Yes. The effect of calling the infield fly rule is simply that the batter is out, whether the infielder catches the ball or not. It is tantamount to a declaration by the umpire that the fielder has caught the ball. However, that does not preclude the base runners from attempting to advance at their own risk, the same as on any fly ball.

5: In the preceding play, say that Nilsson's fly ball was into short right field. Could the Rockies have avoided the effect of the infield fly rule by having the right fielder intentionally drop the ball instead?

No. Based on the definition of the infield fly rule itself, we know that if, in the umpire's judgment, the ball *could* be caught by an infielder "with ordinary effort," it doesn't matter whether another fielder is involved with the play. Also, under the definition of the infield fly rule, all fielders who station themselves on the infield on the play are considered infielders.

6: In the preceding play, if Nilsson had picked up the ball and thrown it to the third baseman in advance of Loretta's arrival, is Loretta out?

No, because it is not a force situation, Loretta would have to be tagged out. In this aspect of the rule, players frequently reveal their ignorance of how the infield fly rule works. In an April 13, 2008, game, Orlando Hudson of the Diamondbacks and Rockies shortstop Clint Barmes both demonstrated their confusion and lack of knowledge of the infield fly rule.

In the bottom of the first inning the D'backs had Orlando Hudson on first and Chris Burke on second with one out when Mark Reynolds lofted a fly ball to first baseman Todd Helton. First-base umpire Sam Holbrook signaled infield fly. Helton lost the ball in the sun and the ball fell to the ground untouched. Reynolds was automatically out. The runners did not have to run but could do so at their own risk.

Hudson, apparently unaware that he was protected by the infield fly rule, took off for second. Helton threw to shortstop Clint Barmes. Barmes, thinking it was a force play, just tagged the bag. Second-base umpire Gerry Davis made no call because Hudson was not forced to run and thus had to be tagged to be retired. Hudson, thinking he was out, ran off the bag. At that point, another Rockies player yelled to Barmes to tag Hudson, which he did, a few feet off the bag on the shortstop side. The odd play thus resulted in Hudson running into a double play.

7: Say Nilsson had tried to bunt the ball instead of hitting the soft fly and Lansing intentionally dropped it. Could he then try to double up Valentín and Nilsson?

No. The infield fly rule would not apply since it specifically excludes bunt attempts. However, under Rule 6.05(l), the umpire can kill any play in which he feels that the infielder intentionally dropped the ball.

8: If the infield fly ball is clearly in foul territory, would the infield fly rule apply?

No. It is treated the same as any foul ball.

9: What if it is near the baseline?

If it's near the baseline, the umpire should call, "Infield fly if fair." If the ball is touched by a fielder in fair territory, or if the ball settles on the ground in fair territory, the infield fly rule is invoked. If a fly ball declared to be an "infield fly if fair" falls untouched in fair territory and rolls into foul territory where it settles or is touched, it is a foul ball.

10: What if a declared infield fly lands in foul territory, but rolls fair before passing first or third base?

Then the infield fly rule applies and the batter is out.

11: Can an umpire's infield fly call (or noncall) be appealed?

No. It's a judgment call.

Not calling an infield fly as an "infield fly" can have interesting consequences. On September 1, 2000, the Orioles were playing the Indians. In the second inning, Cleveland had Travis Fryman on second and Wil Cordero on first with no outs. Sandy Alomar then lifted a pop fly twenty feet behind the dirt between third and second. Shortstop Melvin Mora drifted back to catch the ball. No umpire signaled for an infield fly, though any of them could have. Mora, hearing that nothing had been called, let the ball drop to the ground untouched. He then threw to second baseman Jerry Hairston, who caught the ball with his foot on the bag. With no infield fly in effect, the runner at first, Cordero, was forced at second. Fryman, seeing what was about to transpire, remained fixed to the bag when Hairston took the relay from Mora, who tagged Fryman, an instant after making the force on Cordero. Alomar was out for abandonment. He ran to first but thought the play was over and retreated to the dugout. The result was a called triple play.

12: Aside from whether it was an error by the umpires not to declare an infield fly on the Alomar pop-up, the umpires did make an error on the above play based on the facts as (accurately) described. What was it?

Remember that Cordero was forced out just *before* Fryman was tagged, which means that Fryman was no longer required to go to third base. That being the case, if Fryman got back to second base before being tagged, he would be safe at second. Based on replays, that's exactly what happened. Had Fryman been tagged before Cordero's out, he would have been out, too, because the force would still be in effect and he would still be required to go to third.

13: In the fifth game of the 2008 World Series, Pedro Feliz of the Phillies hit a pop-up to the right side of the infield with runners on first and second and one out. The infield fly rule was not invoked. Given that it was a fair fly ball that was clearly going to land in the infield, why wasn't it?

October 5, 2012, Cards-Braves, one-game playoff. Mayhem is about to ensue. With runners on first and second with one out, Atlanta's Andrelton Simmons hit a pop fly to left. Cards shortstop Pete Kozma drifted back but at the last second moved out of the way. The ball dropped between Kozma and left fielder Matt Holliday. However, instead of bases loaded with one out, the left field umpire ruled it an infield fly. The infuriated Braves fans littered the field with debris. Did the umpire get the call right? *Scott Cunningham/Getty Images*

Because of the windy and swirling conditions. Crew chief Tim Tschida explained that "the infield fly rule requires the umpire's judgment to determine whether or not a ball can be caught with ordinary effort, and that includes wind." The umpire's determination was that in this case no infielder could make the play with "ordinary effort." Some may remember that the weather in Game 5 was so bad that it had to be suspended in the sixth inning and completed several days later. The Phillies won the game to win the Series 4–1.

14: On May 13, 2003, the Giants hosted the Expos. The Giants had the bases loaded with one out in the fifth inning. Barry Bonds hit a

fly ball between home and third. On the play, plate umpire Jim Joyce correctly signaled infield fly, meaning that none of the runners were forced to advance. Thinking he had a force at home, Expos third baseman Fernando Tatís let the ball drop, then picked it up and stepped on the plate. Neifi Pérez, the runner on third, decided to head for home anyway and crossed home plate untouched. Is Pérez out? Has he scored? Does he have to head back to third?

Pérez has scored. Since he was not obligated to run on the play because of the infield fly rule, he had to be tagged to be put out. Anytime a runner is advancing from one base to another when not forced to do so (such as on a stolen base), he must be tagged out. The infield fly rule works the same way.

15: True or false? The infield fly rule requires that the ball be hit in or near the infield.

False. In fact, the definition of "infield fly" makes no reference to where the ball is hit other than requiring it to be fair. A controversial play, which played a key role in ending the 2012 season for the Atlanta Braves, involved an infield-fly-rule call on a ball that was nowhere near the infield. It was also the last game of Chipper Jones's career.

On October 5, 2012, in the first year of baseball's one-game wild-card playoff format, the Braves were playing the Cardinals in Atlanta. With the Braves trailing 6–3 in the eighth inning, with one out and runners on first and second, Atlanta's Andrelton Simmons hit a pop fly to left. Cardinals shortstop Pete Kozma drifted back . . . and back . . . and back a little farther until he was well into the outfield. He was finally camped under the ball, waiting for it to come down, but at the last second he peeled off, apparently assuming that left fielder Matt Holliday, who was a few feet behind him, would make the catch. However, that did not happen, and the ball dropped between them. However, umpire Sam Holbrook, working left field as one of six umpires for the playoff game, ruled it an infield fly.

Therefore, instead of bases loaded, one out, the Braves were left with runners on first and second and two outs. The Atlanta fans were so upset they began littering the field with debris, causing an eighteen-minute delay. Braves manager Fredi González protested the call. Atlanta's next batter, pinch hitter Brian McCann, walked to load the bases, but Michael Bourn struck out to end the inning, and the Braves went on to lose 6–3, and their season was over.

It is not clear what caused Kozma to move away. It could have been the crowd noise or hearing the infield fly call or perhaps assuming that Holliday was calling him off. (Holliday could probably have caught the ball if he kept running, but he stopped presumably because he thought that Kozma would catch the ball.)

The question is, did the umps blow the call? In the media and the blogosphere immediately after the game, opinions were divided. Some said that Kozma was way too far into the outfield for the infield fly rule to apply. Also, the call was not made until the last second, rather than when the ball was at its apex. Others, however, citing the definition of the rule itself, argued that the key issue is not where the infielder is standing, but whether he can catch the ball with "ordinary effort." In fact, the Comment to the definition of "infield fly" provides that "the umpire is to rule whether the ball would ordinarily have been handled by an infielder, not by some arbitrary limitation, such as the grass, or the baselines." That Kozma was facing the infield and momentarily waiting for the ball suggests that it could have been caught by him with ordinary effort.

It was a tough way for Jones's career to end, especially since he had recently railed against the new one-game playoff system.

16: In the previous question, we saw that a ball does not necessarily have to be hit in the infield for the infield fly rule to apply. However, does it at least have to be caught by an infielder?

No. It can be caught by any fielder. The only question is whether the fly ball could be caught by an infielder with ordinary effort.

17: True or false? The rules themselves make no reference to an "infield fly rule."

True. There is merely a definition of "infield fly." The infield fly rule is referenced in a Comment to the definition and in the Approved Ruling to Section 6.05(1), but not in the rules themselves.

Chapter 16

Batting Orders

16.1 Erroneous lineup cards

On May 28, 2010, the Padres were playing the Nationals. The Padres lineup card, signed by manager Bud Black, had Adam Russell as the pitcher. In fact, Russell had been sent to the Padres Triple-A affiliate earlier in the day and wasn't even on the Padres roster. The actual pitcher was Clayton Richard. After Richard pitched a scoreless first inning, Black noticed the error on the lineup card and pointed it out to the umpires. They in turn informed Nationals manager Jim Riggleman, who argued that the Padres had made an illegal substitution. The umpires allowed Richard to stay in the game and the Nationals filed a protest.

1: Did the Nationals have a case under the rules?

Probably not, although the protest was rendered moot since the Nationals won the game. Rule 4.01 addresses batting orders. As to the issue of "obvious" errors in batting orders, the Comment to Rule 4.01 states that if the umpire in chief notices such an error before he calls "Play," he shall bring it to the attention of the manager or captain of the team in error so the mistake can be corrected. It provides that the team should not be "trapped" by inadvertent errors that can be corrected before the game starts.

What is an "obvious" error? Clearly an error in the order of the hitters or any other error that would only be known to the manager would not qualify. The Comment gives two examples: having only eight men in the batting order or two players with the same last name and no identifying initial.

In this case, it is not clear that the error was obvious. The umpires may have had no idea that Russell was not on the Padres roster when the game started. In any event, it was never noticed by the umpires. (Press reports of the game differed as to who noticed the error. For example, the *San Diego Union-Tribune* stated that Riggleman raised the issue. However, the Padres Web site quoted Black as saying, "We inadvertently had Russell on the card as the starting pitcher. We spotted it and told the umpire it was wrong. They told [Riggleman], and from that point we played on.") Therefore, this Comment would not be applicable.

Rule 3.05 also addresses this issue. Rule 3.05(a) requires the pitcher named in the batting order to pitch to at least one batter. This would have been impossible. "There's no way to fulfill that given the fact that the pitcher named is not even in the area code," said crew chief Tim Tschida. Moreover, Rule 3.05(c) provides that if an "improper substitution" is made, then "the improper pitcher becomes the proper pitcher as soon as he makes his first pitch to the batter, or as soon as any runner is put out."

16.2 Batting out of order

On August 16, 2003, the Yankees were playing the Orioles. Orioles manager Mike Hargrove submitted a lineup that had Jay Gibbons batting fourth and Tony Batista fifth. (The lineup card is the official record of the lineup order.) However, the scoreboard had their order reversed. In the bottom of the first inning, with runners on second and third and one out, Batista (batting out of order, perhaps himself confused by the scoreboard) hit a sacrifice fly to center field and the runner on third tagged up, giving the Orioles a 1–0 lead. Then the Yankees, not noticing that Batista had hit out of order, pitched to Gibbons, throwing at least one pitch to him.

1: What is the result of the play under the above circumstances?

No one is out and the run counts because the Yankees didn't bring the situation to the attention of the umpire. None of the consequences from batting out of turn come into play unless the other team appeals before a pitch is made to the next batter. Rule 6.07(c) provides that if an improper batter becomes a runner or is put out, and a pitch is made to the next batter of either team before an appeal is made, the improper batter is now considered the proper batter, and the results of his time at bat become legal. When a proper appeal is made, the batter who failed to bat in turn is out. The defensive team must appeal the improper batter before the next pitch or play.

2: Assume that the Yankees did make the appeal before a pitch was thrown to Gibbons. Which of the following is correct?

A. Gibbons would be out, the run would not count, and Batista would bat again.

B. Batista and Gibbons are both automatically out and the run doesn't count because they both hit out of order.

C. Batista is out because he hit out of turn.

D. No one is out because the Yankees didn't appeal until Batista's at bat was over.

The correct answer is A. Rule 6.07(b) states in part that if an improper batter becomes a runner or is put out, and the defensive team appeals to the umpire *before the first pitch to the next batter of either team*, then the umpire shall (1) declare the proper batter out and (2) nullify any advance or score made because of a ball batted by the improper batter. Accordingly, the other choices are all incorrect. As for choice B, it is true that Gibbons would have been out and the run would not have counted. However, Batista would not have been out as well. He would have been able to hit (again) in his correct fifth spot in the lineup. As for choice C, it is Gibbons who would be out and not Batista.

3: Say the Orioles had realized their error while Batista was still at bat with a 2-1 count. Could Gibbons have come to the plate in the middle of Batista's (improper) at bat and finished the at bat for him? How would the count be affected?

Gibbons could legally complete the at bat. He would inherit the 2-1 count per Rule 6.07(a).

4: If the Yankees noticed Batista's improper at bat when the count was 2-1, could they cause Batista to be declared out right then and there?

No, because the rule requires that "another batter" (in this case Batista) is batting in Gibbons's place, and that batter has to "complete his turn" before Gibbons could be called out. Therefore, in this situation, the result would be the same as in the previous question. The Yankees would thus best be advised to let Batista complete his time at bat.

5: Is there any circumstance under which Batista could be called out for batting out of turn?

No. All of the penalties that can occur fall on Gibbons. If the Yankees appealed the improper at bat on a timely basis, then the results of Batista's at bat would be nullified per Rule 6.07(b), but Batista himself would not be out. For this reason, we know that choices B and C in question 2 above must be wrong, since they both call Batista out.

6: In the actual play, Batista hit a sacrifice fly to score the run from third. Say that Gibbons then came to the plate, but before a pitch has been thrown to him, the pitcher attempts a pickoff throw to second base. Is it too late now for the Yankees to appeal Batista's improper at bat?

Yes. Rule 6.07(b) allows the appeal to be made before the first pitch is thrown or "before any play or attempted play," which would include a pickoff move.

7: Say that the base runner on third had scored on a wild pitch in the middle of Batista's at bat. Then, before the first pitch to Gibbons, the Yankees appealed Batista's improper at bat (i.e., the appeal was timely). Would the run count?

Yes. The Note to Rule 6.07(b) states that if a runner advances on a stolen base, balk, wild pitch, or passed ball while the improper batter is at bat, the advance is legal. This means that even if the other effects of Batista's at bat (such as a hit by him) would be nullified, the run would still count.

8: In the actual situation above, in which the Yankees failed to appeal the batting mix-up, who would bat next, Gibbons or the number 6 hitter?

The number 6 hitter. Rule 6.07(d)(2). Once a pitch was thrown to Gibbons, it legalized Batista's at bat and the number 6 hitter should be at bat. Therefore, if Gibbons had reached base safely, the Yankees could have appealed a batting out of turn, and the number 6 batter would be out for failing to bat in turn.

9: The next time the Orioles work their way through the lineup, who bats first, Gibbons or Batista?

Gibbons. The offensive team's manager can correct the error at any time. That the hitters batted out of order once has no effect on subsequent plate appearances. Such a controversy occurred on August 14, 2002. With one on and one out in the top of the second inning, the Tigers' number 7 hitter, Shane Halter, flied out for the second out. Number 8 hitter Brandon Inge was due up, but number 9 hitter Chris Truby batted instead and struck out. Angels manager Mike Scioscia was immediately aware of the situation. However, as discussed above (quiz number 4), it was not incumbent on him to do anything until Truby completed his at bat. In the fourth inning, Inge followed Halter in the order and finally got his first at bat of the game—an RBI double to give the Tigers a 2–0 lead. That brought Scioscia out of the dugout, claiming Truby was established as the hitter after Halter. "After Inge hits the double, Mike [Scioscia] wants to say they should always bat Truby in front of Inge," crew chief Gary Darling said. "But the lineup card is still the lineup card. You can't change the batting order just because you batted out of order once."

10: If the umpire was aware that Batista was batting out of turn in the actual situation above, what are his obligations?

None. The Comment to Rule 6.07 makes explicit that the umpire "shall not direct the attention of any person to the presence of an improper batter in the batter's box." An interesting situation involving this Comment arose in the Tigers-Angels game discussed above. Recall that Truby, the number 9 hitter, batting out of order, struck out to end the second inning. Because of the strikeout, Angels manager Mike Scioscia did not appeal.

Then before the third inning began, Tigers manager Luis Pujols realized his mistake and went to the umpires to figure out what to do. "He said, 'We batted out of order, who's supposed to hit?' " crew chief Gary Darling said. "We said, 'Well, who's after Truby?' " That was Tigers leadoff hitter Hiram Bocachica, who came up to bat. This got Scioscia out of the dugout and onto the field for a lengthy conversation with all four umpires.

The issue was not whether Bocachica was the proper batter—he was. Rather the Angels' protest was based on the charge the umpires assisted the Tigers. According to Darling, "Mike was upset because we told them who to bat. That was his first protest, that we told the Tigers who was supposed to come up. His protest was that we were coaching them, basically." However, the umpires did not appear to have been prohibited from assisting by the Comment to Rule 6.07. That is, they were not "directing the attention of any person to the presence of an improper batter in the batter's box." Rather, they were simply responding to Pujols's question about who should lead off the third inning.

While the rule requires the manager and players themselves to be vigilant (rather than the umpire), in some situations even the vigilant manager might be penalized by this rule, or the snafu could benefit the team batting out of order even if the other manager was aware of what was going on. In the Tigers-Angels game, even though Scioscia was aware of the batting mix-up, it was to his advantage to let it slide once Truby struck out. However, the effect was that the Tigers were able to skip their number 8 hitter in the lineup the first time around and got to the top of the order more quickly. "If there's a way you can gain an advantage with a mistake in the lineup card, there's something wrong with that," Scioscia said. "They should be penalized, and if anything, they should not be able to gain an advantage by it."

I think Scoscia outsmarted himself. If he wanted Truby to lead off the next inning, he should have appealed the batting out of turn. The number 8 hitter would have been ruled out, and Truby would have led off the next inning.

PART THREE:
THE OFFICIAL SCORER

Chapter 17

Runs Batted In

Let's return to a play we examined earlier in a different context. On August 1, 1971, the Reds were playing the Dodgers in Los Angeles. In the bottom of the eleventh, with the score tied 4–4, the bases were loaded with two outs. Manny Mota was on third base. Willie Crawford was at bat for the Dodgers. On an 0-1 pitch by Reds reliever Joe Gibbon, Crawford swung and missed as Mota broke for home on a steal attempt. Reds catcher Johnny Bench reached for the ball and tagged Mota before he scored. However, home plate umpire Harry Wendelstedt ruled that Bench had interfered with Crawford's attempt to swing at the ball—i.e., catcher's interference. As a result, Crawford was awarded first base, and because the bases were loaded, Mota scored even though he had apparently been put out at home. Game over.

1: Does Crawford get an RBI on the play?

Yes. Rule 10.04(a)(2) specifically provides that the batter gets an RBI in this situation.

2: What if Crawford had been hit by the pitch—would he get an RBI?

Yes, under Rule 10.04(a)(2), again.

Here is another play we examined earlier. On September 15, 1990, the Mets were playing the Phillies. In the sixth inning, the Mets had the bases loaded with one out. Keith Miller was on first base and Howard Johnson was on third. Dave Magadan hit a bouncer to Phils second baseman Randy Ready. With Miller on the move from first, Ready intended to tag Miller and throw to first baseman Ricky Jordan for the inning-ending double play. However, Miller sized up the situation and stopped between first and second, where Ready couldn't readily tag him. Ready then immediately threw to first to retire Magadan, and Jordan then threw to shortstop Dickie Thon, who tagged Miller to complete the double play. Before Miller was tagged, Johnson scored. We saw earlier that this was a "time play" and that Johnson's run counts.

3: Does Magadan get an RBI?

No. Rule 10.04(b)(1) provides that in this situation, the batter does not get credit for an RBI. Why? Because the batter grounded into a "reverse force double play."

4: What is a "reverse force double play"?

This is actually defined in the rules. It occurs when the first out is a force play (in the above situation that would be Magadan being thrown out at first), and the second out is made on a runner for whom the force has been removed because of the first out (that would be Miller). The moment the Phillies retired Magadan at first, Miller was no longer a force-out at second and thus had to be tagged. Thus, Magadan does not get credit for an RBI.

5: Say that there were no outs on the play and the Phillies had turned the double play in conventional fashion, 4-6-3. Would Magadan get an RBI then?

No. Same result. Under Rule 10.04(b)(1), the batter gets no RBI when the run that scores results from a force double play or a reverse force double play.

6: Say that, on the actual play above, there were no outs when the play occurred and that Ready throws to Thon to force Miller for the first out. However, Jordan drops the throw back to first base, allowing Magadan to get on base. Would Magadan get an RBI if Johnson scored?

No. Rule 10.04(b)(2) provides that an RBI is not credited if a fielder muffs a throw at first base that would have completed a force double play.

7: Take the facts of question 6 again—i.e., bases loaded, no outs, and Ready throws to Thon to force Miller for the first out. However, this time Thon's relay throw drags Jordan off the base, and Magadan is safe. Would Magadan get an RBI if Johnson scored?

Yes. The noncrediting of the RBI in the previous situation only applies if the fielder taking the throw (typically, but not always, the first baseman) makes the error. This rule doe not apply if the fielder makes a bad throw on what would otherwise be a force double play (assuming no further advancement by the runner). Therefore, the play would be covered by 10.04(a)(3) (providing for the crediting of an RBI if an error is made with less than two outs on a play on which a runner on third would ordinarily score).

Scorer's Discretion

Some plays that might not be remembered if they occurred in the regular season become historic when they occur in the postseason, especially in the World Series, and even more especially in Game 7 of the World Series (such as Bill Mazeroski's walk-off home run in the 1960 Series). One such play occurred in Game 7 of the 1946 World Series between the Cards and the Red Sox, a game that will live in infamy for Red Sox fans.

With the score tied 3–3 in the eighth, Enos Slaughter of the Cards was on first and Harry Walker was at bat. With Slaughter on the move with the pitch, Walker lined the ball to left-center field. Center fielder Leon Culberson fielded the ball and threw it to Sox shortstop Johnny Pesky as Slaughter rounded third. Slaughter never stopped running. He beat the relay to the plate, helped by Pesky's apparent hesitation before throwing the ball to catcher Roy Partee. The play became known as Slaughter's Mad Dash, and his run was the difference in the game. (To Red Sox fans, it's the Pesky Held the Ball play.) In 1999, this play was named number 10 on the *Sporting News* list of baseball's twenty-five greatest moments ever.

On the actual play, Walker was given credit for the RBI. We will never know for certain whether Slaughter would have been thrown out had Pesky not held on to the ball a second or two too long (if in fact he did—some argue that there was no hesitation at all). But let's assume for argument that Pesky *did* hold on to the ball and that, but for that hesitation, Slaughter would have been out at home. We saw that Rule 10.04(a) covers situations in which the batter is credited with an RBI and 10.04(b) covers situations in which he is not. However, this situation is not directly addressed in either category. It was a safe hit by Walker with no "error" by Pesky, but under our hypothetical, Slaughter should not have scored, and the only reason he did was because of Pesky's "misplay."

1: Would Walker have received credit for the RBI? Would it make any difference if Slaughter had stopped between third and home and took off again when he saw Pesky's hesitation?

Rule 10.04(c) gives the scorer discretion on whether to award an RBI when a fielder holds the ball or throws to the wrong base. The rule provides that "ordinarily" if the runner keeps moving, the scorer should credit an RBI, and if the runner stops and starts when he notices the misplay, the run should be attributable as a fielder's choice. In the above situation, while there was some question about whether Pesky hesitated, there is no question that Slaughter did not hesitate as he rounded third. So Walker would likely get credit for the RBI no matter how long Pesky held on to the ball. Alternatively, if Slaughter stopped and then started again, it would likely be scored as a fielder's choice. In either case, it is ultimately up to the scorer's discretion.

Chapter 18

Base Hits

18.1 When does the batter get credit for a base hit?

The interesting play described below occurred in a minor league game, but the result in the majors would be the same. On October 10, 1969, Ken Papes of the Free Soil (Michigan) Pirates had a no-hitter going against the Mason County Eastern Cardinals. With two outs in the ninth inning, Mason County had Ken Budzynski on first via an error. Bill Chye hit a ground ball that struck Budzynski while he was running from first to second. As we saw earlier, Budzynski is out by virtue of Rule 7.08(f).

1: Would Chye get credit for a base hit?

Yes. Rule 10.05(a)(5) provides in part that the batter gets a hit for a fair ball that has not been touched by a fielder even if it strikes a runner.

2: Given that there were two outs when the play occurred, which takes precedence, the hit or the out, when they necessarily occurred simultaneously?

While the result is obviously more significant when a pitcher has a no-hitter going, the issue still arises anytime it happens with two outs in an inning. The commentators addressing this issue have all said that the no-hitter was lost—and in the above play, Papes *was* ruled to have lost his no-hit bid. However, nothing in the official rules says whether the base hit or the out takes precedence.

A New York Mets fan blogger, writing in 2010 and lamenting that, as of then, the Mets were one of only four teams that had never had a no-hitter, imagined the following scenario, involving this exact same situation:

> Say Johan Santana is mowing down the Phillies and becomes the first Mets pitcher not named Tom Seaver to take a no-hitter into the ninth inning. (What, did you expect it to be Maine or Perez? Neither of them is capable of pitching into the ninth inning, let alone carrying a no-hitter into the ninth.) Santana retires Jimmy Rollins and Placido Polanco to start the ninth inning, making him the first Mets pitcher to come within one out of a no-hitter.
>
> The next batter is Chase Utley, but he draws a walk. The Phillies now have a baserunner, but the no-hitter is still intact as Ryan Howard steps up to the plate. Howard hits a routine grounder towards Luis Castillo that appears to be the third out of the inning, but the ball hits Utley as he's running to second base. The umpires immediately call Utley out for being hit by a batted ball in fair territory and the game is over.
>
> Could it be? Has Johan Santana become the first pitcher in

> Mets history to toss a no-hitter? The players on the field seem to think so, as they're celebrating with Johan on the mound. . . . While Johan Santana and his Merry Men were all celebrating his apparent no-hitter, the official scorer had to give Ryan Howard a base hit [under Rule 10.05(a)(5)]. Therefore, at the exact moment Johan Santana recorded the 27th out of the game, he also lost his no-hitter. Imagine the shock on his face when the scoreboard flashed the "1" in the hit column.

On June 1, 2012, Johan Santana (ironically the same pitcher mentioned in the above hypothetical) actually did finally throw a no-hitter for the Mets in an 8–0 win over the Cardinals. The victory closed out their era as the oldest team without a no-hitter and ended a drought that had lasted 8,019 regular-season and 74 postseason games. Mets pitchers have thrown 36 one-hitters.

3: Would the result change if the runner intentionally let the ball hit him, just to break up the no-hitter?

No. One wonders, however, whether a runner would be so spiteful toward a pitcher and hurt his own team. After all, if the ball doesn't hit him, the fielder still has to make the play. Once the ball hits him, however, it's game over.

4: Let's stick with the Phils-Mets hypothetical above. Say that, rather than hitting Utley, Howard's ball goes into right-center field. Utley, in his haste to get to third, misses second base, and the Mets successfully appeal. Is Howard credited with a hit?

Surprisingly, no, per Rule 10.05(b)(2). The rule provides that the official scorer shall not credit a base hit when a batter "apparently hit safely and a runner who is forced to advance fails to touch the first base to which he is advancing." In this case, third base would not be the first base to which Utley was forced to advance. Presumably the rationale here is that, if Utley never touched second base, he is effectively out on appeal and thus the play is treated like a fielder's choice. So Howard would be charged with an at bat but no hit.

5: Would it make any difference if instead Utley had missed third base while trying to score on Howard's hit?

Yes. If Utley did touch second, then Howard's ball would be treated as a hit because it would have advanced Utley safely to second. Anything that happens to Utley afterward would not deprive Howard of his hit.

6: On October 7, 2007, the Yankees were playing the Indians in the American League Division Series. In the third inning, the Yankees had Hideki Matsui on second with one out. Melky Cabrera hit a swinging bunt that dribbled just a few feet away from home plate. Indians catcher Victor Martínez fielded the ball cleanly and threw to third in an attempt to throw out Matsui. What pieces of information are needed to determine whether Cabrera would be given credit for a hit?

We need to know whether Matsui was safe or out at third (and if safe, if due to an error), and whether, in the scorer's judgment, the batter-runner would have been put out if Martínez had gone to first instead. More specifically:

1. Matsui is safe at third with no fielder's error *and* the official scorer feels that Cabrera could not have been put out "with ordinary effort"—Cabrera gets a hit. Rule 10.05(a)(6).
2. Matsui is out at third—Cabrera does not get a hit. Rule 10.05(b)(3).
3. Matsui is safe at third because of a fielder's error—Cabrera does not get a hit. Rule 10.05(b)(3).

7: Assume that Martínez could have fielded the ball cleanly and thrown Cabrera out at first. Just before Martínez picked up the ball, however, the Indians pitcher rushed over and attempted to throw Cabrera out but failed. Does Cabrera get credit for a hit?

Yes. The Comment to Rule 10.05(a)(2) provides that a hit shall be credited "if the fielder attempting to handle the ball cannot make a play, even if such fielder deflects the ball from or cuts off another fielder who could have put out a runner." Presumably, one doesn't want to penalize the fielder for trying to make a hustle play or take a hit away from the batter-runner.

18.2 Determining the value of base hits

On April 17, 2010, the Indians were playing the White Sox. In the first inning, with one out, Cleveland's Grady Sizemore tripled to left-center and scored when Shin-Soo Choo lined an apparent double to right. However, the White Sox appealed at first base, claiming that Choo missed the bag. First-base umpire Dan Bellino agreed that Choo had missed first base.

1: Does Choo get credit for a hit?

No. Rule 10.06(d).

2: Does Choo get credit for an RBI, and if so, how would his at bat be judged for scorekeeping purposes?

He would get the RBI under Rule 10.04(a)(1) on the basis of an infield out. In essence, it would be no different than if he had hit a routine grounder to shortstop and was thrown out at first.

On September 16, 2008, the Rays were playing the Red Sox. In the bottom of the ninth, with the score tied 1–1, Tampa had runners on second and third. Rays catcher Dioner Navarro hit a fair ball that bounced over the fence. Here he is celebrating his hit. What was the final score of the game and what kind of hit was Navarro credited with? *AP Photo/Mike Carlson*

3: What if there had been two outs when the play occurred—would the run have counted?

No. This is not a time play because any play at first is a force situation, and when the third out is on a force, no run scores, regardless of when the runner on third crosses home plate.

4: What if Choo had hit a triple while there were two outs, but he missed second base. How would his at bat be treated and would the run count?

He would get a single. Rule 10.06(d). The run would count here because, once Choo has reached first base, it is no longer a force situation. Therefore, presuming that Sizemore crossed the plate before Choo missed second (which is highly likely), the run would count.

18.3 Bases awarded for game-ending hit

On September 16, 2008, the Rays were playing the Red Sox. In the bottom of the ninth, and the score tied 1–1, Tampa had runners on second and third. Rays catcher Dioner Navarro hit a book-rule double.

1: What was the final score of the game, and what kind of hit was Navarro credited with?

The final score was 2–1 and Navarro was credited with a single only. On a play like this, the game ends the moment the winning run scores even if other runners are automatically entitled to score by virtue of a book-rule double. As for the scoring of Navarro's hit, Rule 10.06(f) provides that the official scorer shall credit such batter with only as many bases on his hit as are advanced by the runner who scores the winning run, even if with a book-rule double. Since the Rays had a runner on third, who had to advance just one base to score the winning run, Navarro only got a single.

2: Say that the Rays only had a runner on second and that Navarro's hit had instead been a conventional double, such as a gapper to left-center field. Say also that the game-winning run scored before Navarro got to second base. What kind of hit would Navarro be credited with?

He would be credited with a double, so long as he actually reaches second base. The Comment to Rule 10.06(f) provides that the official scorer shall credit the batter with a base touched in the natural course of play, "even if the winning run has scored moments before on the same play." Of course, while not specified in the Comment, this would only apply to the next base that could be touched by the batter-runner. For example, say that while the winning run scored just before Navarro got to second base, he could easily have reached third base "in the natural course of play." Nevertheless the intent is clear that he would only be credited with a double.

3: What if, in question 1 above, Navarro had hit a home run out of the park. What would the final score be then?

Then the final score would be 4–1. Rule 10.06(g), which is an exception to 10.06(f), provides that on a home run "hit out of the playing field" the batter and any runners on base are entitled to score.

Chapter 19

Stolen Bases

Game 3, 1997 ALCS. The Orioles were playing the Indians. Score tied 1–1 in the bottom of the twelfth. With Marquis Grissom on third, the Indians' Omar Vizquel attempted a suicide squeeze. He missed the bunt, but the ball got away from catcher Lenny Webster. The official scorer ruled it a passed ball on Webster. Grissom scored the winning run on the play. Was the official scorer's ruling correct? *AP Photo/Amy Sancetta*

19.1 Stolen bases on wild pitch or passed ball

In Game 3 of the 1997 American League Championship Series, the Orioles were playing the Indians. In the bottom of the twelfth, with the score tied 1–1, the Indians had Marquis Grissom on third base.

Omar Vizquel attempted a suicide squeeze. He missed the bunt, but the ball got away from catcher Lenny Webster. The official scorer ruled it a passed ball on Webster. Grissom scored the winning run on the play.

1: Was the official scorer's ruling correct?

No. It should have been ruled a stolen base for Grissom, even though that was not his intent. Rule 10.07(a)—then 10.08(a)—provides that if a runner starts for the next base before the pitcher delivers the ball, and there is a wild pitch or passed ball on the pitch, the scorer shall credit the runner with a stolen base and shall not charge the misplay. After the game, the initial passed-ball call was changed, and Grissom was credited with the steal of home. Although not relevant for our purposes, a huge controversy surrounded this play because the Orioles strenuously argued that Vizquel had tipped the ball, which would have nullified the play.

2: Say that Grissom's run did not end the game and a runner was on first, not otherwise attempting to steal, who moved to second on the play. How would the runner's advance to second be scored?

It would be a passed ball on the catcher, allowing the runner to move to second.

3: Say that Grissom had been on first base instead of third and was attempting to steal second. After the passed ball, he went to third. How would the play be scored?

The same as the answer to quiz number 2, namely a steal of second by Grissom and a passed ball on the catcher, allowing Grissom to move to third.

19.2 Double steal

On June 1, 2008, Cincinnati was playing Atlanta. In the fifth inning, with one out, the Reds had Jerry Hairston Jr. on second and Jay Bruce on first. They attempted a double steal. Hairston made it safely to third but Bruce was thrown out at second.

1: Does Hairston get credit for a steal?

No. Per Rule 10.07(d), when one runner is thrown out on a double-steal attempt, no other runner gets credit for a steal.

2: Would the result change if Bruce had initially been safe at second but then overslid the bag and was tagged before he could get back?

No, it would make no difference. Under Rule 10.07(d), the runner has to not only reach, but also "hold" the base.

19.3 Effect of oversliding on steal attempt, effect of dropped ball, and effect of wild throw

On September 1, 2000, the Mets were playing the Cards. In the second inning, with no one on base, Cards left fielder Ray Lankford singled. He then attempted to steal second and got there before the throw but overslid the bag.

1: He was tagged before he could return. How is the play scored?

Caught stealing. Rule 10.07(e).

2: **Say that on Lankford's steal attempt, he did not overslide the bag, and the throw from Mets catcher Mike Piazza to shortstop Mike Bordick was in time and on line, but it was dropped by Bordick. How would the play be scored as to Piazza, Bordick, and Lankford?**

It's a good result for Piazza, but bad for Bordick and Lankford. Piazza would get an assist, Bordick would get an error, and Lankford would be charged with "caught stealing," per Rule 10.07(f), even though he would not be out at second.

3: **Say that in quiz 2, Lankford was safe only because Piazza made a poor throw. How would the play be scored as to Lankford and Piazza?**

It would be scored as a stolen base for Lankford and no error for Piazza, per Rule 10.07(b). The rules do not distinguish between bad throws that permit the stolen base and bad throws where the runner would be safe anyway. If, however, another runner advanced because of the wild throw or if Lankford was able to move to third on the play, then Piazza would be charged with an error, per Rule 10.07(b).

19.4 Defensive indifference

On June 26, 2007, the Indians were playing the A's. In the bottom of the ninth, the Indians had Grady Sizemore on first with one out and Victor Martínez at the plate. Sizemore ran to second, and the A's did not attempt to throw him out.

1: **Does Sizemore get credit for a stolen base?**

A. Yes.

B. No, because the catcher did not attempt to throw him out.

C. No, if there was defensive indifference.

D. Not enough information to answer the question.

The correct answer is C. However, whether there was defensive indifference is a judgment call for the official scorer based on the totality of the circumstances, per Rule 10.07(g) and Comment. For example, what was the score at the time? How many outs were there? Was Sizemore being held on first? Had the A's tried to pick him off first? Here, the A's were winning 5–3 with two outs, Sizemore was not being held on, and the A's had not attempted to pick him off. Sizemore was not credited with a stolen base. As it happened, after a walk, a double, another walk, and a 3-run, walk-off homer, the Indians won 8–5.

2: How would the play be scored?

The advancement to second would be due to "defensive indifference" to the runner's advance.

3: The Comment to Rule 10.07(g) states that the defensive team may have a "legitimate strategic motive not to contest the runner's advance," and in that case a stolen base should be credited. What might be an example of such a motive?

If the hitting team has runners on first and third, the defensive team may not contest the advance to second base because they are concerned about the runner on third scoring on the play. In other words, the team is not "indifferent" to the advance; rather, they have a reason to let it occur.

19.5 Caught stealing

On April 28, 1990, the Orioles were playing the Mariners. In the third inning, Phil Bradley of the Orioles was on first. He was charged with caught stealing, yet there was no putout or assist.

1: How is that possible?

It's possible because the term "caught stealing" includes a runner's being picked off while trying to advance to the next base who is put out *or would have been put out on an errorless play*, per Rule 10.07(h). On this play, Bradley was going to be picked off first by Seattle pitcher Matt Young. However, Young's pickoff attempt sailed high and beyond the reach of first baseman Alvin Davis. It rolled to the front of the stands, where a fan grabbed the ball. Bradley was awarded third base. Despite his good fortune, he was nevertheless "caught stealing" under the rule.

2: Assume that the ball skipped away from Mariners catcher Scott Bradley on a pitch and, as a result, the Orioles Phil Bradley (no relation) took off for second but was thrown out on the play. Was he caught stealing?

No, as per the Comment to Rule 10.07(h), which addresses this situation.

3: Would he have been credited with a stolen base if he had been safe?

No. The advancement would be attributed to a passed ball or a wild pitch.

Chapter 20

Sacrifices

20.1 Sacrifice bunts

On May 19, 2010, Toronto was playing Seattle. In the fourth inning, with the Mariners down 1–0, Ichiro Suzuki of the Mariners was on first with one out. The speedy Chone Figgins laid down a bunt that rolled between the mound and home plate. Blue Jays pitcher Brett Cecil threw over to first, retiring Figgins by a step. Suzuki moved to second on the play.

1: Figgins was not credited with a sacrifice bunt but rather was charged with an at bat and an out. Why?

In these situations, the official scorer always has discretion to decide whether the batter is giving himself up to move the runners along or whether he is actually trying for a hit. Rule 10.08(a) provides that in the latter instance, he is safe and the runners advance anyway; that's a bonus. In making this decision, the scorer is supposed to take the totality of the circumstances into account. This game was only in the fourth inning, and Figgins was known to be fast. The scorer concluded that Figgins was trying for a hit rather than a sacrifice.

2: Say that instead of throwing out Figgins at first, Cecil instead tried to throw out Suzuki at second, but was unsuccessful. Which of the following statements is true?

A. The play is scored as an error on Cecil.

B. Figgins is credited with a base hit.

C. Figgins is credited with a sacrifice.

D. It's up to the scorer how to treat Figgins's plate appearance.

The answer is D. The official scorer has to judge whether Figgins would have been out at first if Cecil had gone that way, per Rule 10.08(b). If the scorer feels that Figgins would have been safe, then it's a base hit for Figgins. Otherwise it's treated as a sacrifice.

3: Say that the Mariners also had a runner on second. Figgins laid down his bunt. Cecil threw to second and retired Suzuki. Which of the following statements is true?

A. Figgins is not charged with an at bat and it's a fielder's choice.

B. Figgins is charged with an at bat and it's a fielder's choice.

C. Figgins is credited with a sacrifice.

D. It's the scorer's discretion.

The correct answer is B. Under Rule 10.08(c), the batter is charged with a time at bat.

20.2 Scoring a sacrifice fly

On July 13, 2002, the Tigers hosted the White Sox. In the top of the eighth inning, Chicago had Ray Durham on third and Paul Konerko on first with one out when José Valentín hit a foul fly along the first-base stands. The ball was caught by Tigers first baseman Carlos Peña, who then fell into the seats. The runners both advanced one base, allowing Durham to score on the play. Official scorer Richard Shook credited Valentín with a sacrifice fly.

1: Would that ruling be incorrect when made but correct now, based on amendments to the rules since then, or would it be correct when made but incorrect now, for the same reason?

In 2002, Rule 10.09(e) stated in part that the official scorer shall "score a sacrifice fly when, before two are out, the batter hits a fly ball or a line drive handled by an outfielder or an infielder running in the outfield which is caught, and a runner scores after the catch." In the above play, Peña did not catch the ball in the outfield, but rather in foul territory. For this reason, Shook's call, which was incorrect when made, was later changed. Now, however, it makes no difference where the ball was caught. In addition, the reference to "a fly ball or line drive" has now been simplified to "a ball in flight." Rule 10.08(d), as amended, now credits a sacrifice fly when there are less than two outs, and "the batter hits a ball in flight handled by an outfielder or an infielder running in the outfield in fair or foul territory that is caught, and a runner scores after the catch." So if the play occurred today, Valentín would be properly credited with a sac fly.

2: If the above play occurred today and Peña had dropped the ball, could Durham have scored and would Valentín have been credited with a sacrifice fly?

No to both questions. A runner can only tag up on a foul fly if the ball is caught, not if it is dropped. Rules 10.08(d)(1) and (d)(2).

3: No matter how many baseball games you see in a lifetime, whenever you go to a ballpark, you might still witness something for the first time. That even applies to official scorers. On April 17, 2011, the Nationals were playing the Brewers. In the ninth inning, the Brewers had the bases loaded with one out. Ryan Braun hit a pop-up and was

out. However, Carlos Gómez scored from third on the play. Braun was credited with an RBI but no sacrifice. How is that possible?

On Braun's pop-up, an infield fly was ruled. The wind, though, took the ball away from Nationals' second baseman Danny Espinosa. The ball dropped fifteen feet behind him, allowing Gómez to score from third. The ball wasn't caught, but a run scored because players can advance at their own risk on an infield fly. So the official scorer, Ben Trittipoe, was left with two questions. Should there be an RBI, and should Braun be credited with a sacrifice fly? Trittipoe concluded that the results of Braun's at bat fit within the definition of an RBI under Rule 10.04(a)(1). There was no error on the play; it would be similar to a groundout that brings in a run. As for the sacrifice fly, Trittipoe concluded that it did not fit within Rule 10.08(d)(2), as the ball was neither caught nor dropped by Espinosa.

Chapter 21

Putouts

A number of interesting situations arise about who should be credited with the putout.

21.1 Catching fly ball but fan interference

On August 18, 2003, the Giants were playing the Expos. In the sixth inning, the Expos were batting with one out and José Vidro on third. Orlando Cabrera hit a foul pop-up past first base near the Expos' bullpen mound. Giants first baseman Pedro Feliz didn't catch the ball because a fan reached out and was then ruled to have interfered on Feliz's attempt to catch the ball. Based on Rule 3.16, Cabrera was out.

1: Did Feliz get credit for the putout even though he never touched the ball?

A. Yes, because the rules so provide.

B. No, because the rules so provide.

C. Yes, even though the rules are silent on this issue.

D. No, even though the rules are silent on this issue.

The correct answer is C. Feliz was credited with the putout although the rules do not actually address this situation. However, in several instances a fielder will get credit for a putout even though he never touches the ball, including one runner passing another on the base path, and a runner being hit by a batted ball.

21.2 Batting out of turn

We earlier looked at a situation in a game between the Orioles and the Yankees on August 16, 2003. With runners on second and third with one out, the Orioles number 5 hitter, Tony Batista, batting out of order, hit a sacrifice fly to center fielder Bernie Williams, and the runner on third tagged up, giving the Orioles a 1–0 lead. The proper batter was cleanup hitter Jay Gibbons. The Yankees did not notice that Batista had hit out of order. However, as noted earlier, if the Yankees had noticed the mistake and brought it to the umpires' attention before a pitch was thrown to the next batter, Gibbons would have been out, Batista's at bat would have been nullified, and he would have had to bat again.

1: Does a putout have to be credited to an individual fielder on every out?

Yes.

2: Is there such a thing as a "team putout"?

No.

3: Who then would get credit for the putout of Gibbons?

Center fielder Williams. Under Rule 10.03(d), when a player bats out of turn and is put out and the proper batter is called out before the ball is pitched to the next batter, the at bat is scored as if the correct order had been followed.

4: Who would get credit for the putout of Gibbons if Batista had singled instead?

The catcher. Rule 10.09(b)(6). On many plays where an out is recorded based on an action of the batter other than his actually hitting the ball in fair territory (including a strikeout and bunting foul for a third strike), the catcher gets the putout.

21.3 Infield fly not caught

Let's return to a play we looked at earlier to consider it from another angle. On May 13, 2003, the Giants hosted the Expos. The Giants had the bases loaded with one out in the fifth inning. Barry Bonds hit a fly ball between home and third. On the play, plate umpire Jim Joyce correctly signaled infield fly. Thinking he had a force at home, Expos third baseman Fernando Tatís let the ball drop, then picked it up and stepped on the plate. However, Neifi Pérez, the runner on third, decided to head for home anyway and crossed home plate untouched. We saw earlier that Perez's run counts. Because of the infield fly rule, he had to be tagged, which he wasn't. However, because it was ruled an infield fly, Bonds was out.

1: Who gets credit for the putout of Bonds?

Tatís. Under Rule 10.10(b)(1), in an infield fly situation where the ball is not caught, the putout is credited to the fielder who the scorer believes could have made the catch.

21.4 Ball hitting runner

On April 29, 2004, Tampa Bay was playing Boston. With José Cruz Jr. of the Rays on first base, Tino Martinez ripped a line drive to right field. Home plate umpire Jim Joyce said that the ball grazed Cruz's jersey. As we saw earlier, under Rule 7.08(f), Cruz is out because the ball touched him before touching or passing an infielder.

1: Which fielder gets credit for the putout?

Under Rule 10.09(c)(2), it's the fielder closest to the ball, which in this case was Red Sox first baseman Brian Daubach.

21.5 Passing runner on base paths

On July 29, 1986, Milwaukee was hosting the Yankees. In the bottom of the first, the Brewers had the bases loaded with no one out when Ernie Riles hit a ball to deep left-center. It could have been caught by left fielder Claudell Washington but was misplayed and bounced off the base of the wall. Gorman Thomas had been on first base, but he hesitated between first and second because he wasn't sure if the ball would be caught by Washington. He was then passed on the base path by the hard-running Riles. As discussed previously, under Rule 7.08(h), Riles would be out. Whether he or Thomas is more at fault, it is Riles's obligation to stay behind Thomas.

1: Which fielder gets credit for the putout?

Under Rule 10.09(c)(4), it's the fielder closest to the point of passing, which in this case was Yankee second baseman Willie Randolph. As noted above, although the catcher often gets the putout where an out is recorded based on an action of the batter other than his actually hitting the ball in fair territory, when the out is based on the action of a runner, the putout typically goes to the fielder closest to the runner.

21.6 Interference by preceding runner

We earlier looked at a play where Detroit had Carlos Guillén on first with one out when Pudge Rodríguez hit a ground ball to Kansas City shortstop Ángel Berroa. He flipped the ball to second baseman Desi Relaford, who was trying for the double play on Rodríguez. However, as Relaford was throwing the ball to first, Guillén made a rolling block on him, which was ruled runner interference. Under Rule 6.05(m), the batter-runner, Guillén, is out on the interference.

1: Who gets credit for the putout?

The first baseman. Rule 10.09(c)(7) provides that the first baseman gets credit for the putout when there is interference by a preceding runner.

Chapter 22

Assists

On September 7, 2007, the Mets were playing the Astros. In the second inning, with the bases loaded and one out, Houston's Wandy Rodríguez hit a grounder to Mets shortstop José Reyes. Reyes booted the ball, but deflected it to second baseman Luis Castillo, who turned the double play.

1: Does the scorer have discretion to credit Reyes with an assist on this play?

Yes. Rule 10.10(a)(1) provides that the scorer shall credit an assist to each fielder who throws or deflects a batted or thrown ball in such a way that a putout results or would have resulted but for a subsequent error by a fielder. However, if the scorer considers Reyes's action to be "ineffective contact," then no assist is to be credited. Here, Reyes was not credited with an assist. Any play that follows a "misplay," whether or not the misplay is an error, is a new play, and the fielder making the misplay shall not be credited with an assist unless that fielder takes part in the new play. (As for the distinction between a misplay and an error, see the discussion on errors below.) Interestingly, Rule 10.10(a)(1) provides that an assist *shall* be credited to each fielder who "deflects" a batted ball in such a way that a putout results. Based on that rule, Reyes should have been credited with an assist. Presumably the difference is that 10.10(a)(1) is intended to be limited to deflections that are *not* resulting from "misplays." (The Comment to Rule 10.10(a)(1) notes that "ineffective" contact with the ball is insufficient, and that "'deflect' shall mean to slow down or change the direction of the ball and thereby effectively assist in putting out a runner.")

In addition, this rule, when combined with Rule 10.10(b)(3), means that the room for defining a deflection under Rule 10.10(a)(1) is fairly narrow. The ball must hit the fielder's body or glove and carom in a way that would not be considered a misplay (which is broader than an error because not all misplays are errors). That doesn't happen too often, at least not intentionally. The most common instances would be hard shots that hit the pitcher or his glove too quickly for him to react.

2: Say that Castillo's throw would have been in time to complete the double play but it was dropped by the first baseman. Would Castillo get an assist on the play?

Yes. Under Rule 10.10(a)(1), the fielder who makes a throw that would have led to a putout but for an error on the receiving end of the throw is credited with an assist whether the putout results or not.

3: On July 11, 1963, the Phillies were playing the Giants. In the second inning, with Willie Mays on first, Orlando Cepeda hit a dribbler to second baseman Tony Taylor. Mays was trying to steal second on the play. Mays assumed that Taylor would try to throw out Cepeda at first, and Mays, being Mays, decided to try for third on the play. However, Taylor saw what was happening and threw the ball to third baseman Don Hoak. Mays found himself caught in a rundown. As part of the attempted putout of Mays, the ball then went from Hoak to shortstop Ruben Amaro to pitcher Ray Culp (don't ask), back to Amaro, and finally back to Taylor, who tagged Mays out. At least that's what the official scorer could remember about the play in those pre-instant-replay days. Assuming that the scorer's recollection of the play was accurate, which of the following statements is accurate:

A. The one assist on the play goes to Amaro because he threw the last ball before Mays was tagged out.

B. Taylor, Hoak, and Culp each get one assist on the play, and Amaro gets two because he threw the ball twice.

C. Taylor, Hoak, Culp, and Amaro each get an assist on the play.

D. There are no assists on the play because assists are not awarded in rundown situations.

The correct answer is C—everyone who threw the ball on the play gets an assist. Choice B is not correct because there can be no more than one assist per player per putout.

That a putout has occurred does not mean that the action is over. Consider the following play from a June 29, 1965, game between the White Sox and the Twins. In the fifth inning, the Twins had Harmon Killebrew on second and Don Mincher on first. Jerry Kindall then hit a grounder to second baseman Al Weis, but he booted the ball and Killebrew scored. However, Mincher then got caught in a rundown between catcher John Romano and third baseman Don Buford. The action went 2-5-2, and Romano tagged out Mincher, giving him both an assist (because of his initial throw to Buford) and a putout. While this was going on, Kindall tried to go from first to second. Romano wheeled and threw to shortstop Ron Hansen, who tagged out Kindall. Result—Romano winds up with two assists and a putout as part of the same continuous action. One has to be careful, however, about the use of the word "play," because separate "plays" can be part of the same continuous action. For example, a double play is two "plays." So it would not be accurate to say that Romano was credited with two assists and a putout as part of the same "play."

Chapter 23

Double and Triple Plays

On June 11, 2006, Kansas City was playing Tampa, then known as the Devil Rays. In the second inning, Tampa had Aubrey Huff on third and

Rocco Baldelli on first with no outs. Russell Branyan then lofted a fly ball to shallow center that was caught by David DeJesus, who tossed wildly home in an attempt to throw out Huff, who was tagging from third. The ball sailed over catcher Paul Bako's head but was caught by pitcher Scott Elarton, who was backing up the play. Baldelli tried to tag up from first but was out when Elarton threw to second baseman Mark Grudzielanek, who tagged Baldelli. The Royals then appealed, arguing that Huff left too soon from third, and the ball was thrown by shortstop Ángel Berroa to third baseman Mark Teahen. Umpire Bob Davidson upheld the appeal. DeJesus's throw was not considered a misplay.

1: Would this be considered three individual outs or a double play or a triple play?

It is a triple play. All outs between the time the pitcher throws the pitch and the time the ball next becomes dead or is next in the possession of the pitcher in the pitching position are considered part of the same continuous action, per Rule 10.11. In addition, the Comment to this rule specifically provides that the official scorer shall credit a double play or triple play if an appeal results in an additional out.

2: What are the putouts and assists on the play?

DeJesus gets a putout for his catch. Elarton gets an assist for his throw to second, and Grudzielanek gets a putout on that second out. Finally, Berroa and Teahen get an assist and a putout respectively on the appeal.

3: As noted above, DeJesus's throw was not considered a misplay. Would the answer to the first question have changed if it was considered a misplay?

Yes. There is no crediting of a double play or triple play if an error or misplay occurs between putouts. What constitutes a misplay is discussed in the next chapter. While a wild throw can be considered a misplay, the scorer may have concluded that, since DeJesus's throw was coming from center field, Huff might have scored anyway. With a misplay, the action would still be considered a (rather unusual) double play. It would go, out (DeJesus's catch); misplay (DeJesus's throw); out (Baldelli at second); and out (Huff on the appeal play). Therefore, because no error or misplay occurred between the outs on Baldelli and Huff, that would be considered a double play.

4: Can the team on defense record three outs with no fielder ever touching the ball after the pitch was thrown?

Newsweek columnist and baseball enthusiast George Will came up with just such a hypothetical situation. Runners on first and second, no outs (obviously). The batter hits an infield fly between second and third. The runner on first passes the runner on second, and the ball hits the runner who had been on second. In this situation, the batter is out due to the infield fly rule; the runner on first is out when he passed the runner on second, Rule 7.08(h); and the runner on second is out when the ball hits him, 7.09(k).

5: Can there be a triple play without the batter's hitting the ball?

Yes, and it has happened. On September 2, 2006, the Tampa Bay Devil Rays were playing the Seattle Mariners. In the first inning, the Mariners had José López on third and Adrián Beltré on first. Raúl Ibañez struck out. On the play, Beltré was thrown out trying to steal second, then López got thrown out trying to steal home.

Chapter 24

Errors

Most fans don't give much thought to how most plays will be scored, but an exception to that is with errors. Typically, on multiple plays per game, even fans who have no interest in the scoring rules of baseball will ask, "Will that be ruled a hit or an error?" When a pitcher is going deep into a game with a no-hitter on the line, or a batter has a hitting streak, the scoring of errors becomes all the more important.

24.1 Mental errors and errors generally

Let's return again to the play that keeps on giving. On May 13, 2003, the Giants hosted the Expos. The Giants had the bases loaded with one out in the fifth inning. Barry Bonds hit a fly ball between home and third. On the play, home plate umpire Jim Joyce correctly signaled infield fly. Thinking he had a force at home, Expos third baseman Fernando Tatís let the ball drop, then picked it up and stepped on the plate. However, Neifi Pérez, the runner on third, decided to head for home anyway and crossed home plate untouched.

1: Did Tatís commit an error on the play?

No. The Comment to Rule 10.12(a)(1) provides that mental mistakes or misjudgments are not to be scored as errors unless otherwise provided for in the rules. Mental blunders can lead to errors, but not in this case because no physical misplay occurred such as a bad throw or mishandled ball. The mental blunder was simply in Tatís's not tagging Pérez. However, a mental mistake that leads to a physical misplay can be considered an error.

2: On April 9, 2012, the Phillies were playing the Marlins. In the sixth inning, the first batter for Florida, Emilio Bonifacio, laid down a bunt toward first base. Both pitcher Cole Hamels and first baseman John Mayberry went to field the ball. Second baseman Freddy Galvis was supposed to be covering first but failed to do so. Hamels picked up the ball and immediately threw to first, assuming that Galvis would be there. The ball sailed down the first-base line and Bonifacio wound up at third. Which of the following is correct?

A. Error on Hamels.

B. Error on Galvis.

C. Error on both players.

D. Error on neither player.

The correct answer is A. Galvis committed no error because his mental mistake did not lead to a physical misplay on his part. However, since no one was covering first, Hamels should not have thrown the ball to first.

24.2 Slow handling of ball

On June 28, 2007, Colorado was playing Houston. In the fifth inning, with one out, Craig Biggio laced a sharp grounder toward third base, where Garrett Atkins took two steps to his right and reached across his body to field the ball. After a brief pause, Atkins threw the ball high above first baseman Todd Helton's outstretched glove. The ball hit the wall next to the Astros' dugout, and Biggio advanced to second. Official scorer Trey Wilkinson charged Atkins with an error, but also gave Biggio a hit on the play.

1: How is that possible?

Biggio was credited with a hit because Wilkinson felt that he would have beat out the throw as a result of Atkins's slow handling of the ball, regardless of the poor throw. The Comment to Rule 10.12(a)(1) provides that slow handling of the ball that does not involve a mechanical misplay is not an error. For an error, there must be a misplay (which is defined as a fumble, muff, or wild throw) that prolongs the time at bat or permits a runner to advance one or more bases. Here, in terms of the play on Biggio, Atkins did everything cleanly. He simply held on to the ball too long. (The scorer's ruling on this play was particularly significant because it was career hit number 2,999 for Biggio. Number 3,000—about which there was no dispute—came later in the game.) Note also that the term "misplay" is not officially defined in the rules, except in Rule 10.12(a)(1), which refers to a "misplay (fumble, muff or wild throw)." So if Biggio was credited with a hit, then why was an error charged to Atkins? Because his wild throw allowed Biggio to go to second on the play.

24.3 Dropped foul ball

On April 14, 2010, the Orioles were playing the Rays. In the ninth inning, Orioles left fielder Nolan Reimold hit a pop-up that was dropped by Rays catcher John Jaso in foul territory. Reimold then struck out swinging.

1: Is Jaso charged with an error?

Yes. With errors, the issue is not whether the play allowed the batter to reach base, but whether it prolonged the time at bat, which it did here. If the error/no-error call was dependent on the rest of the at bat, then the ruling would be in limbo until the end of the at bat. There are no instances where the error/no-error call cannot be made immediately.

Jay Bruce of the Reds is attempting to steal second and beat the throw of Indians catcher Mike Redmond. If we stop the action before Bruce gets to second, is there any way that Bruce could wind up with a stolen base *and* Redmond could wind up with an error by the time the play was over?
AP Photo/Tony Dejak

2: **Assume that Jaso dropped the ball with two outs in the ninth inning while the pitcher had a perfect game going. Then Reimold struck out. Would the pitcher get credit for a perfect game despite Jaso's error?**

Yes! People often think of a perfect game as one in which there are no hits, walks, hit batters, or errors. However, all that is required is that no batters reach base. An error doesn't ruin a perfect game so long as it doesn't allow a batter to reach base.

24.4 Failing to tag runner or base

On October 10, 1973, the Mets played the Reds in the final game of the NLCS. In the bottom of the fifth, Wayne Garrett of the Mets doubled. Félix Millan then attempted to sacrifice. He bunted the ball toward the mound, where pitcher Jack Billingham picked up the ball and fired to third baseman Dan Driessen. The throw was in time to get Garrett, but Driessen failed to tag him.

1: Error on Driessen? Would it make any difference if a runner had also been on first when the play started?

The answers are no and yes respectively. The failure to tag a base or a runner is an error but only if it's a force play, per Rule 10.12(a)(4). No force was in effect here on Garrett since no runner was on first. If a runner had been on first, it would have been a force, and thus an error on Driessen.

24.5 Effect of wild throw on stolen base attempt

On May 22, 2010, the Reds were playing the Indians. In the fourth inning, Jay Bruce of the Reds, who was on first, attempted to steal second. Indians catcher Mike Redmond threw to second.

1: If we stop the action before Bruce gets to second, is there any way, assuming Redmond got rid of the ball quickly and cleanly, that Bruce

In the first inning of Game 4 of the 2009 World Series, the Yankees had Johnny Damon on third base with one out when Jorge Posada hit a short fly ball to Phillies left fielder Raúl Ibañez. Damon tagged on the play. Ibañez's throw to catcher Carlos Ruiz was on line but hit Damon in the back. Is Ibañez charged with an error on the play? *AP Photo/Eric Gay*

could wind up with a stolen base *and* Redmond could wind up with an error by the end of the play?

Yes, if a wild throw by Redmond allowed Bruce to go to third (which happened here). Bruce gets credit for the stolen base—even if he would otherwise have been out—because Rule 10.12(a)(5) provides that no error is charged when a catcher makes a wild throw on a steal attempt. However, if the wild throw allows Bruce to take an extra base, Redmond is charged with an error for that advance, per Rule 10.12 (a)(6).

24.6 Throw hitting runner

In the first inning of Game 4 of the 2009 World Series, the Yankees had Johnny Damon on third base with one out when Jorge Posada hit a short fly ball to Phillies left fielder Raúl Ibañez. Damon tagged on the play. Ibañez's throw to catcher Carlos Ruiz was on line but hit Damon in the back.

1: Is Ibañez charged with an error on the play?

Yes. Anytime a throw hits a runner and it permits a runner to advance, it's an error on the fielder, even if the fielder could have done nothing about it and the throw was on line.

2: Say that Posada's fly ball had gone to center fielder Shane Victorino instead and Damon scored because Victorino's throw, though on line to Ruiz, had hit the pitcher's rubber and bounced away. Error on Victorino?

Yes, the same result, again assuming that the throw allowed Damon to advance.

3: Say that Damon scored because Ibañez's throw, though on line to Ruiz, hit a stone on the field and bounced away. Error on Ibañez?

Again, the same result. Anytime a fielder's throw takes an unnatural bounce or touches a base or the pitcher's rubber or a runner, fielder, or umpire, he will be charged with an error if the throw allows the runner to advance, even if he is not at fault and the throw was accurate.

24.7 Error on inteference

Let's return to a play we examined earlier. On July 3, 2007, the Indians were playing the Tigers. In the third inning, Cleveland had Jhonny Peralta on third and Víctor Martínez on first with no outs. Travis Hafner was at the plate. Hafner hit a grounder, and Peralta, trying to score on the play, got caught in a rundown and was tagged out by Tigers catcher Pudge Rodríguez, leaving Martínez on second and Hafner on first. However, home plate umpire Derryl Cousins ruled that Hafner's bat had nicked Rodríguez's mitt on the swing and called catcher's interference. The interference loaded the bases by putting Martínez on second and Hafner on first and leaving Peralta at third.

1: Would Rodríguez be charged with an error on this play?

Yes, per Rule 10.12(c). However, no more than one error can be charged to a fielder for interference or obstruction no matter how many bases the batter, or any runners, advance.

24.8 Error on obstruction

On May 11, 2002, the Pirates were playing the Astros. Pittsburgh's Rob Mackowiak led off the seventh with a grounder to third. Morgan Ensberg fielded the ball and sent a wild throw past Jeff Bagwell at first. On the way to second, Mackowiak smashed into Astros second baseman Craig Biggio. Mackowiak reached second easily anyway, despite the collision, which Biggio got the worse of.

1: Assuming that Biggio obstructed Mackowiak, what are the arguments for and against charging Biggio with an error on the play?

Per Rule 10.12(c), an error should be charged whenever a batter or runner is awarded one or more bases because of interference or obstruction. On the other hand, the Comment provides that no error should be charged if the obstruction does not change the result of the play in the opinion of the scorer. In this case, instead of Ensberg's being charged with a two-base error, he and Biggio were each given one-base errors on the play. The Astros felt that it was a dubious scorer's decision. "When those plays like that happen, it's one error," Ensberg said. "It's not two errors. That was bad. It was not because of Biggio that the guy got to second. Because I threw the ball away, that guy got to second." Biggio laughed about the collision he had with Mackowiak. "I'm fine," Biggio said. "I gave Morgan thanks for putting me on *SportsCenter*."

24.9 Muffed attempt to complete double play

Another play involving the Pirates and the Astros also involved Pittsburgh's Rob Mackowiak and Houston's Craig Biggio. On July 19, 2005, in the seventh inning, Pittsburgh had Humberto Cota on first and Jack Wilson on second with no outs when Mackowiak grounded to second baseman Biggio. He flipped the ball to shortstop Adam Everett for the first out, but Everett made a poor throw to first baseman Lance Berkman, who was unable to come up with it. Assume that (1) the failure to complete the double play was due to Everett's poor throw, (2) a good throw would have beaten Mackowiak, (3) there was no interference with the first baseman by the runner on first, and (4) that Wilson advanced to third on the play.

1: Error on Everett?

No. Rule 10.12(d)(3) provides that no error gets charged to a fielder who makes a wild throw in attempting to complete a double play or a triple play, unless runners advance farther than they would have had the throw not been wild. In this regard, one sometimes hears the expression "you can't assume a double play." However, this is not accurate. True, an error will not be charged if the double play is lost because of the fielder's poor throw. However, if the first baseman simply dropped the ball, that would be E3.

2: Assume instead that, though the throw was off line, Berkman could have come up with it. Error on Berkman?

Yes! In the actual play, this is just what happened. The official scorer originally charged Everett with an error (which would have been impossible as we just saw), then instead charged the error to Berkman. Interestingly, in a bit of discrimination between the thrower and the receiver of the back end of an attempted double play, under Rule 10.12(d)(3), the fielder attempting to catch the ball *is* charged with an error if he "muffs" it, but the thrower is *not* charged with an error for his wild throw if there is no farther advance by a runner.

3: Say that Everett made a good throw and Berkman dropped the ball, so there is no double play. Does Everett get an assist?

Yes again! Under the Comment to Rule 10.12(d)(3), an assist is awarded in this case even though Berkman did not come up with the ball. In accord with Rule 10.10(a)(1), which we examined earlier, a fielder always gets an assist on any play where the fielder throws or deflects a batted ball in such a way that a putout results or would have resulted except for a subsequent error by another fielder.

4: On July 28, 2008, the Mets were playing the Marlins. In the eighth inning, with one out, the Mets had David Wright on third and Car-

los Beltrán on first. Fernando Tatís hit a grounder to Marlins shortstop Hanley Ramírez, which should have been an inning-ending double-play ball. However, after Ramírez flipped to second baseman Dan Uggla for the force on Beltrán, Uggla made a poor throw to first and Tatís was safe. As a result, Wright scored on the play. Assume that (1) the failure to complete the double play was due to Uggla's poor throw, (2) a good throw would have beaten Tatís, and (3) there was no interference by Beltrán. Error on Uggla?

No. As we saw previously, under Rule 10.12(d)(3), an error does not result when the failure to complete the double play is due to a fielder's wild throw. Uggla (like Everett in the first play above) is let off the hook because Beltrán was forced out at second. Note, however, a key difference between this play and that in question 1, which also involved a poor throw to first in an attempt to complete a double play. In that play, there were no outs when the play began, meaning that the runner on second would have made it to third even if the double play was completed. Here, however, Tatís's grounder should have been an inning-ending double play. Rule 10.12(d)(3) provides that no error shall be charged to any fielder who makes a wild throw in attempting to complete a double play or triple play, "unless such wild throw enables any runner to advance beyond the base such runner would have reached had the throw not been wild."

On this play, Uggla's errant throw *did* allow a runner—namely Wright—to advance beyond the base he would have reached had the throw not been wild. In fact, he scored on the play. Nevertheless, a fielder in Uggla's position will not be charged with an error on this type of play. The clause beginning with "unless" is applied to situations where either the batter-runner advances to second on the wild throw or where a runner on first advances to third on the wild throw—in other words, they get an extra base.

24.10 Misplay with recovery for force-out

On September 9, 2009, the Phils were playing the Nationals. In the seventh inning, Washington had runners on first and third with one out when Cristian Guzmán hit a sure double-play grounder to shortstop Jimmy Rollins. However, Rollins bobbled the ball and was only able to force the runner who had been on first. Because the Phils did not turn the double play, the runner on third scored.

1: Error on Rollins?

This is a different situation from those presented in the previous sections because the misplay was not by the fielder attempting to "complete" the double play, but rather by the fielder starting it. In both cases, however, the result is the same—i.e., the runner who was at first is forced out, but there is no double play. Also, in both cases, there is no error charged, although this time, it would be by virtue of Rule 10.12(d)(4), which provides that if a fielder fumbles a grounder or drops a fly ball, no error will be charged if the fielder recovers in time for a force-out.

An analogous play occurred in a minor league game, with the same rules as the major leagues. On August 4, 2009, the Rochester Red Wings were playing the Lehigh Valley IronPigs. In the top of the second inning, Lehigh had runners on first and third, with one out. John Mayberry Jr. hit a pop-up. Each of the runners held his base. Red Wings second baseman Matt Tolbert dropped the ball, allowing the runner on third to score. Tolbert recovered in time to throw to second base for a force-out.

This play created an interesting situation for the official scorer. Rule 10.12(a)(1) requires giving an error to a fielder if his misplay allows a runner to advance one or more bases. However, Rule 10.12(d)(4) provides that the scorer should *not* give an error to a fielder who forces out a runner after misplaying the ball. Both of these situations occurred here. The official scorer charged an error on Tolbert, but that decision was later overturned by the league.

2: On September 15, 1971, the Braves were playing the Astros. In the third inning, the Astros had Joe Morgan on second base and Bob Watson on first with two outs. With the runners on the move, John Mayberry (the father of the player mentioned in the previous problem) hit a grounder to second baseman Félix Millan, who booted the ball. Upon seeing that, Morgan headed for home, where he was thrown out by Millan in a close play at the plate. This was the third out of the inning. Error on Millan?

Yes. On first impression, it would seem that this is analogous to the previous problem. In both cases, there was a misplay, and although the double play was not turned in the previous problem, an out was created on the play. But in the previous problem, the runner on first was out via a force play. Because Rule 10.12(d)(4) only applies to force plays, it would not apply to this situation. One could argue that it doesn't seem appropriate that the result in one play is that no error is charged, while it is in the other. The difference, though, is that in the latter play, Morgan was not forced to run and thus had to be tagged out. The fact that he chose to and was thrown out was basically a fortunate happenstance for Millan, at least in terms of recording the out. It is treated essentially like two separate events.

Chapter 25

Wild Pitches and Passed Balls

A wild pitch is one that cannot be handled with ordinary effort by the catcher. A passed ball is charged to a catcher who does not hold or control a pitch that should have been held or controlled with ordinary effort.

25.1 Wild pitch/passed ball/balk as errors?

On May 13, 2010, the Mets were playing the Marlins. With the score tied 1–1 in the bottom of the ninth, the Marlins had Cody Ross on third base. Pitcher Fernando Nieve threw a wild pitch and Ross scored the game-winning run on the play.

1: Error on Nieve?

No. A wild pitch is not an error, even if the batter reaches first as a result, per Rule 10.12(d)(5).

2: Would the result change if a passed ball had been called on the catcher instead?

No. A passed ball is not an error either.

3: If Ross's run had not been a game-winner, would the result change if the passed ball or wild pitch had allowed the batter to reach first base (as for example with two strikes when the pitch is thrown and the batter swings)?

No, per Rule 10.12(e).

4: Usually a walk-off involves a game-winning hit or perhaps a bases-loaded walk. On May 31, 2010, a different kind of walk-off ended a game between the Dodgers and the Diamondbacks. In the bottom of the ninth, with the score tied 4–4, Casey Blake was on third base for the Dodgers. Relief pitcher Esmerling Vásquez was on the mound for Arizona. The clever veteran Blake took a few steps away from third base for his normal base-runner lead, faked a run for home, and moved back to his regular lead. As Vásquez came to a set position, he reacted by taking the baseball out of his glove and then stepping off the rubber. As first-base umpire Tim Timmons saw this, he called a balk, giving Blake the extra base from third and the Dodgers the 5–4 win. Error on Vasquez?

No. Balks are treated the same as wild pitches and passed balls—no error.

25.2 Advance on wild pitch/passed ball on ball four

On May 3, 2008, the Royals were playing the Indians. In the fourth inning, Cleveland had Víctor Martínez on first and Davis Dellucci on third with one out. With a full count, pitcher Luke Hochevar threw a wild pitch to Travis Hafner. Martínez moved to second and Dellucci scored on the play.

1: How does the play get scored?

It would be scored as a walk on Hafner (since the pitch was thrown with a full count) and a wild pitch on Hochevar (since Dellucci scored).

2: Would the pitcher have been charged with a wild pitch if Dellucci had not been on third base?

No. For there to be a wild pitch or passed ball on ball four, (1) any runner forced to advance must move ahead more than one base, or (2) a runner not forced to advance must move ahead at least one base. If Dellucci had not been on third, neither of those would have been the case. Thus it would have been scored as a walk only, and Hochevar would not have been charged with the wild pitch.

25.3 Wild pitches and passed balls generally

On June 6, 2010, the Cardinals were playing the Brewers. In the fourth inning, on a 2-2 count, Brewers pitcher Manny Parra threw a wild pitch to Yadier Molina, who nevertheless swung at it. However, he beat the throw to first by catcher George Kottaras.

1: Does Parra get credit for a strikeout?

Yes, just as he would with a passed ball, per Rule 10.13. The first two outs of this inning were recorded via strikeout, as was the next out, meaning it was a four-strikeout inning for Parra.

2: On June 15, 1994, the Rangers were playing the Mariners. In the eighth inning, with one out, the Rangers had Iván Rodríguez on first and José Canseco on second with Dean Palmer at the plate. On a 1-2 pitch, Palmer swung and missed, but catcher Dan Wilson did not hold on to the ball.

Canseco then took off for third, where he was thrown out by Wilson for an inning-ending (unusual) double play. Passed ball on Wilson?

No. The Comment to Rule 10.13(b) provides that no passed ball is charged if the catcher is able to throw out a runner on the play.

3: Say that there were no outs when the play occurred, Wilson threw out Canseco, and Rodríguez wound up at second base. Passed ball on Wilson? How is Rodríguez's advance scored?

Still no passed ball on Wilson (since he threw Canseco out), and Rodríguez's advance would be scored as a fielder's choice.

Chapter 26

Pitching

26.1 Bases on balls

On October 14, 2003, the Yankees were playing the Red Sox in Game 5 of the ALCS. In the second inning, Red Sox pitcher Derek Lowe was facing Nick Johnson with a runner on second and two outs. On a 3-0 count, Lowe intentionally missed the strike zone by throwing well wide of the plate for ball four. This was the first pitch of the at bat on which Lowe intentionally missed the strike zone.

1: Would that be considered an intentional walk?

Yes.

2: Say that the situation was reversed and that Lowe intentionally missed with the first three pitches, but then changed his mind and tried to get Johnson out. However, the next pitch missed anyway. Is that an intentional walk?

No. Under Rule 10.14(b), the only pitch that is relevant for determining an intentional walk is the last one.

3: Say that, with the 3-0 count, Lowe intentionally missed the strike zone by throwing the ball in the dirt, but otherwise over the plate. Johnson didn't swing. Intentional walk?

No. For an intentional walk, the pitch must actually be wide of the plate. If a pitch is intentionally high or low, it won't be called an intentional walk if not also wide. Presumably, batters may swing at a bad pitch thrown within the width of the plate no matter how high or low, but not one that is very wide.

Bizarre rule: Some rules cover situations so bizarre that one cannot realistically imagine them occurring. Rule 10.14(c) is an example. It provides that if a batter is awarded a base on balls but refuses to go to first base, then the scorer shall not credit the base on balls but shall charge the batter with a time at bat. This would be scored as a putout credited to the catcher under Rule 10.09(b)(7). One can only try to imagine what might bring this about—having to run to the bathroom?

26.2 Strikeouts

1: Which, if any, of the following would be counted as strikeouts?

A. On June 15, 1994, the Rangers were playing the Mariners. In the eighth inning, with one out, the Rangers had Pudge Rodríguez on first and José Canseco on second with Dean Palmer at the plate. On a 1-2 pitch, Palmer swung and missed, but catcher

Dan Wilson did not hold on to the ball. (This is the same play we examined previously but from a different perspective.)

B. On July 17, 1978, the Royals were playing the Yankees. In the tenth inning, with the score tied 5–5, a runner on first and no outs, Reggie Jackson of the Yankees attempted a bunt with two strikes on him. He popped the ball up in foul territory, where it was caught by Royals catcher Darrell Porter.

C. Both of them are strikeouts.

D. Neither of them is a strikeout.

The correct answer is A. That is a strikeout because Rule 10.15(a)(2) provides that a strikeout occurs when a batter is put out by a third strike not caught when there is a runner on first with less than two outs. Choice B is not a strikeout because Rule 10.15(a)(4) provides that the fielder who catches the foul fly is credited with a putout in this situation.

2: Can a pitcher be credited with striking out a batter he did not face?

Yes. On August 23, 2006, the White Sox were playing the Tigers. In the seventh inning, after issuing a leadoff walk, Tigers reliever Colby Lewis went to a 2-2 count on Scott Podsednik, who was attempting to sacrifice bunt the leadoff runner to second base. Tigers manager Jim Leyland then elected to bring in the southpaw Jamie Walker. White Sox manager Ozzie Guillén countered by sending Brian Anderson to the plate to pinch-hit for Podsednik. Walker delivered one pitch; Anderson swung and missed for a strikeout. Per Rule 10.15(b), the strikeout is credited to Walker, who threw the third strike, but is charged to Podsednik, who had the first two strikes called on him.

3: Would the result be different if Anderson came in with a 2-1 count on Podsednik and Anderson then struck out?

Yes. The above rule only applies if there are two strikes on the replaced hitter. In this case, Anderson would be charged with the strikeout instead of Podsednik.

4: If Anderson came in with a 3-0 count and drew ball four, who would get credit for the walk?

Anderson. Other than in the first situation above, Anderson would be credited (or charged) with whatever happened after he came up.

26.3 Starting pitcher goes less than five innings

Let's return to a situation we considered earlier (section 3.3). On June 1, 2001, the Yankees played the Indians in New York. The line score looked like this:

	1	2	3	4	5	6	R	H	E
Indians	0	0	0	1	4	2	**X**	**10**	**3**
Yankees	1	1	1	1	0	0	**4**	**5**	**2**

The Indians pitching lines looked like this:

	IP	H	R	ER	BB	SO
CC Sabathia	4	4	4	3	5	2
Ricardo Rincón	1	1	0	0	0	0

Indians reliever Ricardo Rincón was pitching to the first batter in the bottom of the sixth when the game was called because of rain. Thus the Yankees did not bat in the bottom of the sixth.

1: We saw earlier that the Indians won the game. Who gets the win for the Indians—Sabathia or Rincón?

Sabathia. To baseball fans, that may seem odd. As baseball columnist Jim Storer wrote in discussing a similar game: "How could [Sabathia] have been credited with a win for pitching only four innings in a game in which he was the starting pitcher? This surely flies in the face of the immutable rule, learned by all fans in their youth, that the starter must go at least five innings to pick up the win. How many times have we watched a starting pitcher nurse a one-run lead, struggling with one or two out in the fifth inning, as his manager nervously fidgets in the dugout, hoping that he can avoid making that fateful call to the bullpen that will deny his starter a chance for the 'W'?"

Under the current version of the rules, a starting pitcher does not always need to pitch five innings to get a win. Sabathia gets the win, despite having pitched only four innings, based on Rules 10.17(a) and 10.17(b) read together. Rule 10.17(a) provides that "the official scorer shall credit as the winning pitcher that pitcher whose team assumes a lead while such pitcher is in the game, or during the inning on offense in which such pitcher is removed from the game, and does not relinquish such lead, unless (1) such pitcher is a starting pitcher and Rule 10.17(b) applies." Rule 10.17(b) in turn provides:

"If the pitcher whose team assumes a lead while such pitcher is in the game, or during the inning on offense in which such pitcher is removed from the game, and does not relinquish such lead, is a starting pitcher who has not completed (1) five innings of a game that lasts six or more innings on defense, or (2) four innings of a game that lasts five innings on defense, then the official scorer shall credit as the winning pitcher the relief pitcher, if there is only one relief pitcher, or the relief pitcher who, in the official scorer's judgment was the most effective, if there is more than one relief pitcher."

So let's apply the rules to the actual game. Does Rule 10.17(b)(1) apply? No, because the game did not last six innings on defense.

Since the Indians were the road team, they only played five innings on defense (plus a few pitches to the Yankees first batter in the sixth), not six full innings. Does Rule 10.17(b)(2) apply? No, because Sabathia *did* pitch four innings of a game that lasted five innings on defense. Therefore we go back to Rule 10.17(a). Recall that the Indians were trailing 4–1 going into the top of the fifth. However, even though Sabathia did not pitch in the bottom of the fifth, he was still the pitcher of record when the Indians scored their four runs in the top of the fifth. Therefore Sabathia gets the win because his team assumed the lead during an inning in which he was removed from the game and did not relinquish it.

2: Would the result be different if the Yankees had completed their at bats in the bottom of the sixth and did not score?

If the game had gone six full innings, and the Yankees did not score (or scored less than three runs), then Rincón would have received credit for the win, not Sabathia. Why? Because now it would be accurate to say that Sabathia did not pitch "five innings of a game that lasts six or more innings on defense," per Rule 10.17(b)(1).

26.4 Who gets the loss?

On April 28, 2006, the Astros were playing the Reds. The line score looked like this:

	1	2	3	4	5	6	7	8	9	R	H	E
Astros	0	0	0	1	0	1	0	0	2	**4**	**9**	**0**
Reds	0	1	0	1	1	0	2	0	X	**5**	**12**	**1**

The Astros pitching lines looked like this:

	IP	H	R	ER	BB	SO
Roy Oswalt	6	8	3	3	3	4
Mike Gallo	0.1	1	1	1	0	1
Chad Qualls	0.2	3	1	1	0	1
Russ Springer	1	0	0	0	2	1

1: Who gets the loss for the Astros?

The answer is Oswalt because, under Rule 10.17(d), he was responsible for the run that gave the Reds a lead that they did not relinquish. Some argue that in a situation like this, the loss should go to Qualls since he gave up the run that turned out to be the deciding run. For example, blogger Bernardo Fallas wrote, "If [Oswalt] would have left trailing 3–2 and the Astros would have never led and lost 15–14, Oswalt would have gotten the loss. Doesn't make sense. The losing pitcher should be the pitcher who gave up the deciding run in any given game. So if the Astros lose 8–1, the pitcher that gave up the second run should get the loss. If they lost 8–7, the pitcher who gave up the eighth run should get the loss, no matter who had the lead earlier in the game."

There is probably something to be said both for the rule as written and for Fallas's argument. In support of the former, while Oswalt was pitching, he knew exactly how many runs his team had scored at all times. Thus, for example, when he was pitching in the bottom of the fifth, he knew his team was trailing 2–1. On the other hand, when Qualls gave up his run, the Astros were already down 4–2 and nobody could have known at the time that the fifth run would turn out to be the difference. That was just happenstance.

In support of Fallas's argument, however, is the fact that wins and losses can be fluky and are often based on future events having nothing to do with the pitcher's performance, especially when he is out of the game. For example, if the Astros took the lead at any point after Oswalt had left the game, he would be off the hook. Therefore, while it's true that neither Qualls nor anyone else had any idea that the fifth run would later turn out to be the game-winner, neither did anyone know that the third run would be the one after which the Reds would not relinquish their lead. In addition, say that the Astros had scored four runs in the top of the eighth to go ahead, and Springer held the Reds scoreless in the eighth and ninth. Suddenly, instead of a loss (under Fallas's proposed rule), Qualls, who left the game before the Astros took the lead, would get the win.

It is also true that a win can turn into a loss under the current rules. Say a pitcher who would otherwise be the winning pitcher, leaves the game in the ninth, ahead by a run, but with two runners on base. If they don't score, he is the winning pitcher. If they do, he loses. Of course, in this case, the pitcher would have some involvement with the loss because he is responsible for the base runners.

26.5 Earned runs allowed

Most times in life, if you earn something, chances are it is something desirable. Not in baseball when it comes to runs allowed by a pitcher. The science (or is it an art?) of determining which runs are earned and which are unearned is often hard work. Let's consider a few examples.

On April 16, 2002, the Cubs played the Expos. In the bottom of the fourth, Juan Cruz was on the mound for the Cubs. The first two Expo batters were retired. Chris Truby then singled and Brad Wilkerson walked. Pitcher Masato Yoshii then reached base on an error by Cubs third baseman Chris Stynes. Truby scored and Wilkerson went to second. Peter Bergeron then doubled, scoring Wilkerson. José Vidro then singled, scoring Yoshii and Bergeron. After a wild pitch moved Vidro to second, Vladimir Guerrero singled, scoring Vidro. No more runs scored.

1: Of the 5 runs scored, how many are earned?

None are earned. Under Rule 10.16, the job of the official scorer in determining earned runs is to reconstruct the inning without errors or passed balls, giving the benefit of the doubt to the pitcher in determining which bases would have been reached by runners had there been errorless play. But for Stynes's error on the Yoshii grounder, none of the runs would have scored because that would have been the third out of the inning.

2: On April 22, 2012, the Angels were playing the Orioles. In the top of the eighth, with one out, Angels starter Dan Haren yielded a single to Matt Wieters and another to Robert Andino, putting Wieters at second. Scott Downs was brought in to relieve Haren. Endy Chávez then singled to load the bases. The next hitter, J.J. Hardy, then hit a grounder to Downs, who threw home for the force, leaving the bases still loaded. Nick Markakis then singled, scoring Andino and Chávez. Andino's run is charged to the starter, Haren. Who is Chávez's run charged to?

Surprisingly, it is charged to Haren as well, even though Chávez was put on base by Downs. Rule 10.16(g) and the Comment provide that what is relevant is the number of runners put on base rather than the individual runners. Haren put two runners on base. The key here is the fielder's choice. Although Wieters was forced at home, two runners were still on base after the play, just as when Haren left the game. Thus, Chávez became Haren's responsibility even though he was put on base by Downs. Had Markakis scored (which he didn't), that run would have been charged to Downs.

3: On July 1, 2009, the Cardinals were playing the Giants in St. Louis. In the bottom of the tenth, with the score tied 1–1, Colby Rasmus hit a foul fly, which was dropped by Giants third baseman Pablo Sandoval.

Rasmus then hit a game-winning walk-off homer. Would this be an earned run or not?

No. Even though Rasmus hit a home run and even though his previous fly ball was foul, Rule 10.16(b)(1) provides that a run scored by a runner whose time at bat is prolonged by a muffed foul fly is not an earned run.

4: Say that Rasmus had reached first on catcher's interference, and the next batter hit a home run. We saw earlier that both runs would count, per Rule 4.11(c). How many of these runs would be earned?

A. Both runs, because a run scored by a player reaching base on catcher's interference is an earned run.

B. Neither run, because but for the catcher's interference, neither run would have scored.

C. One run, namely the home run.

D. It's up to the umpire's discretion.

The answer is C because we do not know for sure what would have happened to Rasmus had the catcher's interference not occurred. Rule 10.16 specifically provides that pitchers are to be given the benefit of the doubt in determining which bases would have been reached by runners had there been errorless play. With catcher's interference, a pitcher would get the benefit of the doubt. However, even though Rasmus's run would not be considered earned, the pitcher is not off the hook for the home run. In calculating earned runs, it is as if Rasmus's at bat had never occurred.

5: On April 7, 2012, the Pirates were playing the Phillies. In the sixth inning, with one out, Yamaico Navarro of the Pirates walked, moved

to second on a single, and to third on a groundout. Cliff Lee threw a wild pitch, scoring Navarro. Andrew McCutchen, the batter, was later retired for the third out. Is an earned run charged to Lee?

Yes, per Rule 10.16(a).

6: Assume instead that McCutchen hit a one-hopper back to Lee, who then overthrew the first baseman for an error, allowing Navarro to score. E1. Is this an earned run to Lee?

No. Rule 10.16(e) provides that an error by the pitcher is treated the same as an error by any other fielder. Although Rule 10.16 provides that an earned run is a run for which the pitcher is held accountable, in this instance no earned run is charged even though the pitcher is at fault. A runner's scoring on a passed ball is also not considered an earned run.

7: Let's return once again to a play we have examined before (which seems to involve half of the rulebook because it raises so many issues). On May 13, 2003, the Giants hosted the Expos. The Giants had the bases loaded with one out in the fifth inning. Barry Bonds hit a fly ball between home and third. On the play, plate umpire Jim Joyce correctly signaled infield fly, meaning that none of the runners were forced to advance. Thinking he had a force at home, Expos third baseman Fernando Tatís let the ball drop, then picked it up and stepped on the plate. However, Neifi Pérez, the runner on third, decided to head for home anyway and crossed home plate untouched. Was the run that Pérez scored an earned run?

Surprisingly, the answer is yes. This is because Tatís's "mental error" is not counted as an error under Rule 10.12. Whether a run is earned is determined by Rule 10.16, which provides that the inning is reconstructed to see who scored as if there were no errors or passed balls. Since no official errors were committed in the inning, Pérez's run is earned.

Let's now examine a particularly nasty half-inning. Fair warning: this is not for the faint of heart. You may want to have a scorecard handy to keep track. Otherwise, if you want to stick with lighter reading, feel free to skip ahead. However, like all the primary plays in this book, it actually happened, and an official scorer had to deal with it—and if he or she did, so can we.

On June 3, 2009, the Brewers were playing the Marlins in an interleague game. In the fifth inning, with Sean West pitching for the Marlins, Casey McGehee led off the inning with a groundout. Ryan Braun was then safe at first on an error by Marlins shortstop Hanley Ramírez. Prince Fielder then singled to center, moving Braun to second. Hayden Penn then entered the game in relief. The next batter, Mike Cameron, walked, moving Braun to third and Fielder to second. J. J. Hardy then hit into a fielder's choice, with third baseman Emilio Bonifacio throwing out Braun at home. Fielder is therefore now at third base, Cameron is at second, and Hardy is at first.

Sean West pitching
One out
Braun safe on error
Fielder singles, Braun to second

Penn replaces West with one out, runners on first and second
Cameron walks, loading bases
Hardy fielder's choice at home, still bases loaded, with two outs

8: True or false? Since two runners were on base when West left the game (Braun and Fielder) and since one of them has now been retired (Braun), West is only liable for one runner, namely Fielder.

False. Relief pitchers are treated as having entered the game with no outs and no one on base. Thus if Penn came in with no one on base, Hardy would have come up with Cameron on first only. Hardy's fielder's choice would then have wiped out Cameron. It's not Penn's fault Braun was on third base to be put out on the fielder's choice. Therefore, Cameron takes Braun's place as West's responsibility. This is covered by Rule 10.16(g), which provides a relief pitcher is not charged with any runs scored by a runner who reaches base on a fielder's choice that puts out a runner left by a preceding pitcher. This is a similar concept to that discussed in question 1 above.

9: The next batter, Bill Hall, walked. Fielder scored, Cameron moved to third, and Hardy moved to second. So now, the bases are loaded with one run across. Who is Fielder's run charged to, and is it earned?

It's charged to West since Fielder got on base when West was pitching. However, it is not an earned run. As noted above, the job of the official scorer is to reconstruct the inning without errors and passed balls. Braun should have been the second out of the inning, but he reached on an error, meaning that Hardy's fielder's choice should have been the third out of the inning.

10: The next batter, Jason Kendall, also walked, scoring Cameron for the second run of the inning. Hardy moved to third and Hall to second. Who is Cameron's run charged to and is it earned?

The answer here is the same as the answer to quiz number 2, namely that the run is charged to West, and again it's unearned. If Fielder's run was unearned, and West is already out of the game, then any subsequent runs would also be unearned as to West. Again, the inning should be over from his perspective. But why is the run charged to him at all? After all, Cameron wasn't even on base when West left the game. The reason is that, after Hardy's fielder's choice, Cameron took Braun's place as West's responsibility.

11: Continuing on a theme of walking and scoring, the next batter, pitcher Braden Looper, also walked, scoring Hardy for the third run of the inning. Hall moved to third, and Kendall to second. Who is Hardy's run charged to and is it earned?

We saw earlier that Hardy reached on a fielder's choice while Penn was pitching. Under Rule 10.16(a), he then becomes Penn's responsibility. The run is also earned. Why, since the inning should already have been over? The reason is because Rule 10.16(i) (examined in greater detail below) provides that, unlike West, Penn does not get the benefit of previous errors. Therefore, from Penn's perspective there should only be two outs, and Hardy's run is earned against him.

12: At this point, Brian Sanches came in the game to replace Penn. Let's examine Sanches's outing. Recall that there were bases loaded and two outs when he entered the game. His first batter, Corey Hart, is safe at first on a throwing error by third baseman Emilio Bonifacio. Continuing their base-by-base march on the walks and errors, Bill Hall scored, Jason Kendall went to third, and Braden Looper to second. At this point, the Brewers have batted around, have a grand total of 1 hit—a single—but have scored 4 runs. Who is Hall's run charged to and is it earned?

Hall's run is charged to Penn, but it is also unearned. But for Bonifacio's error, the inning would be over.

13: McGehee, who led off the inning innocently enough with a groundout, now on his second chance, hit a double to left field, knocking in Kendall and Looper, and sending Hart to third. Who are the runs charged to and are they earned?

Both Kendall and Looper reached because of Penn, so their runs are charged to him. Since the inning should have ended after Hart's at bat, neither run is earned. Both runners are Sanches's now, so close the book on Penn.

14: **Finally, Ryan Braun struck out to end the inning. The total damage? West is responsible for two runs, both unearned. Penn is responsible for four runs, only one of which is earned. Sanches gave up zero runs. Is it therefore accurate to say that there was one team earned run in the inning?**

No. Surprisingly, there were no team earned runs in the inning. To see why, see the discussion of Rule 10.16(i) in section 26.8.

26.6 Which pitcher to charge with a run

1: **True or false? Whether a run is earned or not can always be determined at any given point in time.**

False. As discussed previously, in determining earned runs, we have to reconstruct the inning without errors or passed balls, giving the benefit of the doubt to the pitcher in determining which bases would have been reached by runners had there been errorless play. Say for example, the leadoff batter walks. Then on a passed ball the runner moves to second. The next batter singles, scoring the runner on second. At that point, we don't yet know if the run will be earned or unearned. If the next three batters strike out, it will be unearned. However, if the next batter hits a home run, it will be earned.

2: **On August 31, 1992, the Blue Jays played the White Sox. Charlie Hough was pitching for the White Sox. In the bottom of the fourth, the first batter for the Jays, Ed Sprague, reached on an error on first baseman Frank Thomas. Alfredo Griffin then flied out. Derek Bell then**

tripled, scoring Sprague. Terry Leach was then brought in to replace Hough. He issued an intentional walk to Roberto Alomar, who then stole second. Joe Carter then grounded out for the second out of the inning, with no advancement by the runners. Dave Winfield then hit a 3-run homer, and Candy Maldonado grounded out to end the inning. How many of the runs scored are charged as earned runs against Hough?

None. Sprague's run was unearned because of Thomas's error. Also, but for Thomas's error, Carter's groundout would have been the third out of the inning.

3: How many of the runs scored are charged as earned runs against Leach?

Two, the runs scored by Alomar and Winfield. As noted earlier, relief pitchers are treated as having entered the game with no outs and no one on base. That means that, just as Leach is not charged with existing base runners, so, too, he is not "protected" by Thomas's error. Therefore, since he walked Alomar and yielded Winfield's home run, both of those runs are earned.

4: Is it possible for runs to be unearned as to a team even when those runs are earned as to a particular pitcher?

Yes, and the above play is a perfect example. Carter's groundout should have been the third out of the inning. But for Thomas's error, no runs would have scored. Therefore all four runs scored in the inning are unearned as to the team.

5: Let's consider another situation that is simplified from the actual play. On April 16, 2009, the Angels were playing the Mariners. In the sixth inning, Chris Jakubauskas was pitching for the Mariners. Chone

Figgins led off with a single, followed by a Howie Kendrick flyout to right and a single by Bobby Abreu, moving Figgins to third. Roy Corcoran was brought in to relieve Jakubauskas. The next batter, Torii Hunter, hit a grounder to third baseman Adrián Beltré, who threw out Figgins at home. Assume that Hunter eventually scores with no errors or passed balls. Is his run charged to Jakubauskas or Corcoran?

It might seem as if it would be charged to Corcoran, since Jakubauskas left the game with two runners on and one of them was thrown out at home. But Rule 10.16(g) advises us that when Figgins was thrown out on the fielder's choice, Hunter became Jakubauskas's responsibility.

As noted in the Comment to this rule, "it is the intent of Rule 10.16(g) to charge each pitcher with the number of runners he put on base, rather than with the individual runners." The number of runners is more important than who they are. This makes sense—had Figgins not been on third to begin with, the Mariners would not have had to deal with him when Hunter grounded to the third baseman. Accordingly, the second run is charged to Jakubauskas. Note that if Figgins had been picked off third, then Jakubauskas would have been off the hook for Hunter.

6: Assume that Figgins singled to open the inning and Corcoran was brought in to relieve Jakubauskas at that point. Assume also that Kendrick still flew out and Abreu singled, but that Figgins was thrown out trying to go to third and that Abreu moved to second on the play. The next batter, Hunter, hits a single to score Abreu. The next hitter is retired, leaving Hunter at first. Who is Abreu's run charged to?

An example is given in the Comment to Rule 10.16(g) that essentially presents this exact situation, and it tells us that the run would be charged to Corcoran. This makes sense because Figgins was the only runner on base when Jakubauskas left the game, and he was put out other than by fielder's choice. Therefore all Jakubauskas's runners are gone.

However, let's assume that Figgins had not tried for third. If Abreu had been able to score from second on Hunter's single, it stands to reason that another player on second (especially the fleet Figgins) would have scored as well. While Figgins was thrown out trying for third, Abreu was able to move to second. In other words, while it's not a fielder's choice situation, it is analogous to a fielder's choice because the Mariners had to deal with Figgins's presence on the base paths, and he was Jakubauskas's responsibility. Thus, if Figgins hadn't tried for third, he would have scored from second on Hunter's single (which would obviously have been charged to Jakubauskas), and the fact that he did try for third is what allowed Abreu to go to second. The point is that a run was going to score in this situation no matter what. If a run scored by Figgins from second is going to be charged to Jakubauskas, then consider whether a run scored by Abreu from second should also be charged to him.

26.7 Which pitcher to charge with a walk when a switch is made during an at bat

On April 19, 2005, the Mariners played the Angels. In the third inning, Chris Bootcheck came on in relief of Angels starter Kevin Gregg. Randy Winn was at the plate at the time and had a 3-0 count. He wound up walking.

1: Whom would the walk be charged to—Gregg or Bootcheck?

A. Gregg, no matter what.

B. Bootcheck, no matter what.

C. Gregg, but the answer could be different if the count was different.

D. Bootcheck, but the answer could be different if the count was different.

One of the (many) little-known provisions in the *Official Baseball Rules*, Rule 10.16(h), ascribes responsibility for the batter who walks in this situation based on every possible count. Under (h)(1), on a 3-0 count, the first pitcher is accountable for the runner. Therefore, the answer is C because of the specific count when Gregg left the game.

The opening section of Rule 10.16(h) provides that a relief pitcher shall not be held accountable when the first batter to whom he pitches reaches first base on four called balls if such batter has a "decided advantage in the ball and strike count when pitchers are changed." If one read only to this point, a natural question would be, What is a "decided advantage"? There is no need to answer this question because the remainder of the rule tells us who is charged with the walk in every possible situation. More specifically, Rule 10.16(h)(1) provides that the preceding pitcher is charged with the walk if there are three balls (regardless of the number of strikes) and on 2-0 and 2-1 counts. On every other possible count, the walk would be charged to the relief pitcher, per Rule 10.16(h)(3).

26.8 Relief pitcher not benefited by prior errors

On June 2, 2009, the Cubs were playing the Braves. In the eighth inning, with Randy Wells pitching for the Cubs, Garret Anderson led off the inning with a home run. Martín Prado then reached first on an error by first baseman Derrek Lee. Carlos Mármol was brought in to replace Wells. Jeff Francoeur then walked, and Gregor Blanco lined out for the first out of the inning. Greg Norton was then hit by a pitch to load the bases. Mármol then walked Kelly Johnson to score Prado, moving Francoeur to third and Norton to second. Yunel Escobar then hit a sacrifice fly to right to score Francoeur. Finally, Chipper Jones grounded out to end the inning. Three runs scored in the inning.

To summarize:

Off Wells: Anderson home run and Prado reaches on error

Off Mármol: Walk to Francoeur, out, hit by pitch (bases loaded), walk (scoring Prado with second run), sacrifice (scoring Francoeur with third run)

1: Which run or runs are charged to Wells, which to Mármol, and which are earned runs?

Wells would be charged with one earned run (Anderson's home run) and one unearned run. Prado's run is unearned since he reached on an error, but is charged to Wells since Prado reached while Wells was pitching. Mármol is charged with one earned run, since he put Francoeur on base and Francoeur scored with no errors or passed balls.

This play is another example of the team's not being charged with an earned run even though one of its pitchers was. Rule 10.16(i) tells us that relief pitchers do not get the benefit of "prior outs not accepted" (presumably another way of saying errors) in determining earned runs. So how does this translate to the above play? As a team, the Cubs would have been out of the inning on Escobar's fly ball but for Lee's error. Instead, it was only out number two and Francoeur was able to tag and score on the play. Thus, the run was unearned to the team (and had Wells not come out of the game, Francoeur's run would not have been charged to him). However, once Mármol came in, he did not get the "benefit" of that error, due to Rule 10.16(i). And if he doesn't get the benefit, then Francoeur's run must be charged against him since he was solely responsible for the run (two walks, a hit batsman, and a sacrifice fly). For this situation to occur requires an error, a pitching change, and ineffective pitching by the new pitcher.

26.9 Effective vs. ineffective relief

On August 25, 2007, the Rangers were playing the Mariners. In the top of the seventh, with the score tied 3–3, Seattle had runners on first and second with two outs. Frank Francisco was brought in to pitch for the Rangers. The batter he faced hit a single to left on Francisco's first pitch, but the runner on second was thrown out trying to score from second, for the third out of the inning. Texas then scored two runs in the bottom of the seventh to take a 5–3 lead, which they did not relinquish. Joaquín Benoit then came in to pitch the eighth for Texas and retired the side in order. The official scorer credited Francisco with the win.

1: Which of the following statements is most accurate?

A. The scorer got it right.

B. Benoit gets the win and the scorer got it wrong.

C. In this kind of situation, the scorer has discretion and probably got it right.

D. In this kind of situation, the scorer has discretion and probably got it wrong.

The correct answer is D, and the next day the decision was changed by the league to give Benoit the win. We start again with Rule 10.17(a), which states the general rule about assuming or gaining the lead while a pitcher is in the game. If the analysis was over at this point, then A would be the correct answer, since the Rangers took the lead while Francisco was still the pitcher of record and they never relinquished it. There would be no scorer discretion involved. However, we saw before that there are exceptions to that rule. Rule 10.17(c) provides that a relief pitcher who is ineffective in a brief appearance shall not get credit for the win when at least one succeeding relief pitcher pitches effectively in helping his team maintain its lead.

In this situation, Francisco pitched to only one batter and didn't even get him out. Meanwhile, Benoit retired the side in order in the eighth. It should be noted that the Comment to this rule gives guidance as to what constitutes an "ineffective" appearance: less than one inning pitched and allowing two or more earned runs to score (even if charged to a previous pitcher). Nevertheless, it is a guideline only, and the scorer can make his or her own decision as to what constitutes an ineffective appearance.

Sometimes a similar situation occurs and the official scorer simply goofs. On April 21, 1997, the Royals were playing the Mariners. The line score was as follows:

	1	2	3	4	5	6	7	8	9	R	H	E
Royals	0	0	0	0	0	3	2	0	0	**5**	**7**	**1**
Mariners	1	1	0	0	1	0	3	0	X	**6**	**9**	**1**

The Mariners pitching lines were as follows:

	IP	H	R	ER	BB	SO
Randy Johnson	6	5	3	3	5	5
Bobby Ayala	1	2	2	2	1	1
Scott Sanders	0.2	0	0	0	1	0
Greg McCarthy	0.1	0	0	0	1	0
Norm Charlton	1	0	0	0	1	0

Guess who got the win? Ayala, despite giving up two earned runs in one inning (which is the specific example given in the Comment about an "ineffective appearance"). It is interesting that the official scorer is given discretion on who gets the win in a situation such as this, but no such discretion when a pitcher—especially a starting pitcher—leaves the game with the score tied. Indeed, the Comment to Rule 10.17(a)(1) is explicit on this point: "Whenever the score is tied, the game becomes a new contest insofar as the winning pitcher is concerned. Once the opposing team assumes the lead, all pitchers who have pitched up to that point and have been replaced are excluded from being credited with the victory."

This could lead to an unfair result. Consider the following: On August 25, 2004, the Cubs were playing the Brewers. Greg Maddux pitched 8 full innings for the Cubs and left the game with a 2–1 lead. In the top of the ninth, manager Dusty Baker brought in LaTroy Hawkins to pitch. He gave up an earned run to tie the game. The Cubs went on to win 4–2 in the bottom of the ninth. Guess who gets the win? Hawkins, and the official scorer has no discretion in the matter.

	1	2	3	4	5	6	7	8	9	R	H	E
Brewers	0	0	0	1	0	0	0	0	1	**2**	**6**	**2**
Cubs	0	0	0	0	1	0	0	1	2	**4**	**10**	**0**

The pitching line looked like this:

	IP	H	R	ER	BB	SO
Greg Maddux	8	4	1	1	1	8
LaTroy Hawkins (W)	1	2	1	1	0	1

26.10 Shutouts, no-hitters, and perfect games

1: Can a pitcher who doesn't start a game be credited with a shutout?

Yes. The only requirement is that no batters have been retired before he enters the game, per Rule 10.18. An amazing example of such a situation is presented in the next quiz. While looking at shutouts, let's also take a look at no-hitters and perfect games. Neither term is actually defined in the *Official Baseball Rules*. However, they are defined by Major League Baseball in "MLB Miscellany: Rules, regulations and statistics," which can be found on the MLB Web site.

2: On June 23, 1917, Babe Ruth was pitching for the Red Sox against the Washington Senators. The first batter he faced, Ray Morgan, drew a walk. Ruth then got into an argument over the calls of home plate umpire Brick Owens. Owens promptly ejected Ruth. In came reliever Ernie Shore. Morgan was thrown out trying to steal second. Shore then retired the next 26 Senators he faced. Would this be considered an official perfect game?

No, because a batter reached base, even though that happened before Shore entered the game and even though Morgan was thrown out. It is only an unofficial "perfect game" for Shore. The game is considered a combined no-hitter (and a shutout), making Ruth the only pitcher ever to participate in a combined no-hitter without retiring a single batter.

3: Assume that Ruth had retired Morgan but then had to leave the game because of an injury, and Shore retired the next 26 batters. Is that an official perfect game?

Yes. There is no requirement that only one person pitch in an official perfect game.

4: On May 26, 1959, the Pirates played the Braves. The line score looked like this:

	1	2	3	4	5	6	7	8	9	10	11	12	13	R	H	E
Pirates	0	0	0	0	0	0	0	0	0	0	0	0	0	**0**	**12**	**1**
Braves	0	0	0	0	0	0	0	0	0	0	0	0	1	**1**	**1**	**0**

Harvey Haddix pitched the entire game for the Pirates. No one reached base for the Braves until the thirteenth inning, when a runner reached on an error, was sacrificed to second, and scored on a double by Joe Adcock. Official perfect game for Haddix?

No. Runners reached base, regardless of the inning.

5: On April 21, 1984, the Cards played the Expos. The line score looked like this:

	1	2	3	4	5	6	R	H	E
Expos	3	0	1	0	0	0	**4**	**6**	**0**
Cardinals	0	0	0	0	0	X	**0**	**0**	**1**

The pitching line for Expos pitcher Davis Palmer looked like this:

	IP	H	R	ER	BB	SO
David Palmer	5	0	0	0	0	2

The game was official. But was it an official perfect game for Palmer?

No. The game has to go nine full innings.

6: On April 30, 1967, the Orioles played the Tigers. The line score looked like this:

	1	2	3	4	5	6	7	8	9	R	H	E
Tigers	0	0	0	0	0	0	0	0	2	**2**	**0**	**1**
Orioles	0	0	0	0	0	0	0	1	0	**1**	**2**	**2**

The pitching line for the Orioles pitchers looked like this:

	IP	H	R	ER	BB	SO
Steve Barber	8.2	0	2	1	10	3
Stu Miller	0.1	0	0	0	0	0

Is this an official no-hitter for the Orioles?

Yes. Despite two pitchers, two runs (one of them earned), two errors, ten walks, two hit batsmen, and one wild pitch, not to mention Baltimore's losing the game (!), it still fits within the definition of an official no-hitter. In an even more amazing example of a multipitcher no-hitter, on June 8, 2012, in a 1–0 win over the Los Angeles Dodgers, the pitching line for the Seattle Mariners pitchers looked like this:

	IP	H	R	ER	BB	SO
Kevin Millwood	6	0	0	0	1	6
Charlie Furbush	0.2	0	0	0	0	1
Stephen Pryor	0.1	0	0	0	2	1
Lucas Luetge	0.1	0	0	0	0	0
Brandon League	0.2	0	0	0	0	1
Tom Wilhelmson	1	0	0	0	0	0

Interestingly, Stephen Pryor, the least effective pitcher for Seattle, wound up with the win. After he struck out the last Dodger batter in the top of the seventh, the M's scored their lone run in the bottom half of that inning, so Pryor was the pitcher of record at the time. He then walked the first two Dodger batters in the eighth and was pulled.

26.11 Saves

On May 24, 2009, the Twins played the Brewers. The final line score looked like this:

	1	2	3	4	5	6	7	8	9	R	H	E
Brewers	0	0	0	1	0	0	0	0	2	**3**	**7**	**0**
Twins	1	0	0	1	0	0	4	0	X	**6**	**6**	**0**

Starter Scott Baker yielded two runs to the Brewers in the top of the ninth and left the game with one out and the bases empty. Joe Nathan was brought in for relief duty. The Twins' pitching line looked like this:

	IP	H	R	ER	BB	SO
Scott Baker	8.1	7	3	3	0	6
Joe Nathan	0.2	0	0	0	0	2

1: Does Nathan get the save?

No. He did not pitch for an inning and the tying run wasn't on base, at bat, or on deck.

The line score in this photo reflects an August 27, 2007, game between the Rangers and the Orioles. Is there any way a Texas pitcher could have earned a save in this game? *AP Photo/Nick Wass*

2: Would the answer change if Baker had left a runner on first base?

Yes. If a runner was at first when Nathan entered the game, then the tying run would be on deck in a 3-run game.

3: On August 27, 2007, the Rangers played the Orioles. The final line score looked like this:

	1	2	3	4	5	6	7	8	9	R	H	E
Rangers	0	0	0	5	0	9	0	10	6	**30**	**29**	**1**
Orioles	1	0	2	0	0	0	0	0	0	**3**	**9**	**1**

Is there any way a Rangers pitcher could have earned a save in this game?

Yes, because a pitcher can earn a save if he pitches for the last three innings, regardless of the score. To earn credit for a save, the pitcher must be the finishing pitcher for the winning team. In addition, a pitcher must either (1) enter the game with a lead of no more than three runs and pitch for at least one inning, or (2) enter the game, regardless of the count, with the potential tying run either on base, at bat, or on deck, or (3) pitch for at least the last three innings, per Rule 10.19(d). Many people don't realize that the on-deck hitter is included in the formula.

In the Rangers-Orioles game, a Rangers reliever did earn a save. The pitching line for the Rangers looked like this:

	IP	H	R	ER	BB	SO
Kason Gabbard	6	7	3	3	1	3
Wes Littleton	3	2	0	0	1	1

Despite being ahead 14–3 when Littleton entered the game, he got the save because (1) the Rangers won, (2) Littleton was not the winning pitcher, and (3) he pitched at least three innings. Just to make sure that Littleton did not have to worry about a blown save, his teammates helpfully tacked on 16 more runs in the final two innings.

4: True or false? An official scorer sometimes has discretion as to who gets credit for a win, but no discretion as to who gets credit for a save.

True.

5: True or false? It is possible to get both a win and a save in the same game.

False. One of the requirements for a save is that the pitcher not be the winning pitcher.

Chapter 27

Statistics

27.1 Games played

During the last home stand of the Giants' 2008 season, J. T. Snow signed a one-day contract with the club so he could officially retire as a Giant, where he had played most of his career. His previous last appearance in a major league game was on June 18, 2006, for the Red Sox. He was listed as the starting first baseman in the lineup while taking the infield in a Giants uniform one last time. He then tipped his cap and shook hands as he walked off the field, being replaced at first base before the game started.

1: Is Snow credited with a game played?

Surprisingly, the answer is yes. Per Rule 10.20, as long as a player is listed in the starting lineup, he is credited with a game played. There was, however, a downside to Snow's final bow. Because he last played in a major league game in 2006, he could normally appear on the Hall of Fame ballot in 2012. (Rule 3.C of the Baseball Writers' Association of America [BBWAA] Election Rules states that to be eligible "a player shall have ceased to be an active player in the Major Leagues at least five calendar years preceding the election.") However, because his appearance in 2008 is technically a game played, the BBWAA has indicated that Snow cannot appear on the ballot until 2014.

2: Would Snow's being in the lineup have counted toward a consecutive game streak if Snow had one going at the time?

No. Per Rule 10.23(c), he would have had to play a half-inning on defense or complete a time at bat by reaching base or being put out.

27.2 Batting average champion

1: True or false? To win a batting title, a player needs to have a minimum number of at bats.

False. The relevant number is not at bats, as many people assume, but rather plate appearances. Certain kinds of plate appearances do not count as at bats, namely walks, sacrifices, hit by pitch, and obstruction. However, all appearances at the plate are "plate appearances."

2: In determining the batting champion, how is the minimum number of plate appearances calculated?

You multiply the number of games "scheduled for each club" by 3.1, per rule 10.22(a). If 162 games are scheduled for a team, the minimum number of plate appearances is 162 x 3.1 = 502.2, which rounds down to 502. Interestingly, since the minimum is based on plate appearances and not at bats, then, to take an extreme example, if a player was 1 for 2 on the season and had 500 walks and sacrifces, he would likely win the batting title with an average of .500.

The phrase "scheduled for each club" is also worth noting. It is not unusual for games to be canceled and not replayed if, for example, they occur at the end of a season and are meaningless because they have no playoff ramifications. In such situations, the games were "scheduled"; they were simply not played. Still, it is the original number scheduled that is used to derive the minimum number of plate appearances.

3: In 1996, Tony Gwynn of San Diego had 498 plate appearances and hit .353 for the year. Ellis Burks of Colorado had 685 plate appearances and hit .344 for the year. Although no one had a higher average than Gwynn, he did not have the minimum number of plate appearances to qualify for the batting championship. Of the players who did have the minimum number of plate appearances, Burks had the highest average. Gwynn won the batting title anyway. Why?

Because of an exception in Rule 10.22(a). It essentially provides that if you add enough plate appearances to a player's average to give him the required minimum number of plate appearances, then, if his average is still the highest, he wins the batting title. In this case, Gwynn had 498 plate appearances, 451 at bats, and 159 hits, which rounds to a .353 average. It we assume that he had 4 more plate appearances (which would have put him at the 502 minimum) and was hitless each time, his average would be .349 (159/455), which is still higher than Burks's average.

4: What average is Gwynn actually given for the year?

He is given his actual average of .353, as opposed to his "deemed average" if the exception is factored in.

27.3 Earned run average

To win the award for lowest earned run average, a player needs to have a minimum number of innings pitched.

1: What is that number in Major League Baseball?

It's 162. Based on the Comment to Rule 10.22(b), the number of innings required is equal to the number of games scheduled, which is 162.

We saw that to win a batting-average title a minimum number of plate appearances are required, but that a player can win the title without achieving that minimum. Let's compare that to earned run average. The following statistics are from 1986 in the American League.

Pitcher	Innings Pitched	Earned Runs Allowed	ERA
Roger Clemens	254	70	2.48
Mark Eichhorn	157	30	1.72

2: Who wins the earned run title for 1986 in the AL?

It's Clemens. The batting-average exception does not apply to earned run average. If a player doesn't have enough plate appearances, he can simply be charged with enough outs to reach the minimum. However, if a pitcher doesn't have enough innings pitched, there is no way to calculate what might have happened. Even though Eichhorn was just a few innings short of the minimum, he might have given up any number of runs in the "phantom" extra innings pitched.

3: Say that Eichhorn had pitched 161⅔ innings. Would he then win?

No. The Comment to Rule 10.22(b) tells us that 161⅔ innings does not qualify when 162 games are scheduled.

4: Say that Eichhorn had pitched 161⅔ innings and Toronto only played 161 games that year? Would he win then?

The answer is again no because the standard is based on games "scheduled," and major league teams are scheduled for 162 games. Thus, if a team only plays 161 games, Eichhorn would wind up being penalized for that if, for example, the missed game prevented him from attaining the minimum number of innings.

27.4 Consecutive game/hitting streaks

On May 11, 2010, Kevin Youkilis of the Red Sox had a 9-game hitting streak going. In the game against the Blue Jays that day, Youkilis hit a sacrifice fly for an RBI, was hit by a pitch, walked twice, and hit into a fielder's choice.

1: Did this game terminate Youkilis's streak?

Yes. If Youkilis had not been credited with a base hit in this game but all his plate appearances ended in walks, being hit by a pitch, a sacrifice bunt, or reaching base by virtue of interference or obstruction, the streak would have continued. However, because one of his plate appearances ended in a sac fly, the streak was broken, and even without that, reaching on a fielder's choice would have brought the same result. The fact that Youkilis did not get a base hit is not sufficient to terminate the streak per Rule 10.23(a).

2: If Youkilis had only one plate appearance and hit a sacrifice bunt, would the streak have been terminated?

No. The rules draw a distinction between a sacrifice fly, which does terminate a hitting streak, and a sacrifice bunt, which does not. The distinction is that a sacrifice bunt is more of an intentional act than a sacrifice fly. With a sacrifice bunt, it is clear that the batter is giving himself up, but with a sacrifice fly, it can be ambiguous.

3: On May 4, 2011, Dodgers manager Don Mattingly scratched Andre Ethier from the lineup because of elbow inflammation. At the time, Ethier had a 29-game hitting streak going. Did his sitting out the May 4 game affect his hitting streak?

No. Per Rule 10.23(b), what is relevant are the games in which the player appears, not the games that his team plays.

4: Including his tenure in Japan, Hideki Matsui had played in 1,768 consecutive games. On May 11, 2006, Matsui was in left field for the Yankees. In the top of the first inning Mark Loretta of the Red Sox hit a sinking fly ball to Matsui. For a moment it appeared that Matsui had made a great diving catch, but the ball slipped out of his glove. Matsui broke his wrist on the play and had to leave the game. Is his consecutive game streak intact?

No. Under Rule 10.23(c), a player has to play at least a half inning on defense or have a time at bat. Since Matsui didn't play the full half inning on defense and didn't bat, his playing streak was terminated.

5: What if, instead of Matsui's being injured on the play, a controversy arose over whether he had caught the ball. If he started arguing with the umpire and was ejected from the game, would his streak be intact?

Yes, per Rule 10.23(c), which addresses this exact situation.

6: Outfielder Juan Pierre appeared in 674 consecutive games. However, on June 3, 2005, after playing in 386 consecutive games, he was inserted as a pinch runner for the Marlins, but never appeared in the field. Does that appearance keep the playing streak intact?

No. Per Rule 10.23(c), a pinch-running appearance does not extend the streak.

27.5 On-base percentage vs. batting average

Batting average is defined as number of hits divided by number of at bats. The following are the most common instances that are not considered at bats: walks, hit by pitch, and sacrifice bunts and flies. See Rule 10.02(a)(1). Reaching on an error or on a fielder's choice are considered at bats (and because they are not hits, they lower the batting average).

On-base percentage is roughly defined as the sum of hits, walks, and times hit by pitch divided by at bats, walks, times hit by pitch, and sacrifice flies. Thus, walks and hit by pitch help a player's on-base percentage but do not affect the batting average.

Note that neither sacrifice flies nor sacrifice bunts are considered at bats for purposes of determining batting average. However, a batter's on-base percentage *is* reduced by sacrifice flies but not sacrifice bunts.

1: It would seem virtually impossible for a player's batting average to be higher than his on-base percentage, but it is possible. On August 11, 2010, Domonic Brown of the Phillies entered the game against the Dodgers holding just this statistical anomaly. How is this possible?

Because sacrifice flies are not considered at bats in determining batting average but do count against a batter in determining on-base percentage. In Brown's case, he was 9 for 35, giving him a .257 batting average. However, he also had no walks and 3 sacrifice flies. This meant that his on-base percentage was only .237. For anomalous situations such as Brown's to occur generally requires a small number of at bats because walks are far more common than sacrifice flies.

Chapter 28

Miscellaneous Scoring Rules

28.1 Fielder's choice vs. extra base?

Just for fun, let's focus on a play from that noted hotbed of baseball the Netherlands. The result would be the same in an MLB game. On March 28, 2004, DOOR Neptunus was playing the Amsterdam Pirates. In the fourth inning, with one out, Stijn Gabriëls walked, Maikel Benner singled, and Jeroen Sluijter walked, to load the bases. Shaldimar Daantji then hit a shot to center field, scoring Gabriëls and Benner. Sluijter attempted to score from first, and the speedy Daantji continued to run toward third. The shortstop who took the throw from the outfield felt that he had no chance to get Daantji at third, so the relay throw went to home, where Sluijter was called out.

1: Which of the following statements is accurate?

A. Daantji is credited with a double.

B. Daantji is credited with a triple.

C. Whether Daantji gets credit for a double or triple is based on whether the official scorer determines that it was a legitimate three-base hit or whether he was able to take third on a fielder's choice.

The answer is A. Daantji is credited with a double because Sluijter was thrown out at home. Under Rule 10.06(b) and the accompanying Comment, the batter is not credited with a three-base hit when a pre-

Justin Upton of the Diamondbacks shows his frustration after being tagged out by the Brewers' Felipe López as Upton slid past second base. He had hit a gapper to the outfield and got caught between second and third. Is he credited with a single, a double, or an out? *AP Photo/Ross D. Franklin*

ceding runner is out at home plate (or would have been out but for an error). The batter only gets credit for the last base he touches. Thus, if Sluijter had been thrown out at third instead, Daantji would only get credit for a single if he hadn't yet touched second. If, on the other hand, Sluijter had been safe at home, then the correct answer would be C.

28.2 Oversliding the base

On September 11, 2009, Milwaukee was playing Arizona. In the seventh inning, Justin Upton of the Diamondbacks hit a gapper to the outfield but overslid second base and was tagged before he could get back.

1: What's the ruling regarding his at bat?

It's a single. Per Rule 10.06(c), when a batter-runner overslides a base and is tagged out, he is credited with the last base safely touched, which in this case was first base.

2: Would it have made a difference if Upton had overrun third base instead and was tagged before he could return to the bag?

Yes. In that case, he would be credited with a double. Per Rule 10.06(c), if a batter-runner runs past second or third base and is tagged out trying to return, he is credited with the last base safely touched (here, second base).

28.3 Escaping a rundown

On September 7, 1985, the Yankees were playing the A's. In the sixth inning, the Yanks had Dave Winfield on third base. With one out, Billy Sample attempted a suicide squeeze, but he missed the ball and Winfield got caught in a rundown between third and home. However, he avoided the tag of A's pitcher Tommy John at home plate.

1: How is the play scored?

Under Rule 10.07(c), Winfield gets credit for a steal of home. If a runner is attempting to steal or gets caught in a rundown, he gets credit for a stolen base if he evades being put out and advances to the next base without the benefit of an error. One may ask whether the rule would still apply in this play given that Winfield was not attempting to steal a base. The answer is yes. The moment the catcher caught the ball and Winfield was between third and home, he had to decide whether to head back to third or try for home. If he winds up at home without being tagged, then it's a stolen base. The fact that stealing was not his intent when the play started (or during the play) is not relevant.

2: What if Winfield had been safe at home because he was hit in the back with the ball before it got to John?

Then there would simply be an error on the play and no stolen base. A runner who has been picked off but advances to the next base gets credit for a stolen base only if there is no error on the play, per Rule 10.07(c).

3: Say that a base runner was on first base on the play who advanced to second while Winfield was escaping the rundown. No attempt was made to throw him out. Does he get credit for a stolen base?

Yes, again per Rule 10.07(c).

4: If in the previous situation Winfield instead returned safely to third, would the runner advancing from first to second still get credit for a stolen base?

Yes, as long as there was no error on the play, per Rule 10.07(c).

28.4 Catcher's interference

On May 29, 2008, the Mets were playing the Dodgers. In the Mets' fourth inning, with Brad Penny pitching for the Dodgers, the first two batters were out after a double play. The next batter, pitcher Claudio Vargas, appeared to have been thrown out at first after a grounder to shortstop, but he was awarded first base after a catcher's interference call on Russell Martin of the Dodgers. José Reyes then singled Vargas to second. Luis Castillo then doubled to left field, scoring Vargas and Reyes. David Wright then homered, giving the Mets 4 runs for the inning. No further runs were scored.

1: Is the catcher's interference considered an error in the first place?

Yes. Rule 10.12(c).

2: If Vargas reached base due to an error (catcher's interference), are any of the runs scored by the Mets in the inning earned, and if so, how many?

This is tricky. Based on Rule 10.16, despite being booked as an error, the catcher's interference does not preclude subsequent runs from being charged as earned runs to the pitcher (though a passed ball, which is not scored as an error, does result in runs counting as unearned).

The Comment to Rule 10.16(a) then provides in part that a run scored by a batter who gets on base via catcher's interference is not counted as an earned run. This is exactly what happened with Vargas, so his run was unearned. But what about the other runs? The problem is that we don't know what Vargas would have done had there not been catcher's interference (putting aside the fact that he was a pitcher with a .000 batting average). The Comment to Rule 10.16(a) recognizes this: "Because such batter never had a chance to complete his time at bat, it is unknown how such batter would have fared absent the catcher's interference." The official scorer is thus instructed not to assume that the batter would have made an out absent the catcher's interference ("unlike, for example, situations in which a batter-runner reaches first base safely because of a fielder's misplay of a ball for an error").

Accordingly, to determine whether subsequent runs are earned ("subsequent" because we already saw that Vargas's run is unearned), one must evaluate the inning not only as if the catcher's interference never occurred, but as if the at bat itself never occurred. Viewed in that manner, the answer to the question becomes easy. After the catcher's interference, Reyes singled, Castillo doubled, and Wright homered. So, for the inning as a whole, Penny was charged with four runs, three of them earned.

28.5 Reaching on a muffed foul pop

On July 4, 2009, the Mets were playing the Phillies. In the sixth inning, the Phils had runners on first and second with two outs. Shane Victorino hit a foul pop that was dropped by catcher Omir Santos for an error. Victorino then singled to knock in a run.

1: Is an earned run charged on this play?

No. To calculate whether a run is earned, the inning gets reconstructed as if there were no errors or passed balls. Therefore, Victorino's foul pop should have been the third out of the inning, and any runs that score afterward are unearned. Rule 10.16(b)(1) specifically provides that no earned run is charged when the error occurs in foul territory.

28.6 Advance aided by an error

On April 20, 2010, the White Sox were playing the Rays. In the second inning, with one out, Alex Ríos of the White Sox tripled to deep right-center. He scored on the play on a throwing error by Rays shortstop Jason Bartlett, who tried to throw out Ríos at third. Mark Teahen then flied out to left field, and Alexei Ramírez flied out to center field.

1: Is Ríos's run earned?

A. Yes.

B. No, because he scored on an error.

C. It's up to the official scorer.

The answer is C. At the moment Ríos scored, the run would not have been considered earned. However, earned runs are one statistic that sometimes cannot be determined until after the inning is complete because, as noted in Rule 10.16, the official scorer is required to reconstruct the inning after it is over whenever a run is scored after an error or a passed ball. Under Rule 10.16(d), the official scorer is given discretion to determine what would have happened absent a misplay. In this case, though Teahen's fly ball was not too deep, the official scorer decided that it was deep enough to allow Ríos to score on the play. Thus the run was ruled earned.

SOURCES

Sources are keyed to chapter number, section number, and question number. Thus in the first source below, *1.1.Q3* refers to chapter 1, section 1, question 3.

Chapter 1: Equipment

1.1.Q3: Dawn Klemish, "Notes: Nolasco to Rest on Disabled List," MLB.com, May 5, 2007.

1.1.Q5: Jeff Horgan, "Deion Setting the Style for Reds," *Cincinnati Post*, April 11, 1997; and Ken Davidoff, "No Magic in Babe's Hat," *Record* (Bergen County, NJ), June 29, 1997.

Chapter 2: Definitions

2.3.Q4: "A Dove Gives Its All, Sets Baseball Record," United Press International, April 13, 1987.

2.3.Q6: "Yankees Beat Up on Royals (In Mo We Trust)," http://www.inmowetrust.com/baseball/yankees-beat-up-on-royals.php, August 3, 2007.

Chapter 3: Starting and Ending the Game

3.1.Q1: Miles D. Seligman, "Game Called," *Village Voice*, May 29, 2001.

3.2.Q1: Bill Price, "Ya Gotta Believe, Huh?," *New York Daily News*, June 19, 2009.

3.3.Q3: Gordon Edes, "Selig's Unilateral Rule Change Prompts Questions," *Yahoo! Sports*, October 28, 2008.

3.5.Q1: Bob Hertzel, "Rain Delays Yanks' Victory," *Record* (Bergen County, NJ), June 26, 1994.

3.7.Q1: Steve Popper, "Mets Get the Short End on the Field of Streams," *Record* (Bergen County, NJ), May 2, 2005.

Chapter 4: Putting the Ball in Play

4.1.Q1: Sheldon Ocker, "Did John Hart Know It Was Time to Go?," Knight Ridder/Tribune News Service, April 27, 2002.

Chapter 5: The Batter

5.1.Q1: http://www.signonsandiego.com/sports/padres/xtra/2007/06/score_with_julie_back_to_the_b.html; and Rich Marazzi, *The Rules and Lore of Baseball* (Stein and Day, 1980).

5.3.Q1: Greg Johns, "Baek, Bloomquist and Rulebook Lift Mariners to Win over Royals," *Seattle Post-Intelligencer*, April 30, 2007.

5.10.Q1: Paul Sullivan, "Apologetic Sosa: 'I Picked the Wrong Bat'; Says Corked Bat Meant for Practice," *Chicago Tribune*, June 4, 2003.

5.10.Q4: Mythbusters (2007 season), *Wikipedia*; and "Corked bat," *Wikipedia*.

5.12.Q2: Craig Burley, http://www.hardballtimes.com/main/article/the-call, October 13, 2005. Reproduced with permission.

5.13.Q1: Joel Achenbach, "Out of the Park and Right into the Rulebook," *Washington Post*, October 19, 1999; and "What Was It? Ventura's Shot a Perfect Ending to Bizarre Game," cnnsi.com, October 18, 1999.

5.14.Q1: Joe Goddard, "Cub Loss Is Fruit of Vines—Scoreless 12th Costs Game," *Chicago Sun-Times*, June 15, 1995.

Chapter 6: The Runner

6.5.Q2: Erin Murphy, "Wahlert Win a Hit," *Dubuque* (IA) *Telegraph Herald*, June 27, 2007.

6.7.Q1: "Around the Major Leagues," *Washington Post*, July 3, 1989.

6.11.Q1: "Reds Overcome Blunder, Beat Pirates 5–4," AP Online, August 31, 2007.

Chapter 7: The Fielder

7.2.Q2: "Yankees Bail Out Wells with Some Timely Hits," *New York Times*, September 16, 1997.

7.5.Q1: "Thome's Injured Hand Doesn't Stop Hitting Streak," *Philadelphia Inquirer*, April 22, 2004.

7.6.Q1: "Rays' Longoria Ends a Boston Marathon on a High Note," TBO.com (Tampa Bay Online), August 5, 2009.

Chapter 8: The Pitcher

8.1.Q1: Clary's comment: *Pittsburgh Post-Gazette*, August 18, 1978.

8.6.Q1: Tim Sullivan, "Foreign or Domestic, Peavy Doesn't Need a Helping Hand,"*San Diego Union-Tribune*, April 12, 2008.

8.7.Q1: Steve Fainaru, "Umpire's Call One for the Books," *Boston Globe*, July 16, 1989.

Chapter 9: The Umpire

9.1.Q3: http://www.hardballtalk.nbcsports.com/2011/09/27/umpire-ejected-russell-martin-for-making-a-joke-last-night/.

9.2.Q1: Michael Cunningham, "Many Factors in a Manager-Ump Blow-Up," *South Florida Sun-Sentinel*, July 3, 2008.

9.2.Q4: Jack Curry, "A Confusing Day Results in Disappointing Calls," *New York Times*, August 25, 1998.

9.3.Q1: midwestump.blogspot.com/ . . . /john-kibler-nl-umpire-1928-2010.

Chapter 10: Other Situations

10.1.Q1: "Dodgers Still Have the St. Louis Blues," *Los Angeles Daily News*, August 7, 2008.

10.2.Q1: Tim Brown, "Bowa Thinks outside the Box," *Yahoo! Sports*, April 3, 2008.

10.3.Q1: Jesse Sanchez, "Red Sox Jackets Prompt Fan Cheers," MLB.com, October 4, 2003.

10.5.Q1: John Powers, "Red Sox Go Down Fighting; Williams Ejected before Spirited Rally Falls Short," *Boston Globe*, June 1, 2000; and Tony Massarotti, "Jimy Not the Puppeteer; Coach Takes Blame for Nomar, Everett Moves," *Boston Herald*, June 2, 2000.

10.12.Q1: Jeff Horrigan, "Sox Play Subpar—Damon Cards Hole-in-One as Athletics Take 6–1 Win," *Boston Herald*, August 9, 2001; and Malcolm Moran, "Umpire's Reversal Gives Yankees a Loss," *New York Times*, May 10, 1997.

Chapter 11: Interference

11.1A.Q2: Peter May, "A-Rod a Bigger Villain in One Swipe," *Boston Globe*, October 20, 2004; and John Powers, "Game Delayed by Unruly Crowd," *Boston Globe*, October 12, 2007.

11.3C.Q1: Gregory Schutta, "Mets Lose One by the Book," *Record* (Bergen County, NJ), August 4, 1995.

11.8.Q1: "Alou Says He Wouldn't Have Caught Bartman Ball in 2003 NLCS," ESPN.com, Baseball, April 1, 2008; and "Report: Alou Says He Would Have Caught Bartman Ball," ESPN.com, December 27, 2008, http://www.sports.espn.go.com/espn/print?id=3423732&type=story.

11.9A.Q1: La Velle Neal, "Twins Insider; Touch-and-Go Ninth Inning,"*Minneapolis Star-Tribune*, September 6, 2010.

11.9B.Q1: Steve Fainaru, "Morgan Gets First Ejection," *Boston Globe*, May 27, 1989.

Chapter 12: Obstruction

12.1.Q4: Michael C. Dorf, "America's Favorite Pastime Exposes a Necessary Evil in the Legal System: Harmless Error in Baseball, and in Law," http://www.writ.news.findlaw.com/dorf/20031013.html.

12.2.Q1: Bob Hohler, "Traffic Came to a Standstill," *Boston Globe*, October 5, 2003.

Chapter 13: Time Plays

13.1.Q1: Rich Marazzi, "'Time Plays' Can Cause Confusion among Players, Managers, and Occasionally Umpires," *Baseball Digest*, August 2007.

Chapter 14: What is a Legal Catch?

14.1.Q5: "Postgame Interview with Milwaukee," MLB.com, October 4, 2008, http://mlb.mlb.com/news/article.jsp?ymd=20081004&content_id=3591775&vkey=news_mil&fext=.jsp&c_id=mil.

Chapter 15: The Infield Fly Rule

15.1.Q1: William Stevens, "Aside: The Common Law Origins of the Infield Fly Rule," *University of Pennsylvania Law Review* 123 (1975): 1474; John J. Flynn, "Further Aside: A Comment on the Common Law Origins of the Infield Fly Rule," *Journal of Contemporary Law* 4 (1978): 241; Margaret Berger, "Rethinking the Applicability of Evidentiary Rules at Sentencing: Of Relevant Conduct and Hearsay and the Need for an Infield Fly Rule," *Federal Sentencing Report* 5 (1992): 96; Mark W. Cochran, "The Infield Fly Rule and the Internal Revenue Code: An Even Further Aside," *William and Mary Law Review* 29 (1988): 567; Charles Yablon, "On the Contribution of Baseball to American Legal Theory," *Yale Law*

Journal 104 (1994): 227; Neil B. Cohen and Spencer Weber Waller, "Taking Pop-Ups Seriously: The Jurisprudence of the Infield Fly Rule," *Washington University Law Quarterly* 82 (2004): 453; and Anthony D'Amato, "The Contribution of the Infield Fly Rule to Western Civilization (and Vice Versa)," *Northwestern University Law Review* 100 (2006): 194 (reproduced with permission).

Chapter 16: Batting Orders

16.1.Q1: http://www.sandiego.padres.mlb.com/news/article.jsp?ymd; and http://www.signonsandiego.com/ . . . /cabrera-back-on-dl-zawadzki-up-again.

16.2.Q9: Joe Haakenson, "Protest Moot After Victory, Angels 5, Detroit 4," *Los Angeles Daily News*, August 15, 2002.

Chapter 18: Base Hits

18.1.Q2: Ed Leyro, metsmerizedonline.com/ . . . /the-worst-way-for-the-mets-to-lose-a-no-hitter, March 13, 2010. Reproduced with permission.

Chapter 19: Stolen Bases

19.5.Q1: "'Caught Stealing,' but He Wasn't Out," Associated Press, April 29, 1990.

Chapter 20: Sacrifices

20.2.Q3: Lacy Lusk, "An RBI Infield Fly, but No Sacrifice Fly," http://www.washingtonpost.com/blogs/baseball-insider/post/an-rbi-infield-fly-but-no-sacrifice-fly/2011/04/22/AFHHMQOE_blog.html.

Chapter 24: Errors

24.1.Q1: http://www.examiner.com/x-18250-Rochester-Red-Wings-Examiner~y2009m8d7-Wild-week-for-official-scorer-in-Rochester.

24.2.Q1: Alyson Footer, "Biggio Reaches 3,000-Hit Milestone, Seventh-Inning Single Historic Knock in Five-Hit Performance," MLB.com, June 29, 2007.

24.8.Q1: Jose de Jesus Ortiz, "Astros Summary," *Houston Chronicle*, 3 STAR edition, Sports section, May 13, 2002, 4.

Chapter 25: Wild Pitches and Passed Balls

25.1.Q4: Romi Ezzo, "Casey Blake's Balk-Off Wins Ballgame for Bleeding Blue," bleacherreport.com.

Chapter 26: Pitching

26.3.Q1: Jim Storer, "Winning Pitcher: Luebbers: Starting Pitchers' Wins of Less Than Five Innings," *Baseball Research Journal*, January 1, 2001.

26.4.Q1: http://www.blogs.chron.com/baseballblog/archives/2006/04/.

26.5.Q8: http://www.brewcrewball.com/2009/6/4/ . . . /earned-and-unearned-runs-in-the-fifth-inning-last-night.

26.8.Q1: http://www.reconditebaseball.blogspot.com/ . . . /2009-team-unearned-runs.

Chapter 27: Statistics

27.1.Q1: http://www.baseballthinkfactory.org/files/newsstand/discussion/j.t._snow_Rule_10.20_and_the_hall_of_fame/.

27.2.Q2: http://www.verywellthen.com/ . . . /joe-mauers-batting-title-average-an-ephemeral-stat/.

Chapter 28: Miscellaneous Scoring Rules

28.4.Q1: Eric Simon, http://www.amazinavenue.com/2008/5/30/542442/e-2, May 30, 2008.

INDEX

Page numbers in *italics* refer to illustrations.